RABBI DAVID

A Documentary Catalogue

Jacob Neusner

Studies in Judaism

University Press of America,® Inc.
Lanham · Boulder · New York · Toronto · Plymouth, UK

Copyright © 2012 by
University Press of America,® Inc.
4501 Forbes Boulevard
Suite 200
Lanham, Maryland 20706
UPA Acquisitions Department (301) 459-3366

10 Thornbury Road
Plymouth PL6 7PP
United Kingdom

Library of Congress Control Number: 2012931187
ISBN: 978-0-7618-5847-8 (paperback : alk. paper)

Studies in Judaism

CONTENTS

Preface

Rabbinic documents of David, progenitor of the Messiah, carry forward the scriptural narrative of David the king. But he also is turned by Rabbinic writings of late antiquity — from the Mishnah through the Yerushalmi and the Bavli —into a sage. Consequently the Rabbis' Messiah is a Rabbi. How did this transformation come about? Of what kinds of writings does it consist? What sequence of writings conveyed the transformation? And most important: what do we learn about the movement from one set of Israelite writings to take over, or submit to the values of, another set of writings? These are the questions answered here for David, king of Israel.

Here I carry forward a number of prior monographs. The translations are all mine. See the following:

Jeremiah in Talmud and Midrash. A Source Book. Lanham, 2006: University Press of America STUDIES IN JUDAISM SERIES

Rabbi Jeremiah. . Lanham, 2006: University Press of America STUDIES IN JUDAISM SERIES

Amos in Talmud and Midrash. A Source Book. Lanham, 2007: University Press of America STUDIES IN JUDAISM SERIES

Hosea in Talmud and Midrash. A Source Book. Lanham, 2007: University Press of America STUDIES IN JUDAISM SERIES

Micah and Joel in Talmud and Midrash. A Source Book. Lanham: University Press of America STUDIES IN JUDAISM SERIES

Habakkuk, Jonah, Nahum, and Obadiah in Talmud and Midrash. A Source Book. Lanham, 2007: University Press of America STUDIES IN JUDAISM SERIES

Zephaniah, Haggai, Zechariah, and Malachi in Talmud and Midrash. A Source Book. Lanham, 2007: University Press of America STUDIES IN JUDAISM SERIES

Ezekiel in Talmud and Midrash. A Source Book. Lanham, 2007: University Press of America STUDIES IN JUDAISM SERIES

Isaiah in Talmud and Midrash. A Source Book. A. *Mishnah, Tosefta, Tannaite Midrash-Compilations, Yerushalmi and Associated Midrash-Compilations.* Lanham, 2007: University Press of America STUDIES IN JUDAISM SERIES.

Isaiah in Talmud and Midrash. A Source Book. B. *The Later Midrash-Compilations and the Bavli.* Lanham, 2007: University Press of America STUDIES IN JUDAISM SERIES.

The Rabbis, the Law, and the Prophets, Lanham, 2007: University Press of America STUDIES IN JUDAISM SERIES

Rabbinic Theology and Israelite Prophecy. Primacy of the Torah, Narrative of the World to Come, Doctrine of Repentance and Atonement, and the Systematization of Theology in the Rabbis' Reading of the Prophets Lanham, 2007: University Press of America STUDIES IN JUDAISM SERIES.

My thanks go to Bard College for longtime support of my research and to Professor Bruce Chilton for sharing his erudition and insight.

JACOB NEUSNER

DISTINGUISHED SERVICE PROFESSOR OF THE HISTORY AND THEOLOGY OF JUDAISM
SENIOR FELLOW, INSTITUTE OF ADVANCED THEOLOGY
BARD COLLEGE
ANNANDALE-ON-HUDSON, NEW YORK, 12504

NEUSNER@BARD.EDU

Introduction

Joining "Rabbi" and "David" in making a catalogue of the references to David in the late antique Rabbinic documents, which is what I do in these pages, yields an oxymoron. That is "Rabbi + David. " If "rabbi" then how come David? And if David, then whence rabbi"? Scripture's David was no sage, and no sage in the Mishnah or the Tosefta was celebrated as the king of Israel. The components of the formative canon of Rabbinic Judaism — the Mishnah for example — know no sage called "Rabbi David."

Let me supply a case to illustrate the expository narrative of David. It is a protracted comment on Psalm 145, David's psalm of praise.

COMPOSITE ON PSALM 145

III.3.A.   Said R. Eleazar bar Abina, "Whoever says the Psalm, 'Praise of David' (Ps. 145) three times a day may be assured that he belongs to the world to come."

    B.   *What is the scriptural basis for that view?*

    C.   *If you should say that it is because the Psalm follows the order of the alphabet, there also is the Psalm,* "Happy are they that are upright in the way" (Ps. 119) *which goes through the alphabet eight times [and should be a preferred choice on that account]. Rather, it is because, in Ps. 145, there is the sentence,* "You open your hand and satisfy every living thing with favor" (Ps. 145:16).

    D.   *If that is the case, then in the Great Hallel (Ps. 136), we find the phrase,* "Who gives food to all flesh" (Ps. 136:25), *which one would do better to recite.*

    E.   *Rather, it is because [in Ps. 145] there are both considerations [namely, the entire alphabet and the statement that God provides.]*

III.4.A.   [Referring to Ps. 145], said R. Yohanan, "On what account is there no verse beginning with an N is Psalm 145?

    B.   "It is because the N starts the verse referring to the fall of (the enemies of) Israel.

    C.   "For it is written, 'Fallen (NPLH), no more to rise, is the virgin of Israel' (Amos 5:2)."

    D.   *In the West [the Land of Israel] the verse at hand is laid out in this way:* "Fallen, and no more to fall, the virgin of Israel will arise."

    E.   *Said R. Nahman bar Isaac, "Even so, David went and by the Holy Spirit brought together the N with the following letter of the alphabet, S:* 'The Lord upholds (SMK) all those who fall (NPL) (Ps. 145:14)."

III.45.A. And R. Yohanan said in the name of R. Simeon b. Yohai, "Bringing a child up badly is worse in a person's house than the war of Gog and Magog.

B. "For it is said, 'A Psalm of David, when he fled from Absalom, his son' (Ps. 3:1), after which it is written, 'Lord how many are my adversaries become, many are they that rise up against me' (Ps. 3:2).

C. "By contrast, in regard to the war of Gog and Magog it is written, 'Why are the nations in an uproar? And why do the peoples mutter in vain' (Ps. 2:1).

D. "But it is not written in that connection, 'How many are my adversaries become.'"

E. "A Psalm of David, when he fled from Absalom, his son" (Ps. 3:1):

F. "A Psalm of David"? *It should be,* "A lamentation of David"!

G. Said R. Simeon b. Abishalom, "The matter may be compared to the case of a man, against whom an outstanding bond was issued. Before he had paid it, he was sad. After he had paid it, he was glad.

H. "So too with David, when he the Holy One had said to him, 'Behold, I will raise up evil against you out of your own house,' (2 Sam. 2:11), he was sad.

I. "He thought to himself, 'Perhaps it will be a slave or a bastard child, who will not have pity on me.

J. "When he saw that it was Absalom, he was happy. On that account, he said a psalm."

BAVLI SANHEDRIN 2:4E

I.3.A. Said R. Judah said Rab, "David had four hundred sons, all of them born of beautiful captive women. All grew long locks plaited down the back. All of them seated in golden chariots. And they went forth at the head of troops, and they were the powerful figures in the house of David."

B. And R. Judah said Rab said, "Tamar was the daughter of a beautiful captive woman. For it is said, 'Now, therefore, I pray you, speak to the king, for he will not withhold me from you' (2 Sam. 13:13). Now if you hold that she was the daughter of a valid marriage, would the king ever have permitted [Amnon] to marry his sister? But, it follows, she was the daughter of a beautiful captive woman."

C. "And Amnon had a friend, whose name was Jonadab, son of Shimeah, David's brother, and Jonadab was a very subtle man" (2 Sam. 13:3): Said R. Judah said Rab, "He was subtle about doing evil."

D. "And he said to him, Why, son of the king, are you thus becoming leaner... And Jonadab said to him, Lay down on your bed and pretend to be sick... and she will prepare the food in my sight... and she took the pan and poured [the cakes] out before him" (2 Sam. 13:4ff.): Said R. Judah said Rab, "They were some sort of pancakes."

E. "Then Amnon hated her with a very great hatred" (2 Sam. 13:15): *What was the reason?*

F. Said R. Isaac, "One of his hairs got caught [around his penis and cut it off] making him one whose penis had been cut off."

G. *But was she the one who had tied the hair around his penis? What had she done?*

H. *Rather, say,* she had tied a hair around his penis and made him into one whose penis had been cut off.

I. *Is this true? And did not Raba explain, "What is the sense of the verse, 'And your renown went forth among the nations for your beauty' (Ez. 16:14)? It is that Israelite women do not have armpit or pubic hair."*

J. *Tamar was different, because she was the daughter of a beautiful captive woman.*

K. "And Tamar put ashes on her head and tore her garment of many colors" (2 Sam. 13:19):

L. *It was taught on Tannaite authority in the name of R. Joshua b. Qorhah,* "Tamar established a high wall at that time [protecting chastity]. People said, 'If such could happen to princesses, all the more so can it happen to ordinary women.' If such could happen to virtuous women, all the more so can it happen to wanton ones!"

M. Said R. Judah said Rab, "At that time they made a decree [21B] against a man's being alone with any woman [married or] unmarried."

N. *But the rule against a man's being along with [a married woman] derives from the authority of the Torah [and not from the authority of rabbis later on]. For R. Yohanan said in the name of R. Simeon b. Yehosedeq,* "Whence in the Torah do we find an indication against a man's being alone [with a married woman]? As it is said, 'If your brother, of your mother, entice you' (Deut. 13:7). And is it the fact that the son of one's mother can entice, but the son of the father cannot entice? Rather, it is to tell you that a son may be alone with his mother, and no one else may be alone with any of the consanguineous female relations listed in the Torah."

O. Rather, they made a decree against a man's being alone with an unmarried woman.

P. "And Adonijah, son of Haggith, exalts himself, saying, I will be king" (1 Kgs. 1:5):

Q. Said R. Judah said Rab, "This teaches that he tried to fit [the crown on his head], but it would not fit."

R. "And he prepares chariots and horses and fifty men to run before him" (1 Kgs. 1:5):

S. So what was new [about princes' having retinues]?

T. *Said R. Judah said Rab,* "All of them had had their spleen removed [believed to make them faster runners] and the flesh of the soles of their feet cut off [Schachter, p. 115, n. 12: so that they might be fleet of foot and impervious to briars and thorns]."

BAVLI SANHEDRIN 2:5

I.2.A.   *And what is the story of Abishag [and Bath Sheba]?*

    B.   It is written, "King David was old, stricken in years... His servants said to him, Let there be sought..." And it is written, "They sought for him a pretty girl..." and it is written, "And the girl was very fair, and she became a companion to the king and ministered to him" (1 Kgs. 1:1-5).

    C.   *She said to him, "Let's get married."*

    D.   *He said to her, "You are forbidden to me."*

    E.   *She said to him, "When the thief fears for his life, he seizes virtue."*

    F.   He said to them, "Call Bath Sheba to me."

    G.   And it is written, "And Bath Sheba went into the king to the chamber" (1 Kgs. 1:15).

    H.   Said R. Judah said Rab, "At that time [having had sexual relations with David] Bath Sheba wiped herself with thirteen cloths [to show that he was hardly impotent, contrary to Abishag's accusation]."

    I.   Said R. Shemen bar Abba, "Come and take note of how difficult is an act of divorce. For lo, they permitted King David to be alone [with the woman], but they did not permit him to divorce [one of his other wives]."

BAVLI SANHEDRIN 2:5

IV.3. A.   *What is a conspiracy of wicked men?*

    B.   *Shebna gave expositions before thirteen myriads, while Hezekiah gave expositions before eleven myriads. When Sennacherib came and besieged Jerusalem, Shebna wrote a message and shot it on an arrow: "Shebna and his associates are prepared to make peace, Hezekiah and his followers are not prepared to make peace."*

    C.   For it is said, "For lo, the wicked bend the bow, they make ready their arrow upon the string" (Ps. 11:2).

    D.   *Hezekiah was afraid. He said, "Is it possible — God forbid — that the opinion of the Holy One, blessed be he, follows the majority. Since the majority are ready to give up, should we too give up?"*

    E.   The prophet came and said to him, "Do not say a conspiracy, concerning all of whom this people do say, A conspiracy" (Is. 8:12).

    F.   "It is a conspiracy of the wicked, and a conspiracy of the wicked does not come under consideration [to make a decision]."

    G.   [When Shebna] went to carve out a sepulchre for himself among the graves of the house of David, the prophet came and said to him, "What have you here and whom have you here, that you have hewn here a sepulchre? Behold, the Lord will hurl you down as a man is hurled" (Is. 22:16). ["You will go away into exile."]

I do not find a comparable Aggadic composite devoted to King David in any prior Rabbinic document, David again forms the focus of a formidable exegetical project. Now we turn to the Halakhic exposition of King David in the Rabbinic canon.

BAVLI SANHEDRIN 1:5

XXIV.1.A. **They bring forth the army to a war fought by choice only on the instructions of a court of seventy-one [M. 1:5B]:**

B. *What is the scriptural source for this rule?*

C. Said R. Abbahu, "Scripture says, 'And he shall stand before Eleazar the priest, [who shall inquire for him by the judgment of the Urim before the Lord. At his word shall they go out and at his word they shall come in, both he and all the children of Israel with him, even all the congregation]' (Num. 27:21-22).

D. "'He' speaks of the king.

E. "'And all the children of Israel with him' refers to the priest anointed for war.

F. "'And even all the congregation' refers to the sanhedrin."

G. *But perhaps it is the sanhedrin that is instructed by the All-Merciful to inquire of the Urim and Thummim?*

H. *But perhaps it is the sanhedrin that is instructed by the All-Merciful to inquire of the Urim and Thummim?*

I. *Rather, the proof derives from what R. Aha bar Bizna said R. Simeon the Pious said,* "There was a harp suspended over David's bed. At midnight a north wind would blow through it, and it would play on its own. David would get up right away and take up Torah-study until dawn. At dawn the sages of Israel would come in to him. They said to him, 'Our lord, king, your people Israel need sustenance.'

J "He said to them, 'Make a living off one another.'

K. "They said to him, 'A handful of meal is not enough for a lion, and a pit cannot be filled up by its own dirt.'

L. "He said to them, 'Go and organize marauders.'

M. "Forthwith they took counsel with Ahitophel and ask advice of the sanhedrin and address questions to the Urim and Thummim."

N. *Said R. Joseph, "What verse of Scripture shows this?*

O. "'[16B] 'And after Ahitophel was Benaiah, son of Jehoiada, and Abiathar, and the captain of the king's host was Joab' (1 Chr. 27:34).

P. "'Ahitophel' is the adviser, and so it is written, 'And the counsel of Ahitophel which he counseled in those days was as if a man inquired from the word of God' (2 Sam. 16:23).

Q. "'Benaiah son of Jehoiada' speaks of the Sanhedrin.

R. "'Abiathar' refers to the Urim and Thummim.

S. "And so it is written, 'And Benaiah, son of Jehoiada, supervised the Kerethites and Pelethites' (1 Chr. 18:17).

T. "Why were they called 'Kerethites' and 'Pelethites'?

U. "Because they gave definite instructions [a play on the word KRT, which is the root for cut, hence, 'speak decisively,' and also for the name of the group], and because they did wonderful deeds [a play on the root PL', wonder], respectively.

V. "After this: 'And the captain of the king's host was Joab'" (1 Chr. 27:34). [Schachter, p. 80, n. 13: Only after the Sanhedrin had authorized a war was there any need for Joab, the chief general.]"

W.   *Said R. Isaac, son of R. Ada, and some say R. Isaac bar Abodimi,*
     "What verse of Scripture, [supports the view that there was a harp
     over David's bed]? 'Awake my glory, awake psaltery and harp, I*
     will wake the dawn' (Ps. 57:9)."*

BAVLI SANHEDRIN 4:2

I.67 .A.   "And Ishbi-benob, who was of the sons of the giant, the weight of
           whose spear weighed three hundred shekels of brass in weight,
           being girded with a new sword, thought to have slain David" (2
           Sam. 21:16):

B.   *What is the sense of "Ishbi-be-nob"?*

C.   Said R. Judah said Rab, "It was a man [ish] who came on account
     of the matter of [the sin committed at] Nob.

D.   "Said the Holy One, blessed be he, to David, 'How long will the
     sin committed [against Nob] be concealed in your hand. On your
     account, Nob was put to death, the city of priests, on your account,
     Doeg the Edomite was sent into exile; on your account, Saul and
     his three sons were killed.

E.   "'Do you

BAVLI SANHEDRIN 11:4 KING DAVID: HIS SIN AND ATONEMENT

XII.12. A.   R. Dosetai of Biri interpreted Scripture, "To what may David be
             likened? To a Samaritan merchant.

B.   "Said David before the Holy One, blessed be he, 'Lord of the world,
     "Who can understand his errors?" (Ps. 19:13).'

C.   *"He said to him, 'They are remitted for you.'*

D.   ""' Cleanse me of hidden faults" (Ps. 19:13).'

E.   *" 'They are remitted to you.'*

F.   ""'Keep back your servant also from presumptuous sins" (Ps.
     19:13).'

G.   *" 'They are remitted to you.'*

H.   ""'Let them not have dominion over me, then I shall be upright"
     (Ps. 19:13), *so that the rabbis will not hold me up as an example.'*

I.   *" 'They are remitted to you.'*

J.   ""'And I shall be innocent of great transgression" (Ps. 19:13), *so*
     that they will not write down my ruin.'

K.   "He said to him, 'That is not possible. Now if the Y that I took
     away from the name of Sarah [changing it from Sarah to Sarah]
     stood crying for so many years until Joshua came and I added the
     Y [removed from Sarah's name] to his name, as it is said, "And
     Moses called Oshea, the son of Nun, Jehoshua" (Num. 13:16),
     how much the more will a complete passage of Scripture [cry out
     if I remove that passage from its rightful place]!'"

BAVLI SANHEDRIN 11:4 KING DAVID: HIS SIN AND ATONEMENT

XII.13.A.   "And I shall be innocent from great transgression: (Ps. 19:13):

B.   He said before him, "Lord of the world, forgive me for the whole
     of that sin [as though I had never done it]."

C. He said to him, "Solomon, your son, even now is destined to say in his wisdom, 'Can a man take fire in his bosom, and his clothes not be burned? Can one go upon hot coals, and his feet not be burned? So he who goes in to his neighbor's wife, whoever touches her shall not be innocent' (Prov. 6:27-29)."

D. *He said to him, "Will I be so deeply troubled?"*

E. He said to him, "Accept suffering [as atonement]."

F. He accepted the suffering.

BAVLI SANHEDRIN 11:4 KING DAVID: HIS SIN AND ATONEMENT

XII.14. A. Said R. Judah said Rab, "For six months David was afflicted with saraat, and the Presence of God left him, and the sanhedrin abandoned him.

B. "He was afflicted with saraat, as it is written, 'Purge me with hyssop and I shall be clean, wash me and I shall be whiter than snow/ (Ps. 51:9).

C. "The Presence of God left him, as it is written, 'Restore to me the joy of your salvation and uphold me with your free spirit' (Ps. 51:14).

D. "The sanhedrin abandoned him, as it is written, 'Let those who fear you turn to me and those who have known your testimonies' (Ps. 119:79).

E. "How do we know that this lasted for six months? As it is written, 'And the days that David rules over Israel were forty years: [107B] Seven years he reigned in Hebron, and thirty-three years he reigned in Jerusalem' (1 Kgs. 2:11).

F. "Elsewhere it is written, 'In Hebron he reigned over Judah seven years and six months' (2 Sam. 5:5).

G. *"So the six months were not taken into account. Accordingly, he was afflicted with saraat [for such a one is regarded as a corpse].*

H. "He said before him, 'Lord of the world, forgive me for that sin.'

I. "'It is forgiven to you.'

J. "'"Then show me a token for good, that they who hate me may see it and be ashamed, because you, Lord, have helped me and comforted me" (Ps. 86:17).'

K. "He said to him, 'While you are alive, I shall not reveal [the fact that you are forgiven], but I shall reveal it in the lifetime of your son, Solomon.'

L. "When Solomon had built the house of the sanctuary, he tried to bring the ark into the house of the Holy of Holies. The gates cleaved to one another. He recited twenty-four prayers [Freedman, p. 734, n. 4: in 2 Chr. 6 words for prayer, supplication and hymn occur twenty-four times], but was not answered.

M. "He said, 'Lift up your head, O you gates, and be lifted up, you everlasting doors, and the King of glory shall come in. Who is this King of glory? The Lord strong and might, the Lord mighty in battle' (Ps. 24:7ff.).

N.   "And it is further said, 'Lift up your heads, O you gates even lift
      them up, you everlasting doors/ (Ps. 24:7).

O.   "But he was not answered.

P.   "When he said, 'Lord God, turn not away the face of your anointed,
      remember the mercies of David, your servant'(2 Chr. 6:42),
      forthwith he was answered.

Q.   "At that moment the faces of David's enemies turned as black as
      the bottom of a pot, for all Israel knew that the Holy One, blessed
      be he, had forgiven him for that sin."

David emerges here in a manner lacking a counterpart in the Rabbinic
canon. So I ask the question, how and where does the transformation of the royal
Messiah into a rabbi take place? Where do we find a protracted and systematic
account of the royal Messiah?   It is in the Bavli. I show in these pages that the
Messiah acquires his own program of exegesis in the pages of the Bavli and not
much before the closure of that document. My tedious assembly of references to
David document by document only in the Bavli yields a formal program particular
to the Messiah king sage. The documents that reached closure prior to the Bavli
produce formal programs matching the forms of the documents from the Mishnah
to the Yerushalmi, in no way marked by distinctive formal traits.

That is to say, before the Bavli's discussion of the Messiah in law and
theology conformed to the discussions of other legal or theological propositions in
the same document, the Messiah followed the formal patterns of the several
documents in which the Messiah's materials are formulated. Discussion of the figure
of David follows the formal norms of other subjects in the same document.
References to King David in the Mishnah follow the patterns of references to other
figures in the Mishnah. In the documents prior to the Bavli the Messiah exhibits the
formal traits of the program of the document subject to canonical exposition. When
we reach the Bavli we come to a form of discussion that is particular to David.
Prior to the Bavli In the Rabbinic documents the Messiah is not expounded in this
particular form. Here we find the treatment of the royal Messiah in accord with
formal norms that differ from the established documentary ones. I do not know at
this point whether result of this survey is particular to its topic — whether the Bavli
alone formed the setting for a radical shift to the exposition of persons or institutions
such as the Messiah. It suffices at this point to show that the Bavli signifies the
advent of the sage-Messiah with all that that formulation signifies,

In examining the bulk of references to David in the Rabbinic canon, I
follow a simple repertoire of questions. These emerge from the program of definition
that animates the inquiry document by document.

[1] Is David an active player or a routine and scarcely animate one? The
Rabbinic sages represent sages in both manners, sometimes as the exemplary and
original actor and sometimes as a routine example of a fixed rule. How are matters
with David in the successive documents, and do we discern shifts from document
to document?

[2] What components of the collection make routine glosses of the received Scriptures and which ones provide more than minor glosses of the tradition?

[3] Can we identify a pronounced bias or a polemical program in the unfolding entries that transform David king of Israel into Rabbi David? Or are the entries that clarify Scripture through the contrast with tradition scattered without pattern in the Rabbinic canon?

[4] How is David comparable to sages in this document? How else may we classify the figure of David if not as a sage in this document?

Each chapter takes up allusions to David in a particular document. I survey the greater part of the references to David in the Rabbinic canon but omit some of the more trivial allusions. I present the outcome of my survey of a particular document at the outset and then review the references to David in a particular document.

1

David in Abot and the Mishnah

Tractate Abot on David draws on the biblical narratives and does not change their program.

MISHNAH ABOT 3:7

A. R. Eleazar of Bartota says, "Give him what is his, for you and yours are his.

B. "For so does it say about David, 'For all things come of you, and of your own have we given you' (I Chron. 29:14)."

MISHNAH ABOT 5:16

1 A. [In] any loving relationship that depends upon something, [when] that thing is gone, the love is gone.

B. But any that does not depend upon something will never come to an end.

C. What is a loving relationship that depends upon something? That is the love of Amnon and Tamar [11 Sam. 13:15].

D. And one which does not depend upon something? That is the love of David and Jonathan.

A scriptural figure subject to narrative, David in Abot takes an exemplary path in the exposition of proper conduct. He is alluded to in the exposition of the saying of Eleazar of Bartota but has no saying comparable to other sages' sayings. He is a scriptural figure pure and simple. Tractate Abot has little in common with David in the Mishnah.

David in the Mishnah occurs casually and never is reworked into the figure of a sage. The Mishnah makes reference to a small number of narratives involving David. These validate details of the law subject to debate.

MISHNAH MEGILLAH 4:10

A.   The tale of Reuben [Gen. 35:22] is read but not translated.

B.   The tale of Tamar [Gen. 38:1ff.1 is read and translated.

C.   The first tale of the calf [Ex. 32:1-20] is read and translated.

D.   The second one [Ex. 32:21ff.] is read but not translated.

E.   The blessing of the priests [Num. 6:24-26], the story of David [II Sam. 11:2ff.] and of Amnon [II Sam. 13:1ff.], are not read and not translated.

MISHNAH SANHEDRIN 2:2

G.   [Others] do not marry his widow.

H.   R. Judah says, "A king may marry the widow of a king.

I.   "For so we find in the case of David that he married the widow of Saul, For it is said, 'And I gave you your master's house and your master's wives into your embrace' (11 Sam. 12:8)."

MISHNAH SANHEDRIN 2:3

A.   (5) [If] he suffers a death in his family, he does not leave the gate of his palace.

B.   R. Judah says, "If he wants to go out after the bier, he goes out,

C.   "for thus we find in the case of David, that he went out after the bier of Abner,

D.   "since it is said, 'And King David followed the bier' (11 Sam. 3:31)."

E.   They said to him, "This action was only to appease the people."

MISHNAH TAANIT 2:4

G.   For the seventh he says, "He who answered David and Solomon, his son in Jerusalem, will answer you and hear the sound of your cry this day. Blessed are you, O Lord, who has mercy on the Land."

David in Abot and in the Mishnah supplies facts of both a narrative and a normative legal character.

[1] IS DAVID AN ACTIVE PLAYER OR A ROUTINE AND SCARCELY ANIMATE ONE? David supplies norms of interpretation and of law. He does not originate laws but illustrates them. He occasionally defines the norm of Rabbinic conduct in law. The purpose is not to invent laws but to confirm them. We cannot classify him as either active or inanimate. But he does not participate in the legal debates, he only contributes to the exposition of the normative law.

[2] WHAT COMPONENTS OF THE COLLECTION MAKE ROUTINE GLOSSES OF THE RECEIVED SCRIPTURES and which ones provide more than minor glosses of the tradition? This is not the issue, exegesis of Scripture is not intended to extend Scripture's program but only to prove facts deriving from that program.

[3] CAN WE IDENTIFY A PRONOUNCED BIAS OR A POLEMICAL BIAS in the Mishnah's utilization of David? David is not a controversial figure in the Mishnah. He occurs only casually. He is not differentiated from rabbis. He keeps the law and helps define its norms. If we did not know that David's heir would be the Messiah, we should not have drawn the conclusion that David was only another minor rabbi.

But in general the Messiah is not a major figure in the Mishnah. We are left with odds and ends,

[4] HOW IS DAVID COMPARABLE TO OTHER SAGES IN THIS DOCUMENT? The standard sage of the Mishnah takes a key part in the exposition of the law and participates in disputes on matters of law. How else may we classify the figure of David if not as a sage in this document? In the Mishnah David is preserved in his scriptural roles, and he is not redefined into a sage in the model of other Mishnah-sages.

The first document of Rabbinic Judaism, the Mishnah together with tractate Abot does not transform David from king to sage and does not invoke David in the model of the sage. To state matters simply, the Mishnah knows the biblical David and nothing more.

2

David in the Tosefta

The Tosefta, a legal complement and a supplement to the Mishnah, presents three types of writing, ordinarily in this order: [1] a verbatim citation of a rule of the Mishnah and gloss of the cited rule [2] passages that for a full interpretation depend on the Mishnah but that cite the Mishnah only implicitly, and [3] writing that does not cite or gloss the Mishnah but that stands independent of the initial document. David in the Tosefta is accorded a much larger volume of stories and sayings than David in the Mishnah. But the *type* of materials involving David in the Tosefta does not materially differ from the types of writings that refer to David in the Mishnah.

The important development in the Tosefta is the identification of David with the quotation of specified Psalms. The references are to Ps. 55:18, Ps. 122:2. *Ps.* 106:6.

TOSEFTA BERAKHOT 3:6

D. Lest one think that he may recite all of the three daily Prayers at one time, Scripture specifies [to the contrary] in the case of David, as it says, *Evening and morning and noon I utter my complaint and moan* (Ps. 55:18):

E. *evening* — this *is* the evening Prayer; *morning* — this *is* the morning Prayer; *noon* — this *is* the afternoon Prayer.

David's composition of Psalms is taken for granted as the passage is cited and glossed. The same pattern persists in the following, where David proves a proposition on the strength of Scripture.

Tosefta Sotah 11:14

A. Similarly do you say: *Now Saul heard that David was discovered, and the men who were with him. Saul was sitting at Gibeah, under the tamarisk tree in Ramah with his spear in his hand (1* Sam. 22:6).

B. If he was in Gibeah, he was not in Ramah, and if he was in Ramah, he was not in Gibeah.

C. But who upholds the foot of Saul in Gibeah? The court of Samuel of Ramah.

Tosefta Sotah 11:15

A. Similarly do you say: *Our feet have been standing within your gates, O Jerusalem (Ps. 122:2].*

B. It is not possible to say so [that all of them were standing within the gates of Jerusalem].

C. But who supports our feet in war? It is the courts of David that are in session at the gates of Jerusalem.

Tosefta Sotah 11:18

A. His disciples asked R. Yosé, "How did David marry the sister of his wife?"

B. He said to them, "After the death of Merab did he marry her."

Tosefta Sotah 11:19

A. R. Joshua b. Qorha says, "For his act of betrothal was not deemed a completely valid betrothal, as it is said, *Give me my wife, Michal, whom I betrothed at a price of a hundred foreskins of the Philistines* (11 Sam. 3: 14).

B. "Just as his act of betrothal was not a completely valid betrothal, so his marriage was not a completely valid marriage."

Tosefta Sotah 11:12:3

A. *Jehoram was thirty-two years old when he became king, and he reigned eight years in Jerusalem* (11 Kings 21:5).

B. And in the case of Ahaziah, his son, what does it say? *Ahaziah was forty-two years old when he began to reign, and he reigned one year in Jerusalem* (11 Chron. 22:2).

C. Yet in another place it says, *Ahaziah was twenty-two years old when he began to reign* (11 Kings 8:26).

D. Said R. Yosé, "Now how is it possible for a son to be two years older than his father? But when Asa, king of Judah, married off the daughter of Omri, king of Israel, to his son, Jehoshaphat, the decree was issued that the royal house of David will perish with the house of Ahab, as it is said, *But it was ordained by God that the downfall of Ahaziah should come about through his going to visit Joram* (11 Chron. 22:7).

E. Both of them fell on the same day with one another.

Tosefta Sotah 13:2

A. When the first Temple was destroyed, the kingship was removed from the House of David.

B. The Urim and Thummim ceased [M. Sot. 9:12A].

C. The cities of refuge came to an end,

D. as it is said, *The governor told them that they were not to partake of the most holy food until there should be a priest to consult the Urim and Thummim* (Ezra 2:63).

We find a series of allusions to acts of David or involving him and explanations of the result of those actions. I discern no independent thought of David but only harmonization of David's ideas with statements of scriptural law.

TOSEFTA YOMA 2:1

A. How does he state the confession?

G. *"'O Lord, I have committed in4uity, transgressed, and sinned before you . . .'*

H. *"And they respond to him, 'Blessed is the name of the glory of his kingdom forever and ever'* [M. Yoma 3:8F-H].

I. "For we see that all who confess make confession thus.

J. "David said, *'Both we and our fathers have sinned, we have committed iniquity, we have done wickedly' (Ps.* 106:6).

K. "Solomon said, *'We have sinned, we have transgressed, we have done wickedly' (I* Kings 8:47).

L. "Daniel said, *'we have sinned, we have transgressed, we have done wickedly'* (Dan. 9:5)."

TOSEFTA MEGILLAH 3:38

A. The story of David and Bath Sheba is not read or translated [M. Meg. 4:10E].

B. But the teacher teaches it in the usual way.

Allusions to what scriptural figures stated are amplified. The clarifications over details, I discern no program or proposition that imparts coherence to the entire composite,

TOSEFTA SHABBAT 17:19

A. R. Simeon b. Eleazar says, "He who wants to close the eyes of a corpse on the Sabbath blows wine into his nose and puts oil on the two eyelids and they will close on their own" [cf. M. Shab. 23:5K].

B. And so did R. Simeon b. Eleazar say, "Even a child one day old who is alive — they violate the restrictions of the Sabbath on his account [to save his life].

C. "But even David, King of Israel, when dead — they do not violate the restrictions of the Sabbath on his account [to take care of his corpse].

D. "For so long as a man is alive, he engages in religious requirements. Therefore they violate the Sabbath on his account.

E. "But when he dies, he is exempt from religious requirements. Therefore they do not violate the Sabbath on his account."

The allusion to David invokes the contrast between the dead monarch and the living child. Here we find no active engagement with the name of David. We could readily invoke Solomon/child or Moses/child. So Child/David does not signal an active engagement with David in particular.

TOSEFTA ABODAH ZARAH 3:19

G. All graves are subject to removal except for the grave of a king and the grave of a prophet.

H. R. 'Aqiba says, "Also the grave of a king and the grave of a prophet are subject to removal."

I. They said to him, "Now were not the graves of the house of David and the grave of Huldah the prophetess in Jerusalem, and no one ever laid a hand on them [to remove them]."

J. He said to them, "What proof is there from the fact? In point of fact they had underground channels, and it would remove uncleanness to the Qidron Brook."

David supplies an illustrative fact. In the Tosefta he supplies a name.

TOSEFTA HORAYOT 2:2

A. Who is a ruler? It is a ruler of Israel, not a ruler of the tribes.

B. [If there is] a ruler of Israel [and] one from the House of David —

C. This one brings an offering on his own account, and that one brings an offering on his own account.

TOSEFTA HORAYOT 2:9

A. A king takes precedence over a high priest,

B. as it is said, *And the king said to them, Take with you the servants of your lord, and cause Solomon my son to ride on my own mule, and bring him down to Gihon.*

C. And the high priest takes precedence over the prophet, as it is said, *And let Zadok the priest and Nathan the prophet there anoint him king over Israel (1 Kings 1:33-34).*

D. [David] gave precedence to Zadok over Nathan.

TOSEFTA KILAYIM 5:6

A. Isi the Babylonian says, "It is prohibited to ride on the back of a mule [cf. M. Kil. 8:1H-I],

B. "[as we learn] from an argument *a fortiori*: If, in a case in which it is permitted to wear two garments [i.e., one of wool and one of linen] as one [together], lo, it is prohibited in respect to [wearing a garment composed of] their mixture [i.e., a mixture of the two materials], in a case in which it is prohibited to lead two animals [of different kinds] as one [together], is it not logical that it should be prohibited in respect to [using an animal composed of] their mixture [i.e., a hybrid offspring of the two kinds of animals]?"

C. They said to him, "Lo, it [i.e., Scripture] says, *Take with you the servants of your Lord, and cause Solomon my son to ride on my own mule, and bring him down to Gihon (I* Kings *1:33)."*

D. He said to them, "They do not respond from Tekoa [i.e., they do not rule on the basis of the practices of townspeople such as David, who was not a legal authority]."

E. They said to him, "Lo, it [i.e., Scripture] says, *And David did what was right in the eyes of the Lord, and did not turn aside from anything that he commanded him all the days of his life, except in the matter of Uriah the Hittite (I* Kings 15:5)."

Tosefta Sanhedrin 1:3

D. R. Joshua b. Qor4a says, "It is a religious duty to arbitrate, as it is said, *Execute the judgment of truth and peace in your gates* (Zech. 8:16).

E. "Now is it not so that in any case in which there is a judgment of truth, there is no peace, and in any case in which there is peace, there is no judgment of truth?

F. "So what is the judgment of truth which also contains peace?

G. "You have to say, This is arbitration."

What follows is a fine case in which David supplies a fact in support of a law.

H. And so it says in the case of David, *And David acted with judgment and charity to all his people* (II Sam. 8:15).

I. Now is it not so that in any case in which there is judgment, there is no charity, and in any case in which there is charity, there is no judgment?

J. So what is the judgment in which there also is charity?

K. You have to say, This is arbitration.

Tosefta Sanhedrin 4:2

A. An Israelite king does not stand in line to receive comfort [in the time of bereavement],

B. nor does he stand in line to give comfort to others.

C. And he does not go to provide a funeral meal for others.

D. But others come to him to give him a funeral meal [M. San. 2:3F],

E. as it is said, *And the people went to provide a funeral meal for David.*

Tosefta Sanhedrin 4:7

A. *And he writes for himself a scroll of the Torah* (Deut. 17:17) —

I. [When] he goes to war, it is with him, when he comes back, it is with him [cf. M. San. 2:4Ml]; when he goes to court it is with him; when he goes to the urinal, it waits for him [outside] at the door,

J. and so does David say, *I have set God always before me and he is on my right hand (Ps.* 16:8).

Tosefta Sanhedrin 4:11

A. They anoint kings only on account of civil strife.

H.   And they anoint kings only from a horn.

I.   Saul and Jehu were anointed from a flask, because their rule was destined to be broken.

J.   David and Solomon were anointed from a horn, because their dominion is an eternal dominion.

TOSEFTA SANHEDRIN 9:9

A.   *There were two graveyards made ready for the use of the court one for those who were beheaded or strangled, and one for those who were stoned or burned* [M. San. 6:5F].

B.   And so David says, *Do not gather my soul with the sinners (Ps. 26 9)*

Of the three types of writing in the Tosefta only the first, the citation and gloss of the Mishnah or of scripture, enjoys a prominent standing in David-compositions. We now turn to our formal program of questions.

[1] IS DAVID AN ACTIVE PLAYER OR A ROUTINE AND SCARCELY ANIMATE ONE? This question takes for granted that an active player is in the model of a rabbi. But here David is primarily a biblical figure who supplies important facts for the exposition of Scripture. There is no hint at the transformation of David into a sage. He is an authority of the law to be sure, but that is by reason of his role in Scripture's narrative and in other compositions.

[2] WHAT COMPONENTS OF THE COLLECTION MAKE ROUTINE GLOSSES OF THE RECEIVED SCRIPTURES and which ones provide more than minor glosses of the tradition? Most of to he references to David are routine glosses. The Tosefta does not introduce narratives of David.

[3] CAN WE IDENTIFY A PRONOUNCED BIAS OR A POLEMIC in the utilization of David? The bias is to that of Scripture, there is no point of the inclusion of Rabbinic innovation.

[4] HOW IS DAVID COMPARABLE TO OTHER SAGES IN THIS DOCUMENT? He is a king but an exemplary one. When he dies, he is like any other man. The death scenes of the holy rabbis have no counterpart here in the Davidic setting.

The Tosefta brings to David the established program of deriving from a biblical figure a lesson that supports a Rabbinic rule. David is a source of facts. There is no coherent program that characterizes the bulk of the references to things David said or did. David is not compared with rabbis or treated as other than a secular figure. In the Tosefta David is not a holy man like a sage. David is a more elaborate figure than his counterpart in the Mishnah, but both the Mishnah's and the Tosefta's Davids ignore David as a holy man and are satisfied with the secular and this-worldly portrait of an exemplary political figure. In the Tosefta I see no evidence of a process of Rabbinization of David.

3

David in Sifra

Sifra sets forth a comprehensive commentary to Leviticus, repeatedly demonstrating that propositions based on reason and not on proof-texts from Scripture lack reliability. Where David registers, Sifra cites a passage of Scripture or glosses one as a proof-text. We note the occurrence of verses of Psalms attributed to David's authorship: Ps. 37:7. David is one of two anointed, along with Aaron. David acknowledged the justice of the divine decree, as it is said, "My wounds grow foul and fester because of my foolishness"(Ps. 38:5). Sifra's David is a diverse mixture of exegetical cases. No polemic is tied to David, and no program links the references to David into a coherent onstruction. IWe shall fnd that that defines the pattern in many of the Midrash-docunents.

Sifra XCVII:I
2. A.   R. Judah says, "Might one suppose that Aaron and his sons require anointing oil in the time to come?

B.   "Scripture says, 'This is the anointing of Aaron and of his sons.'

C.   "Then how shall I explain the verse, 'These are the two anointed who stand by the Lord of the whole earth' (Zech. 4:14)?

D.   "This refers to Aaron and David."

Sifra XCIX:IV.
7. A.   The righteous as a matter of fact are accustomed to acknowledge the justice of the divine decree.

B.   Abraham acknowledged the justice of the divine decree, as it is said, "And I am but dust and ashes" (Gen. 18:27).

C.   Jacob acknowledged the justice of the divine decree, as it is said, "I am not worthy of the least of all the steadfast love and all the faithfulness which you have shown to your servant" (Gen. 32:10).

    D. David acknowledged the justice of the divine decree, as it is said, "My wounds grow foul and fester because of my foolishness"(Ps. 38:5).

SIFRA XCIX:VI

10. A. On this basis sages have said:

    B. Whoever accepts [suffering] and remains silent – it is a good omen for him.

    C. Through David, Scripture says, "Be still before the Lord and wait patiently for him" (Ps. 37:7).

    D. And through Solomon: "...a time to keep silence, and a time to speak" (Qoh. 3:7).

    E. There are times for everything, times for one to keep silence, and times for one to speak.

SIFRA CLXXVI:I 6

    E. "For so do we find that it is the way of all those who confess to say the confession in this way.

    F. "David said, 'Both we and our fathers have sinned, we have committed iniquity, we have done wickedly' (Ps. 106:6).

    G. "Solomon his son said, 'We have sinned, have transgressed, we have done wickedly' (1 Kgs. 8:47).

    H. "Daniel said, 'We have sinned, we have transgressed, we have done wickedly, we have rebelled' (Dan. 9:5).

SIFRA CCX:II

19. A. "...for you are strangers and sojourners with me":

    B. Do not treat yourselves as principal.

    C. And so Scripture says, "For we are strangers before you and sojourners, as all our fathers were; our days on the earth are like a shadow, and there is no abiding" (1 Chr. 29:15).

    D. And so David says, "For I am your passing guest, a sojourner, like all my fathers" (Ps. 39:12).

Sifra's references to David invoke Psalms more than any other book of Scripture.

[1] IS DAVID AN ACTIVE PLAYER OR A ROUTINE AND SCARCELY ANIMATE ONE? Sifra's David is not the subject of an elaborate narrative. He supplies proof-texts for theological compositions. No elaborate theological program lends coherence to David's corpus of sayings.

[2] WHAT COMPONENTS OF THE COLLECTION MAKE ROUTINE GLOSSES OF THE RECEIVED SCRIPTURES and which ones provide more than minor glosses of the tradition? I discern only routine glosses of a few verses.

[3] CAN WE IDENTIFY A PRONOUNCED BIAS OR A POLEMIC in the utilization of David? David's allusions to Psalms mark him as a pious Israelite. But there are no consequences for the classification of David as a holy man.

[4] HOW IS DAVID COMPARABLE TO OTHER SAGES IN THIS DOCUMENT? David is not a sage of the legal tradition but a pious king. Sifra sets out to validate to the

written Torah as a necessity David is not party to that proposition. He is a standard Israelite and not a distinguished disiple of the sages or otherwise a saint.

4

David in Sifré to Numbers and Sifré Zutta to Numbers

Sifré to Numbers and Sifré Zutta to Numbers follow the program of Scripture and systematically comment on successive verses in the book of Numbers. I discern no exegetical program that predominates. No coherent expositions guide the reading of successive programs. The occasional items on David follow suit.

SIFRÉ TO NUMBERS XLII:III1

A. "...and give you peace:"

B. When you come in, peace, and when you go out, peace, peace with every person.

C. R. Hananiah, prefect of the priests, says, "'...and give you peace:' in your house."

D. R. Nathan says, "'...and give you peace:' this refers to the peace of the house of David, as it is said, 'Of the increase of his government and of peace there will be no end' (Is. 9:6)."

David's successor figures in the exegesis. The house of David is the source of peace. David is not the center of the exposition.

SIFRÉ TO NUMBERS XLVI:II.1.

A. "He gave none to the Kohathites, because the service laid upon them was that of the holy things: these they had to carry themselves on their shoulders" (Num. 7:9):

B. R. Nathan, "On the basis of what is said here we see what David missed, for the Levites did not bear the ark, but they bore the wagon, as it is said, 'They mounted the ark of God on a new cart and conveyed it from the house of Abinadab on the hill' (1 Sam. 6:3).

C.   "'The Lord was angry with Uzzah and struck him down there for his rash act, so he died there beside the ark of God' (2 Sam. 6:7).

D.   "'David was vexed because the Lord's anger had broken out upon Uzzah, and he called the place Perez-uzzah, the name it still bears' (2 Sam 6:8).

E.   "Ahitophel said to David, 'Should you not have learned the lesson of Moses, your master, for the Levites bore the ark only on their shoulders, as it says, "He gave none to the Kohathites, because the service laid upon them was that of the holy things: these they had to carry themselves on their shoulders."'

F.   "Lo, David then sent and had it carried by shoulder, as it is said, 'And David summoned Zadok and Abiathar the priests, together with the Levites, Uriel, Asaiah, Joel, Shemaiah, Eliel, and Amminadab, and said to them, You who are heads of families of the Levites, hallow yourselves, you and your kinsmen, and bring up the ark of the Lord, the God of Israel, to the place which I have prepared for it...So the priests and the Levites hallowed themselves to bring up the ark of the Lord, the God of Israel, and the Levites carried the ark of God, bearing it on their shoulders with poles, as Moses had prescribed at the command of the Lord' (1 Chr. 15:11-15)."

David provides for the transport of the ark.

Sifré to Numbers CXIX:II

1. A.   And the Lord said to Aaron, "You shall have no inheritance in their land" — at the time of the division of the land;

   B.   "neither shall you have any portion among them" — in the spoil.

2. A.   "I am your portion and your inheritance among the people of Israel:"

   K.   Scripture says, "In the house of my dwelling" (Ps. 119:54).

   L.   In caves and traps, and so it says, "When he fled from before Saul in a cave" (Ps. 57:1).

   M.   And so Scripture says, "My soul was in a perpetual quandary, but your Torah have I not forgotten" (Ps. 119:119).

   N.   But once David had studied Torah and found himself at home in it, what does he then say? "More valuable to me is the Torah of your instruction than thousands of pieces of gold and silver" (Ps. 57:72). For gold and silver take a man out of this world and from the world to come, but Torah brings a man into the life of this world and into the life of the world to come.

   O.   That is in line with what is written: "How valuable are your friends, God, how strong are their heads" (Ps. 139:16).

   P.   And it says, "This is the Torah of Lord God" (2 Samuel 7:19).

This final item introduces the theme of Torah-study for David. Knowledge of the Torah brings just rewards. The documentary preference for David's readings of Psalms surfaces here, with a random sample of verses from Psalms: s. 119:54, Ps. 57:1, Ps. 119:119, Ps. 57:72, Ps. 139:16. In Sifra ns the two Sifrés David remaos well within the limits of David as portrayed in Scripture.

SIFRÉ ZUTTA TO NUMBERS

No formal differences mark Sifré Zutta to Numbers apart from Sifré to Numbers.

SIFRÉ ZUTTA TO NUMBERS BEHA 'ALOTEKHA XI:II.I.

4. A. "and the fire of the Lord burned among them:"

B. Rabban Gamaliel says, "Because the Israelites defamed the Holy One, blessed be he, and said, 'Can God set a table in the wilderness?' (Ps. 68:19), the Holy One blessed be he saw that he defamed his honor, and his honor is consuming fire, [so] he sent fire against them and it consumed them, as it is said, 'and the fire of the Lord burned among them.'"

C. From this matter you learn that whoever defames his fellow in secret has no healing, as it is said, "Him who slanders his fellow in secret shall I destroy" (Ps. 101:5).

D. Twelve times fire descended from heaven, six were praiseworthy, and these are they: first, and it came to pass on the eighth day, the second was in the time of Gideon, the third in the time of Manoah, the fourth in the time of David, as it is said, "And he called to the Lord and he answered him in fire from heaven" (1 Chr. 21:26), the fifth in the time of Solomon, as it is said, "And fire came down from heaven" (2 Chr. 7:2), the sixth at Mount Carmel. And six were not praiseworthy, and these are they: the first was in the time of Nadab and Abihu, the second in the time of the complainers, the third in the time of Korach, the fourth in the time of Job, "And the fire of God fell from heaven" (Job 1:16), the fifth and the sixth in the time of Elijah when the messengers of Ahaziah came to him.

David marks an occasion on a list of events.

SIFRÉ ZUTTA TO NUMBERS PINHAS XXVII:XIV:I.I

1 A. "because you rebelled against my word in the wilderness of Zin during the strife of the congregation, to sanctify me at the waters before their eyes:"

B. Moses said before the Omnipresent, "My Lord, how come it is written on what account I was punished?"

C. Said to him the Omnipresent, "I have written that it came about only for nothing, as it is said, 'He still holds fast his integrity although you moved me against him to destroy him without cause' (Job 2:3)."

D.   David said before the Omnipresent, "Do not write down on what account you have exacted a penalty from me."

E.   Said to him the Omnipresent, "It is not worthwhile for you, so that people will not be saying, 'Many transgressions were on David's hands, but the Omnipresent did not write them all down.' But I shall write the matter down, that there was only one, as it is said, 'David did that which was upright in the eyes of the Lord, except only the matter of Uriah the Hittite.'"

David's misdeed is recorded. I see no extension of the narrative,

Sifré Zutta to Numbers Pinhas XXVII:XVII:I.1

1 A.   "who shall go out before them:" that he should not act like the kings of the nations of the world who bring out the troops to battle and go and sit down in their palaces but that will "go forth before them and come in before them," and so Scripture stays of David, "And all Israel and Judah loved David because he went forth before them and came in before them" (1 Sam. 18:15).

B.   "who shall lead them out and bring them in:" that he should not lead out cohorts of ten thousand and bring back remnants of one thousand, lead out thousands and bring back hundreds.

C.   For so Scripture says of David, "In times past when Saul was king over us, it was you that led out and brought in Israel and the Lord said to you, 'You shall be shepherd of people Israel'" (2 Sam. 5:2). Thus what you lead out you bring home.

D.   "that the congregation of the Lord may not be as sheep which have no shepherd:"

The verses of Numbers are clarified but no body of fresh ideas about David emerges.

[1] IS DAVID AN ACTIVE PLAYER OR A ROUTINE AND SCARCELY ANIMATE ONE? David does not define the center of interest of this document. There is no pattern either formal or doctrinal.

[2] WHAT COMPONENTS OF THE COLLECTION MAKE ROUTINE GLOSSES OF THE RECEIVED SCRIPTURES and which ones provide more than minor glosses of the tradition? In dialogue with Ahitophel David makes minor exegetical glosses.

[3] CAN WE IDENTIFY A PRONOUNCED BIAS OR A POLEMIC in the utilization of David? The Rabbinic bias in favor of Torah-study registers in a single passage: "once David had studied Torah and found himself at home in it, what does he then say? "More valuable to me is the Torah of your instruction than thousands of pieces of gold and silver'" (Ps. 57:72).

[4] HOW IS DAVID COMPARABLE TO OTHER SAGES IN THIS DOCUMENT? David in these compilations does not figure in fresh narratives. He registers episodically. No propositions recur. David figures where Scripture introduces him. David does not embody a principal figure or stimulate a protracted inquiry. The miscellaneous

character of Sifré to Numbers and Sifré Zutta to Numbers matches the random quality of the collection of references to David in the same setting. The presentation of large-scale expositions on the theme of David will have to await another generation of exegetes, which will pursue the theme of David far beyond the limits observed in the earlier collections of exegesis,

5

David in Sifré to Deuteronomy

The documentary hypothesis of the Rabbinic canon holds that the document imposes its program on the individual units of discourse compiled therein. Sifré to Deuteronomy presents a striking case of the imposition of a documentary program upon the representation of individual entries. Aiming at the generalization of the particular case, Sifré to Deuteronomy favors the composition of lists of comparable cases. All of them point toward a common pattern. The documentary program thus governs the free standing compositions.

The documentary program of Sifré to Deuteronomy favors transforming cases into generalizations. David is subordinated to a set of generalizations in which several heroic names figure. We find several instances of the documentary dominance over the individual pieces of writing in connection with David in Sifré to Deuteronomy This process is typical of the document. David is only one example of the de-individuation of a named individual. Nor can we suppose all the individuals who contribute generalizations exemplify virtue.

SIFRÉ TO DEUTERONOMY I:I1.

A. "These are the words that Moses spoke to all Israel in Transjordan, in the wilderness, that is to say in the Arabah, opposite Suph, between Paran on the one side and Tophel, Laban, Hazeroth, and Dizahab, on the other" (Dt. 1:1):

4. A. So too you may point to the following:

B. "And these are the last words of David" (2 Sam. 23:1).

C. And did David prophesy only these alone? And has it furthermore not been said, "The spirit of the Lord spoke through me, and his word was on my tongue" (2 Sam. 23:2)?

D. Why then does it say, "And these are the last words of David" (2 Sam. 23:1)?

E.   It teaches that, [when the verse says, "And these are the last words of David" (2 Sam. 23:1)], it refers to words of admonition.

F.   And how do we know that they were words of admonition?

G.   In accord with this verse: "But the ungodly are as thorns thrust away, all of them, for they cannot be taken with the hand" (2 Sam. 23:6).

5. A.   So too you may point to the following:).

B.   "The words of Qohelet, son of David, king in Jerusalem" (Qoh. 1:1).

C.   Now did Solomon prophesy only these words? Did he not write three and a half scrolls of his wisdom in proverbs?

D.   Why then does it say, "The words of Qohelet, son of David, king in Jerusalem" (Qoh. 1:1)?

E.   It teaches that [when the verse says, "The words of Qohelet, son of David, king in Jerusalem" (Qoh. 1:1)], it refers to words of admonition.

F.   And how do we know that they were words of admonition?

G.   In accord with this verse: "The sun also rises, and the sun goes down...the wind goes toward the south and turns around to the north, it turns round continually in its circuit, and the wind returns again – that is, east and west [to its circuits]. All the rivers run into the sea" (Qoh. 1:5-7).

H.   [Solomon] calls the wicked sun, moon, and sea, for [the wicked] have no reward [coming back to them].

A dominant pattern covering a number of scriptural figures, of which I cite only two entries to show the dominance of the pattern over a number of figures.

SIFRÉ TO DEUTERONOMY II:III

1. A.   Another matter concerning the verse, "On the first day of the eleventh month of the fortieth year, [after the defeat of Sihon, king of the Amorites, who ruled in Heshbon, and the defeat at Edrei of Og, king of Bashan, who ruled in Ashtaroth, Moses repeated to the Israelites all the commands that the Lord had given him for them]" (Dt. 1:3-4):

B.   This teaches that he admonished them only when he was near death.

C.   From whom did he learn that lesson? It was from Jacob, who admonished his sons only when he was near death, as it is said, "And Jacob called his sons and said, 'Gather yourselves together, that I may tell you what will happen to you in the end of days'" (Gen. 49:1).

8. A.   So you find in the case of David that he admonished Solomon only when he was near death.

B.   For it says, Now the days of David drew near that he should die, and he commanded Solomon, his son, saying, 'I go the way of all the earth'" (1 Kgs. 2:1).

Here again David contributes the exemplification of a pattern and goes through the motions.

SIFRÉ TO DEUTERONOMY VIII:II.

A. "...to assign the land.

B. "...and to their offspring" refers to their children.

C. "...after them'" (Dt. 1:8) refers to those parts of the land that were conquered by David and Jeroboam.

D. So it is said, "He restored the border of Israel from the entrance of Hamath..." (2 Kgs. 12:25).

David's conquests are casually alluded to.

SIFRÉ TO DEUTERONOMY XXVI:I

1. C. Israel had two truly excellent leaders, Moses and David, king of Israel, and their deeds were sufficient to sustain the whole world. Nonetheless, they pleaded the Holy One, blessed be He, only for naught [but grace, without appealing to their own merit].

D. And that produces an argument *a fortiori*:

E. If these two, whose deeds were sufficient to sustain the whole world, pleaded with the Holy One, blessed be He, only for naught [but grace, without appealing to their own meritorious achievements], one who is only no more than one thousand-thousand-thousandth or ten-thousand-ten-thousandth part of the disciples of their disciples should also plead with the Holy One, blessed be He, only for naught [but grace, without appealing to their own meritorious achievements].

David and Moses are paired.

SIFRÉ TO DEUTERONOMY XXVII:III

1. A. "...to show your servant the first works of your greatness":

B. There are [1] those who called themselves servants, and the Holy One, blessed be He, called them servants, and [2] there are those who called themselves servants, and the Holy One, blessed be He, did not call them servants, and [3] there are those who did not call themselves servants, but the Holy One, blessed be He, called them servants:

[1] C. Abraham called himself a servant: "Do not pass away, I ask, from your servant" (Gen. 18:3), and the Holy One, blessed be He, called him a servant: "For my servant Abrahams sake" (Gen. 26:24).

D. Jacob called himself a servant: "I am not worthy of all the mercies, and of all the truth, which you have shown to your servant" (Gen. 32:11), and God called him a servant: "But you, Israel, my servant" Is. 41:8).

E.   Moses called himself a servant: "To show your servant...," and the Holy One, blessed be He, also called him a servant: "My servant, Moses, is not so" (Num. 12:7).

F.   David called himself a servant: "I am your servant, the son of your servant-girl" (Ps. 116:16), and the Holy One, blessed be He, also called him a servant: "For I will defend this city to save it for my own sake and for the sake of my servant, David" (12 Kgs. 19:34), "And David my servant shall be their prince for ever" (Ez. 37:25).

G.   Isaiah called himself a servant: "And now says the Lord who formed me from the womb to be his servant" (Is. 49:5), and the Holy One, blessed be He, also called him a servant: "Like my servant Isaiah has walked naked and barefoot" (Is. 20:3).

[2]H.   Samuel called himself a servant: "Then Samuel said, 'Speak, for your servant is listening'" (1 Sam. 3:10), but the Holy One, blessed be He, did not call him a servant.

I.   Samson called himself a servant: "You have given this great deliverance by the hand of your servant" (Judges. 115:18), but the Holy One, blessed be He, did not call him servant.

J.   Solomon called himself a servant: "Give your servant, therefore, an understanding heart" (1 Kgs. 3:9), but the Holy One, blessed be He, did not call him servant, but rather made him depend upon his father. David: "For David my servant's sake" (1 Kgs. 11:13).

[3]K.   Job did not call himself a servant, but the Holy One, blessed be He, called him a servant: "You have considered my servant Job?" (Job 2:3).

L.   Joshua did not call himself a servant, but the Holy One, blessed be He, called him a servant: "Joshua the son of Nun, the servant of the Lord, died" (Josh. 24:29).

M.   Caleb did not call himself a servant, but the Holy One, blessed be He, called him a servant: "But my servant, Caleb" (Num. 14:24).

N.   Eliakim did not call himself a servant, but the Holy One, blessed be He, called him a servant: "That I will call my servant Eliakim" (Is. 22:20).

O.   Zerubbabel did not call himself a servant, but the Holy One, blessed be He, called him a servant: "In that day, says the Lord of hosts, will I take you, O Zerubbabel, my servant, son of Shealtiel, and I will make you as a signet, for I have chosen you, says the Lord of hosts" (Hag. 2:23).

P.   Daniel did not call himself a servant, but the Holy One, blessed be He, called him a servant: "O Daniel, servant of the living God" (Dan. 6:21).

Q.   Hananiah, Mishael, and Azariah did not call themselves servants, but the Holy One, blessed be He, called them servants: "Shadrach, Meshach, and Abed-nego, you servants of God Most High, come forth and come here" (Dan. 3:26).

R.   The former prophets did not call themselves servants, but the Holy One, blessed be He, called them servants: "For the Lord God will

do nothing unless he tells his plan to his servants the prophets"
(Amos 3:7).

David figures in a massive and closely patterned construction. The pattern
is repeated for a range of biblical personalities, all of them serving the systematic
program. The same patterning of noteworthy biblical figures is repeated. David is
not distinguished from others in the same pattern. This patterning of biblical saints
treats Dvid as undistinguished but integral,

SIFRÉ TO DEUTERONOMY XXVIII:I.

1. A. "...that good hill country":
   B. Everyone called it "hill country."
   C. Abraham called it hill-country, as it is said, "In the mount where
        the Lord is seen" (Gen. 22:14).
   D. Moses called it hill country, as it is said, "That goodly mountain."
   E. David called it hill country, as it is said, "Who shall ascend the
        mountain of the Lord" (Ps. 24:3).
   F. Isaiah called it hill country, as it is said, "And it shall come to pass
        in the end of days that the mountain of the Lord's house shall be
        established" (Is. 2:2).
   G. The nations called it hill country, as it is said, "And many peoples
        shall go and say, 'Come and let us go up to the mountain of the
        Lord'" (Is. 2:3).

David is a case to make a point common to a number of scriptural figures.
Everyone called the territory "hill country" with the land then joined to a list of
names.

SIFRÉ TO DEUTERONOMY XXXIII:III

1. A. "...upon your heart":
   B. On the basis of this phrase did R. Josiah say, "A person has to
        impose an oath upon his impulse to do evil.
   C. "For so you find that in every setting righteous ones impose an
        oath upon their impulse to do evil.
   D. "In connection with Abraham, Scripture says, 'I have lifted up my
        hand to the Lord, God most high, maker of heaven and earth, that
        I will not take a thread or a shoe-latched nor anything that is yours'
        (Gen. 14:22-23).
   E. "In the case of Boaz: 'Then I will carry out the part of a kinsman to
        you, as the Lord lives, lie down until the morning' (Ruth 3:13).
   F. "In the case of David: 'And David said, "As the Lord lives, no, but
        the Lord shall smite him, or his day shall come to die, or he shall
        go down into battle and be swept away. God forbid me to put my
        hand against the Lord's anointed"' (1 Sam. 26:10-11).
   G. "In the case of Elisha: 'As the Lord lives before whom I stand, I
        shall receive none' (2 Kgs. 5:16).

H.   "And just as the righteous impose an oath upon their impulse to
       do evil that they not do evil, so the wicked impose an oath that
       they do evil: 'As the Lord lives, I will surely run after him and take
       something of him' (2 Kgs. 5:20)."

A variety of cases prove the same proposition. David contributes another
case in the model of Scripture,

Sifré to Deuteronomy LI:I

3. A.   Lo, if they have conquered areas outside of the land, how on the
         basis of Scripture do we know that the religious duties [incumbent
         upon the land] apply there?
   B.   You may construct the following argument: the word "will be" is
         used in one context as well as in the other. Just as the word "will
         be" in the one context indicates that the religious duties do apply,
         so when the word is used here, it indicates that the religious duties
         do apply.
   C.   And if you should say, "Then why did David conquer Aram-naharim
         and Aram-Zobah, where the religious duties do not apply?" you
         may say that David acted not in accord with the law of the Torah.
   D.   The Torah has said only after you have conquered the land of Israel
         will you have the option of conquering areas outside of the land.
   E.   But he did not do it that way. Rather he went and conquered Aram-
         naharim and Aram-Zobah, but the Jebusites, near Jerusalem, he
         did not dispossess.
   F.   Said to him the Omnipresent, "The Jebusites, near your palace,
         you did not dispossess! How are you going to go and conquer
         Aram-naharim and Aram-Zobah?"
4. A.   Along these same lines: "Then sang Moses and the children of
         Israel this song" (Ex. 15:1).
   B.   Moses was covered by the original statement, and why was he
         singled out? To teach that he was worth the rest of them put together.
5. A.   Along these same lines: "And David spoke to the Lord the words
         of this song [in the day that the Lord delivered him out of the hand
         of all his enemies and out of the hand of Saul" (2 Sam. 22:1).
   B.   Saul was covered by the original statement, and why was he singled
         out? To teach that he was worth the rest of them put together.
6. A.   Along these same lines: "There lacked of David's servants nineteen
         men and Assail" (2 Sam. 2:30).
   B.   Assail was covered by the original statement, and why was he
         singled out? To teach that he was as intimidating the rest of them
         put together.

David is in the model of Moses and repeats a familiar pattern.

Sifré to Deuteronomy LXII:I

1. A.	"...but look only to the site that the Lord your God will choose amidst all your tribes " (Dt. 12:5-7):
   B.	Look only to a prophet.
   C.	Is it possible to suppose that you should wait until a prophet instructs you?
   D.	Scripture says, "As his habitation there you are to go."
   E.	Seek and find, and afterward a prophet will instruct you.
2. A.	Along these same lines you find the following in regard to David:
   B.	"Lord, remember for David all his afflictions, how he swore to the Lord and vowed to the Mighty One of Jacob, 'Surely I will not go to the tent of my house nor go up into the bed that is spread for me; I will not give sleep to my eyes nor slumber to my eyelids, until I find out a place for the Lord, a dwelling place for the Mighty One of Jacob'" (Ps. 132:1-5).
   C.	How on the basis of Scripture that he acted only on the instruction of a prophet?
   D.	As it is said, "And Gad came that day to David and said to him, 'Go up, raise an altar to the Lord in the threshing floor of Araunah the Jebusite'" (2 Sam. 24:18).
   E.	And Scripture says, ""Then Solomon began to build the house of the Lord at Jerusalem in Mount Moriah, where the Lord had appeared to David his father, for which provision had been made in the place of David, in the threshing floor of Araunah the Jebusite" (2 Chr. 3:1).

The pattern of scriptural exegesis with David as exemplary repeats itself.

Sifré to Deuteronomy CLXXIII:II

1. A.	"You must be wholehearted with the Lord your God":
   B.	When you are wholehearted, then your share is with the Lord your God.
   C.	And so David said, "But as for me, I will walk in my wholeheartedness, redeem me and be gracious to me" (Ps. 26:112).
   D.	"And as for me, you uphold me because of my wholeheartedness and set me before your face forever" (Ps. 41:13).

David cites Psalms, of which he constitutes a primary author.

Sifré to Deuteronomy CCCVII:II

1. A.	Another comment concerning the verse, "The Rock – [his deeds are perfect. Yes, all his ways are just; a faithful God, never false, true and upright is he]":
2. A.	"...his deeds are perfect":
   B.	What he does is entirely perfect with all those who are in the world, and none may complain against his deeds, even the most minor nitpicking.

C.   Nor may anyone look askance and say, "Why did the generation of the flood drown in water?" "Why did the generation of the tower of Babylon get dispersed to the ends of the world?" "Why did the people of Sodom drown in fire and brimstone?" "Why did Aaron take the priesthood?" "Why did David take the monarchy?" "Why did Korah and his conspiracy get swallowed up by the earth?"

D.   Scripture says, "...his deeds are perfect."

David is one of a list of figures that make the same point. But he is one of a list of dubious characters, and the composite is peculiar.

Sifré to Deuteronomy CCXXXIV:III

1. A.   "...Hosea son of Nun":

    B.   Why do I need this information? And is it not stated in any event, "Moses called Hosea son of Nun Joshua" (Num. 13:16)?

    C.   Why then does it says, "He is Hosea son of Nun"?

    D.   It is to tell you how righteous was Joshua.

    E.   Specifically, I might have supposed that once he was appointed the principal authority, he grew proud. Scripture then says, "...Hosea son of Nun."

    F.   He remained the same Hosea in his righteousness, even though he was appointed the one in charge of sustaining Israel, he remained firm in his righteousness.

2. A.   Along these same lines you may note the following:

    B.   "And Joseph was in Egypt already" (Ex. 1:5).

    C.   Now don't we know that Joseph was already in Egypt? But Scripture serves to tell you the righteousness of Joseph, who was shepherding the flock of his father, and even though he was appointed king in Egypt, he remained Joseph in his righteousness'

3. A.   Along these same lines:

    B.   "David was the youngest" (1 Sam. 13:14).

    C.   Don't we know that David was the youngest? But Scripture serves to tell you the righteousness of David, who was shepherding the flock of his father, and even though he was appointed king over Israel, he remained David in his being the youngest [and modest despite the monarchy].

Here is another example of how David exemplifies a case characteristic of a given rule. Sifré to Deuteronomy favors lists of cases that illustrate a rule in common. In the net entry we have list of ten who were called men of God.

Sifré to Deuteronomy CCCXLII:IV.

1. A   "...the man of God":

    B.   He was one of ten who were called "a man of God."

    C.   Moses was called a man of God: "A prayer of Moses, the man of God" (Ps. 90:1).

D. Elkanah: "And there came a man of God to Eli" (1 Sam. 2:27).
E. Samuel: "Behold now, there is in this city a man of God" (1 Sam. 9:6).
F. David: "According to the commandment of David the man of God" (Neh. 12:24).
G. Shemaiah: "But the word of God came to Shemaiah the man of God saying" (1 Kgs. 12:22).
H. Iddo: "And behold there came a man of God out of Judah by the word of the Lord" (1 Kgs. 13:1).
I. Elijah: "O man of God, I pray you, let me life be precious" (2 Kgs. 1:13).
J. Elisha: "Behold now, I perceive that this is a holy man of God" (2 Kgs. 4:9).
L. Micah: "And a man of God came near and spoke to the king of Israel" (1 Kgs. 20:28).
M. Amoz: "But there came a man of God to him, saying, 'O king, let not the army of Israel go with you'" (2 Chr. 25:7).

The catalogue of men of God encompasses David, The list is not particularly distinguished except for the title common to all of the entries.

Sifré to Deuteronomy CCCXLIII:I

3. A. So too King David commenced by praising the Omnipresent: "Hallelujah, sing to the Lord a new song" (Ps. 149:1).
   B. Then he commenced praising Israel too: "For the Lord has taken pleasure in his people" (Ps. 149:4).
   C. And he concluded with praise of the Omnipresent: "Praise God in his sanctuary" (Ps. 150:1).
4. A. So too Solomon his son commenced by praising the Omnipresent: "There is no God like you in heaven or on earth, who keeps the agreement and mercy" (2 Chr. 6:14).
   B. Then he commenced praising Israel too: ""If there is famine in the land" (2 Chr. 6:28).
   C. And he concluded with praise of the Omnipresent: "Now, therefore, arise O Lord God, to your resting place" (2 Chr. 6:41).

David and his son follow the same pattern — praise God, Israel, God. David is not singled out but rather Solomon and David are linked to a common program. David is the opposite of a unique figure. He exhibits a common pattern.

Sifré to Deuteronomy CCCXLIV:II

1. A "...their hallowed are all in your hand":
   B. These are the ones who sustain Israel, who are ready to give their lives for Israel.
   C. Concerning Moses Scripture says, "And now, if you will forgive their sin – but if not, blot me out of the book that you have written" (Ex. 32:32).

D.   In the case of David: "Is it not I that commanded the people to be
numbered?...[Let your hand, I ask, Lord my God, be against me
and against my father's house but not against your people]" (1
Chr. 21:17).

David once more invokes by exhibiting traits in common for taxonomic
purposes.

SIFRÉ TO DEUTERONOMY CCCXLVIII:IV

1. A.   "And this he said of Judah: [Hear, O Lord, the voice of Judah]":
   B.   This teaches that Moses prayed in behalf of David, king of Israel,
and said before him, "Lord of the age, whenever David, king of
Israel, is embroiled in anguish and prays before you, you raise him
up from that suffering."
2. A.   "...and restore him to his people":
   B.   That you bring him back in peace to his brethren.
3. A.   "Though his own hands strive for him":
   B.   when he killed Goliath.
4. A.   "...help him against his foes":
   B.   when he said, "I lift up my eyes to the hills, whence will my help
come?" (Ps. 121:1).

The interpretation of the cited verses presents no surprises,

SIFRÉ TO DEUTERONOMY CCCXLVIII:V

1 A.   "And this he said of Judah: [Hear, O Lord, the voice of Judah]":
   B.   This teaches that Moses prayed in behalf of the kings of the house
of David, and said before him, "Lord of the age, whenever the
kings of the house of David are embroiled in anguish and prays
before you, you raise him up from that suffering."

SIFRÉ TO DEUTERONOMY CCCLVII:I

1. A.   ["Moses went up from the steppes of Moab to Mount Nebo:"
2. A.   "...from the steppes of Moab":
   B.   This teaches that the Holy One, blessed be He, showed him the
dynasty of kings that was destined to derive from Ruth the Moabite,
that is, David and his seed.

SIFRÉ TO DEUTERONOMY CCCLVII:V

9. A.   Another teaching concerning the phrase, "...the whole land of
Judah":
   B.   This teaches that he showed him David in the time of his reign.
   C.   For it is said, "And all the land of Judah," and elsewhere: "Howbeit
the Lord, the God of Israel, chose me out of all the house of my
father to be king over all Israel for ever..." (1 Chr. 28:4).

Moses matches David.

[1] IS DAVID AN ACTIVE PLAYER OR A ROUTINE AND SCARCELY ANIMATE ONE? What registers here is the preference of Sifré to Deuteronomy to the classification of common traits of lists of things. David is not an active player but only marginally animate one. David is the outcome of the examination of Scripture and the identification of compositions of parallel facts.

[2] WHAT COMPONENTS OF THE COLLECTION MAKE ROUTINE GLOSSES OF THE RECEIVED SCRIPTURES and which ones provide more than minor glosses of the tradition? The demonstration of general propositions is the outcome of the documentary program. David loses all specificity and serves as an instrument of Scripture's patterns.

[3] CAN WE IDENTIFY A PRONOUNCED BIAS OR A POLEMIC in the utilization of David? David does not emerge as the embodiment of a particular principle.

[4] HOW IS DAVID COMPARABLE TO OTHER SAGES IN THIS DOCUMENT? He is comparable to Moses. And the traits in common are specified in Scripture's parallels. That is not the outcome of the program of sages but of the program of Scripture. The best example produces the following: There are [1] those who called themselves servants, and the Holy One, blessed be He, called them servants, and [2] there are those who called themselves servants, and the Holy One, blessed be He, did not call them servants, and [3] there are those who did not call themselves servants, but the Holy One, blessed be He, called them servants.

Sifré to Deuteronomy signals its program of generalization with such formulas as "in every setting" and "Along these same lines you may note the following." To generalize: these lists of traits in common prove propositions through the repetition of traits and function in Sifré to Deuteronomy. They register instances in which David participates in a list of probative cases in common. Some of the combinations are odd.

6

David in Mekhilta Attributed to R. Ishmael

Studies elsewhere have shown that Mekhilta deR. Ishmael does not offer support to the documentary hypothesis. But Mekhilta deR. Ishmael does make room for formalization of language and for propositional compositions. The question is, is the process that builds rabbis out of prophets or holy men in operation here?

MEKHILTA DER. ISHMAEL I:I

2. A. Now before the land of Israel was selected, all lands were suitable for acts of speech. But once the land of Israel was selected, all of the other lands were excluded.

   B. Before Jerusalem was selected, all of the land of Israel was suitable for altars. Once Jerusalem was selected, the rest of the land of Israel was excluded [for that purpose],

   C. as it is said, "Take heed not to offer your burnt offerings in every place that you see but only in the place which the Lord shall choose" (Dt. 12:13-14).

   D. Before the eternal house was selected, Jerusalem was suitable for the Divine Presence. Once the eternal house was selected, the rest of Jerusalem was excluded,

   E. as it is said, "For the Lord has chosen Zion, he has desired it for his habitation. This is my resting place for ever" (Ps. 132:13-14).

   F. Before Aaron was chosen, all Israelites were suitable for acts of priestly service. Once Aaron was chosen, the other Israelites were excluded from performing acts of priestly service,

   G. as it is said, "It is an eternal covenant, signified by salt, before the Lord, with you and with your descendants with you" (Num. 18:19; "And it shall belong to him and to his descendants afterward, the covenant of an eternal priesthood" (Num. 2:13).

H.   Before David was chosen, all Israelites were suitable to assume
     the throne. Once David was chosen, the rest of the Israelites were
     excluded,
I.   as it is said, "Should you not know that the Lord, God of Israel,
     handed the kingdom over Israel to David forever, even to him and
     his sons by a covenant signified by salt" (2 Chr. 13:5).

A rigid pattern imposes on a series of examples a particular proposition.
Conforming to the form and supplying a propositional statement in the same pattern
as other sages, David is one of many instances of the same phenomenon.

Mekhilta deR. Ishmael I.I.
8. A.   And so you find that the patriarchs and prophets gave their lives
        for Israel.
   B.   What is said in connection with Moses? "Yet now, if you will
        forgive their sin...and if not, blot me out, I ask, of the book which
        you have written" (Ex. 32:32); "And if you deal this way with me,
        kill me, I ask, right away, and do not let me see my wretchedness"
        (Num. 11:15).
   C.   "And David spoke to the Lord when he saw the angel that smote
        the people and said, 'Lo, I have sinned and done iniquitously, but
        these sheep — what have they done? Let your hand, I ask, go
        against me and against my father's house'" (2 Sam. 24:17).
   D.   Lo, in every passage you find that the patriarchs and prophets gave
        their lives for Israel.

David is once more comparable to Moses, and the governing generalization
is articulated.

Mekhilta deR. Ishmael LXXV:I.
5. G   Guarding is noted in regard to Israel: "Behold, he who guards
        Israel neither slumbers nor sleeps" (Ps. 121:4), and guarding is
        noted in regard to strangers: "The Lord guards the strangers" (Ps.
        146:9).
   H.   Abraham called himself a stranger: "I am a stranger and a sojourner
        with you" (Gen. 23:4).
   I.   David called himself a stranger: "I am a stranger in the earth" (Ps.
        119:19); "For we are strangers before you and sojourners, as all
        our fathers were; our days on the earth are as a shadow and there is
        no abiding" (1 Chr. 29:15); "For I am a stranger with you, a
        sojourner, as all my fathers were" (Ps. 39:13).

David is now comparable to Abraham. A clear pattern governs both cases.

Mekhilta deR. Ishmael LXXV:I.

6. A.   R. Nathan says, "Greater is the covenant that was made with Jonadab b. Rahab than the one made with David.

B.   "For the covenant made with David was made with him only conditionally: 'If your children keep my covenant' (Ps. 132:12), and if not: 'Then I will visit their transgression with the rod' (Ps. 89:33).

C.   "But the covenant made with Jonadab b. Rechab was not conditional: 'To the Rechabites Jeremiah said, "These are the words of the Lord of Hosts, the God of Israel: 'Because you have kept the command of Jonadab your ancestor and obeyed all his instructions and carried out all that he told you to do, therefore these are the words of the Lord of Hosts, the God of Israel: Jonadab son of Rahab shall not want a descendant to stand before me for all time"'' (Jer. 35:18-19)."

3. A.   "and recite it in the ears of Joshua:"

B.   "This indicates that on that day Joshua was anointed," the words of R. Joshua.

C.   R. Eleazar the Modiite says, "This is one of four righteous men to whom a hint [of what was coming] was given. Two of them perceived, and two of them did not perceive it.

D.   "To Moses a hint was given, but he did not perceive it.

E.   "To Jacob a hint was given, but he did not perceive it.

F.   "To David and Mordecai hints were given, and they perceived them."

34. A.   "To David a hint was given, and he did perceive it:"

B.   "Your servant smote both the lion and the bear" (1 Sam. 17:36):

C.   Thought David, "Why am I so special that I could smite these noxious beasts? It is because in the future something is going to happen to Israel and they are destined to be rescued by me."

35. A.   "To Mordecai a hint was given, and he did perceive it:"

B.   "And Mordecai walked every day" (Est. 2:11):

C.   Mordecai thought, "Is it possible that that pious woman should be married to a wicked, uncircumcised man such as that! It is because in the future something is going to happen to Israel and they are destined to be rescued by her."

Jonadab b. Rahab is compared with David.

Mekhilta deR. Ishmael XLIV:I.

1. A. "And the Lord said to Moses, 'Write this as a memorial in a book:"

3. A.   "and recite it in the ears of Joshua:"

B.   "This indicates that on that day Joshua was anointed," the words of R. Joshua.

C.   R. Eleazar the Modiite says, "This is one of four righteous men to whom a hint [of what was coming] was given. Two of them perceived, and two of them did not perceive it.

D. "To Moses a hint was given, but he did not perceive it.

E. "To Jacob a hint was given, but he did not perceive it.

F. "To David and Mordecai hints were given, and they perceived them."

4. A. "To David a hint was given, and he did perceive it:"

B. "Your servant smote both the lion and the bear" (1 Sam. 17:36):

C. Thought David, "Why am I so special that I could smite these noxious beasts? It is because in the future something is going to happen to Israel and they are destined to be rescued by me."

35. A. "To Mordecai a hint was given, and he did perceive it:"

B. "And Mordecai walked every day" (Est. 2:11):

C. Mordecai thought, "Is it possible that that pious woman should be married to a wicked, uncircumcised man such as that! It is because in the future something is going to happen to Israel and they are destined to be rescued by her."

Moses, Jacob, David and Mordecai form a list of names with shared traits.

MEKHILTA deR. ISHMAEL XXVI:I.

1. A. "Then [Moses and the people of Israel sang this song to the Lord, saying, 'I will sing to the Lord, for he has triumphed gloriously; the horse and his rider he has thrown into the sea]:"

I. the seventh said by David: "And David spoke to the Lord the words of this song" (2 Sam. 22:1);

J. the eighth, said by Solomon: "A Psalm, a song at the dedication of the house of David" (Ps. 30:1). [The catalogue is now interrupted for an exposition of this matter. It resumes below, No. 10.]

6. A. Now did David build it? Did not Solomon build it, as it is said, "And Solomon built the house and finished it" (1 Kgs. 6:14).

B. So why does Scripture say, ""A Psalm, a song at the dedication of the house of David" (Ps. 30:1)?

C. Since David was prepared to give his life for the project to build it, it was named for him, and so Scripture says, "Lord, remember for David all his affliction, how he swore to the Lord and vowed to the Mighty One of Jacob, Surely I will not come into the tent of my house...until I find out a place for the Lord...Lo, we heard of it as being in Ephrath" (Ps. 132:1-6).

D. And elsewhere: "Now, see to your own house, David" (1 Kgs. 12:16).

E. Accordingly, since David was prepared to give his life for the project to build it, it was named for him.

7. A. And so you find that any matter for which a person is prepared to give his life is named for him.

14. A. "I will sing to the Lord, for he has triumphed gloriously:"

B. "Greatness is fitting for the Lord, might is fitting for the Lord, glory and victory and majesty are fitting for the Lord."

    C.   So David says, "To the Lord are greatness, might, glory and victory and majesty" (1 Chr. 29:11).

16. A.   "I will sing to the Lord:"

    B.   for he is excellent, praiseworthy, and none is like him: "For who in the skies can be compared to the Lord...a God dread in the great 'council of the holy ones" (Ps. 89:7-8); "O Lord, God of hosts, who is a might one like you" (Ps. 89:9).

    C.   What is the sense of "hosts"?

    D.   He is the ensign among his host.

    E.   So too: "And he came from the myriads holy" (Dt. 33:3), meaning, he is the ensign among his holy myriads.

    F.   And so David says, "There is none like you, among the gods, O Lord" (Ps. 86:8), "My beloved is white and ruddy...his head is as the most fine gold...his eyes are like doves...his cheeks are as a bed of spices...his hands are as rods of gold...his legs are as pillars of marble" (Song 5:10-15).

The generalization takes up several illustrative cases and yields an eternal truth.

[1] Is DAVID AN ACTIVE PLAYER OR A ROUTINE AND SCARCELY ANIMATE ONE?

David in Mekhilta serves as participant in a number of composites. He has traits in common with other biblical figures. He is important because he is like others, not because he is different from to them. All of them prove the same proposition and contribute to the same demonstration. He is not an active player. No Rabbinic figure differs. Mekhilta wants all the different figures to share in equal terms in the governing system.

[2] WHAT COMPONENTS OF THE COLLECTION MAKE ROUTINE GLOSSES OF THE RECEIVED SCRIPTURES and which ones provide more than minor glosses of the tradition?

This is not a relevant question, because David's role is not to comment on received verses of Scripture and their exegesis The named authorities of the Mekhilta share a common burden.

[3] CAN WE IDENTIFY A PRONOUNCED BIAS OR A POLEMIC in the utilization of David?

No, the Rabbinization of David is not what is at issue. He cites scriptural proof-texts like other sages, and he set forth propositions endorsed by other ages,

[4] HOW IS DAVID COMPARABLE TO OTHER SAGES IN THIS DOCUMENT? The propositions endorsed or illustrated by sages in Mekhilta deR. Ishmael are common to David and Moses, "Before David was chosen, all Israelites were suitable to assume the throne. Once David was chosen, the rest of the Israelites were excluded." The norm derives from the comparison of Abraham and David or Moses and David.

We cannot speak here of a *Rabbi* David. The figure of David remained in its scriptural model. More to the point, David is not an important figure in Mekhilta deR. Ishmael. In this document David occurs episodically. There is no sustained effort to Rabbinize of the figure of David. We must call into question the notion that the Rabbinic sages of Mekhilta deR. Ishmael conducted a systematic program of exegesis and transformed the scriptural figures into something they defined in their model.

7

David in Genesis Rabbah

Genesis Rabbah provides comments on the book of Genesis, verse by verse. No exegetical program encompasses the figure of David, all we find are miscellaneous observations. I discern no Rabbinic polemic — of any other polemic for that matter.

3. A.   [Contrasting the fear and dread of animals for living persons with their indifference to corpses,] R. Simeon b. Eleazar taught on Tannaite authority: "In the case of a one-day-old infant, people violate the Sabbath on his account [to save his life]. But in the case even of David, king of Israel, lying dead, people may not violate the Sabbath on his account."

The allusion to the dead David contains no message particular to David. Any number of others can serve for the same purpose. David is chosen to introduce a great name in Israelite life.

1. A.   R. Yudan and R. Aibu in the name of R. Yohanan: "Two men said the same thing, Abraham and David.
   B.   "Abraham said, "'O Lord God'" (Gen. 15:2). He said before him, 'Lord of the age, If I am going to produce children who will cause you anger, it is better for me "that I go childless" (Gen. 15:2).'
   C.   "David said, "'Search me God and know my heart, try me and know my thoughts" (Ps. 139:23). Know my branches. [Thus the word for thoughts is read as the word for branches.] "See if there be any way in me that is grievous, and lead me in the way

39

everlasting" (Ps. 139:24). Lord of the Universe, If I am going to produce children who will cause you anger, it is better for me that you lead me in the everlasting path [of death].'"

David goes over the same ground as Abraham.

GENESIS RABBAH XXXIX:X.

1. A. R. Berekhiah b. R. Simon in the name of R. Nehemiah: "The matter may be compared to the case of a king who was traveling from place to place, and a pearl fell out of his crown. The king stopped there and held up his retinue there, collected sand in heaps and brought sieves. He had the first pile sifted and did not find the pearl. So he did with the second and did not find it. But in the third heap he found it. People said, 'The king has found his pearl.'

   B. "So said the Holy One, blessed be he, to Abraham, 'Why did I have to spell out the descent of Shem, Arpachshad, Shelah, Eber, Peleg, Reu, Serug, Nahor, and Terah? Was it not entirely for you?'

   C. "'And he *found* his heart faithful before you' (Neh. 9:8). [Freedman, p. 319, n. 2: He was the pearl that God found.]

   D. "So said the Holy One, blessed be he, to David, 'Why did I have to spell out the descent of Perez, Hezron, Ram, Aminadab, Nachshon, Shalomon, Boaz, Obed, and Jesse? Was it not entirely for you?'

   E. "Thus: 'I have *found* David my servant, with my holy oil have I anointed him' (Ps. 89:21)."

David is once again compared to Abraham, and the motif is established that David like Abraham relies upon genealogy for authority.

GENESIS RABBAH XXXIX:XI.

5. A. R. Berekhiah in the name of R. Helbo: "[The promise that God will make Abram great] refers to the fact that his coinage had circulated in the world.

   B. "There were four whose coinage circulated in the world.

   C. "Abraham: 'And I will make you' (Gen. 12:2). And what image appeared on his coinage? An old man and an old woman on the obverse side, a boy and a girl on the reverse [Abraham, Sarah, Isaac and Rebekah].

   D. "Joshua: 'So the Lord was with Joshua and his fame was in all the land' (Josh. 6:27). That is, his coinage circulated in the world. And what image appeared on his coinage? An ox on the obverse, a wild-ox on the reverse: 'His firstling bullock, majesty is his, and his horns are the horns of a wild ox' (Deut 33:17). [Joshua descended from Joseph.]

   E. "David: 'And the fame of David went out into all lands' (1 Chr. 14:17). That is, his coinage circulated in the world. And what image appeared on his coinage? A staff and a wallet on the obverse, a

tower on the reverse: 'Your neck is like the tower of David, built
with turrets' (Song 4:4).

F.   "Mordecai: 'For Mordecai was great in the king's house, and his
fame went forth throughout all the provinces' (Est. 9:4). That is,
his coinage circulated in the world. And what image appeared on
his coinage? Sackcloth and ashes on the obverse, a golden crown
on the reverse."

Abraham, Joshua, David, and Mordecai share the trait of fame. The point
that names circulate like coins is attached to the four names.

GENESIS RABBAH LXIII:VIII.

1. A.   "When her days to be delivered were fulfilled, [behold, there were
twins in her womb. The first came forth red, all his body like a
hairy mantle, so they called his name Esau. Afterward his brother
came forth, and his hand had taken hold of Esau's heel, so his
name was called Jacob. Isaac was sixty years old when she bore
them]"(Gen. 25:24-26)
6. A.   "The first came forth red:"
   B.   R. Abba bar Kahana, "[He was red] because he was entirely a
shedder of blood.
   C.   "When Samuel saw that David was red, as it is written, 'And he
sent and brought him in. Now he was ruddy' (1 Sam. 16:12), he
feared, saying, perhaps this one too is a shedder of blood.
   D.   "Said the Holy One, blessed be he, to him, 'Withal of beautiful
eyes' (1 Sam. 16:12), that is to say, Esau killed out of his own will
and consent, but this one puts people to death only upon the decision
of the sanhedrin."

The comparison of Esau and David is that both men were ruddy. But
David's was a virtuous ruddiness, and that distinguished him from Esau.

GENESIS RABBAH LXVII:VIII.

1. A.   "Now Esau hated Jacob [because of the blessing with which his
father had blessed him, and Esau said to himself, 'The days of
mourning for my father are approaching; then I will kill my brother
Jacob]'" (Gen. 27:41):
2. A.   "...and Esau said to his heart:"
   B.   [Reading the word "to his heart" to refer to someone in control of
his heart, we interpret as follows:] The wicked exist subject to the
domain of their heart.
   C.   "The fool has said *in* his heart" (Ps. 14:1). "And Esau said *in* his
heart" (Gen. 27:41). "And Jeroboam said in *his* heart" (1 Kgs.
12:25). "Now Haman said *in* his heart" (Est. 6:6).
   D.   But the righteous maintain their heart subject to their domain
[speaking *to* their heart, as God does, and telling their heart what
to do, rather than be governed by their heart's impulses, thus]:

E.   "Now Hannah spoke upon her heart" (1 Sam. 1:13). "And David said to his heart" (1 Sam. 27:1). "But Daniel placed upon his heart" (Dan. 1:8).

F.   "And the Lord said to his heart" (Gen. 8:21).

Hannah, David and Daniel share in common the power to govern their thoughts rather than being governed by them.

GENESIS RABBAH LXXV:I. 1.

C.   R. Phineas in the name of R. Reuben said, "There are five passages in the first book of Psalms in which David asks the Holy One, blessed be he, to rise: 'Arise O Lord, save me O my god' (Ps. 3:8); 'Arise, O Lord, in your anger' (Ps. 7:7); 'Arise, O Lord, O God, lift up your hand' (Ps. 10:12); 'Arise, O Lord, let not man prevail' (Ps. 9:20).

D.   "'Arise, O Lord, confront him:'

E.   "Said the Holy One, blessed be he, to him, 'David, my son, even if you ask me to rise a thousand times, I shall not arise. When shall I arise? When you see the poor oppressed and the needy groaning.'

F.   "'For the oppression of the poor, for the sighing of the needy, now I will arise, says the Lord' (Ps. 12:6)."

God responds not to the pleading of man but to the sighing of the poor. Ps. 3:8, 7:7, 10:12, and 9:20 are invoked.

GENESIS RABBAH LXXVIII:XIII.

1. A.   "[Then Esau said, 'Let us journey on our way, and I will go before you.'] But Jacob said to him, 'My lord knows [that the children are frail, and that the flocks and herds giving suck are a care to me; and if they are overdriven for one day, all the flocks will die. Let my lord pass on before his servant, and I will lead on slowly, according to the pace of the cattle which are before me and according to the pace of the children, until I come to my lord in Seir']" (Gen. 33:12-14):

B.   Said R. Berekhiah, "'My lord knows that the children are frail' refers to Moses and Aaron.

E.   R. Berekhiah in the name of R. Levi: "'My lord knows that the children are frail' speaks of David and Solomon.

Moses and Aaron compare with David and Solomon.

GENESIS RABBAH LXXIX:VII.

1. A.   "And from the sons of Hamor, Shechem's father, he bought for a hundred pieces of money the piece of land on which he had pitched

his tent. There he erected an altar and called it El-Elohe-Israel"
(Gen. 33:19-20):

B. Said R. Yudan bar Simon, "This is one of three passages on the basis of which the nations of the world cannot ridicule Israel, saying, 'You have stolen property.'

C. "They are, first, the cave at Machpelah, second, the site of the Temple, and third, the sepulchre of Joseph.

D. "The cave at Machpelah: 'And Abraham weighed to Ephron the silver' (Gen. 23:16).

E. "...second, the site of the Temple: 'So David gave to Ornan for the place six hundred shekels of gold' (1 Chr. 21:25).

F. "...and third, the sepulchre of Joseph: 'he bought for a hundred pieces of money the piece of land on which he had pitched his tent.'"

David bought the land for the temple.

[1] Is DAVID AN ACTIVE PLAYER OR A ROUTINE AND SCARCELY ANIMATE ONE? David is not a particularly animate voice. There is no effort at telling stories about an active hero. David stands for a deceased monarch, he is party to a list along with Abraham, Mordecai, Hannah, David and Daniel. All this is random.

[2] WHAT COMPONENTS OF THE COLLECTION MAKE ROUTINE GLOSSES OF THE RECEIVED SCRIPTURES and which ones provide more than minor glosses of the tradition? Typical of a minor gloss is the reading of Moses and Aaron with David and Solomon. I find no evidence of a systematic program of exegesis of David's record,

[3] CAN WE IDENTIFY A PRONOUNCED BIAS OR A POLEMIC in the utilization of David? David is an established hero, but his role as the progenitor of the Messiah scarcely pays a part in the reading of Scriopture,

[4] HOW IS DAVID COMPARABLE TO OTHER SAGES IN THIS DOCUMENT? David is not comparable to any of the sages in Genesis Rabbah. He is preserved in his scriptural narrative role.

8

David in Leviticus Rabbah

Leviticus Rabbah presents propositional compositions and registers these propositions through selective exegesis. It does not engage in verse-by-verse exegesis in the manner of Genesis Rabbah let alone Sifra and the two Sifrés. It establishes a proposition and proves its validity. David speaks through Psalms in this document. Ps. 89:20, establishes the initial focus of exposition. Ps. 51:19-21 defines the next one.

LEVITICUS RABBAH I:IV

1. A.   R. Abin in the name of R. Berekhiah the Elder opened [discourse by citing the following verse]: "Of old you spoke in a vision to your faithful ones, saying, "I have set the crown upon one who is mighty, I have exalted one chosen from the people" [Ps. 89:20].

4. A.   ["I have exalted one chosen from the people" (Ps. 89:20)] speaks of David, with whom God spoke both in speech and in vision.

   B.   That is in line with the following verse of Scripture: "In accord with all these words and in accord with this entire vision, so did Nathan speak to David" (2 Sam. 7:17).

   C.   "To your faithful one" (Ps. 89:20) [refers] to David, [in line with the following verse:] "Keep my soul, for I am faithful" (Ps. 86:2).

   D.   " . . . saying, I have set the crown upon one who is mighty," (Ps. 89:20) —

   E.   R. Abba bar Kahana and rabbis:

   F.   R. Abba bar Kahana said, "David made thirteen wars."

   G.   And rabbis say, "Eighteen."

   H.   But they do not really differ. The party who said thirteen wars [refers only to those that were fought] in behalf of the need of Israel [overall], while the one who held that [he fought] eighteen

includes five [more, that David fought] for his own need, along
with the thirteen [that he fought] for the need of Israel [at large].

I.   "I have exalted one chosen from the people" (Ps. 89:20) — "And
he chose David, his servant, and he took him . . . " (Ps. 78:70).

5. A.   ["Of old you spoke in a vision to your faithful one . . . "] speaks of
Moses, with whom [God] spoke in both speech and vision, in line
with the following verse of Scripture: "With him do I speak mouth
to mouth [in a vision and not in dark speeches]" (Num. 12:8).

Psalm 89 has God speak of David and Moses. The dispute of E introduces
a trivial question.

LEVITICUS RABBAH VII:II

1. A.   "[O Lord, open my lips, and my mouth shall show forth your praise.
For you have no delight in sacrifice; were I to give a burnt offering,
you would not be pleased.] The sacrifice acceptable to God is a
broken spirit, [a broken and contrite heart, O God, you will not
despise. Do good to Zion in your good pleasure; rebuild the walls
of Jerusalem, then will you delight in right sacrifices, in burnt
offerings and whole burnt offerings; then bulls will be offered on
your altar" (Ps. 51:19-21 [RSV: 15-19]).

B.   Zabdi [Zebedee] son of Levi and R. Yosé b. Petros [Peter] and
rabbis:

C.   The first of them [Zabdi] said, "David said before the Holy One,
blessed be he, Lord of the world, If you accept me back as a penitent
[of my sin with Bath Sheba], then I shall know that Solomon, my
son, will build the house of the sanctuary and will build the altar
and offer on it all of the sacrifices specified in the Torah.

D.   "[And it was from] the following verse of Scripture [that he derived
the answer]: The sacrifice acceptable to God is a broken spirit. "
[So God did accept David s penitence.]

E.   The second [Yosé] said, "How do we know concerning one who
has repented [his sin], that [Scripture] credits it to him as if he had
gone up to Jerusalem, rebuilt the house of the sanctuary, built the
altar, and offered on it all of the sacrifices that are specified in the
Torah?

F.   "It is from the following verse of Scripture: The sacrifice acceptable
to God is a broken spirit. "

G   And rabbis say, "How do we know that the one who goes before
the ark [to lead the congregation in prayer] must make mention of
the Temple service and kneel [at that point], as is done in saying
this blessing: Accept, O Lord, our God and dwell in, Zion, your
city?

H.   "There is he who wishes to derive the answer from the verse: The
sacrifice acceptable to God is a broken spirit, [a broken and contrite
heart, O God, you will not despise. Do good to Zion in your good
pleasure; rebuild the walls of Jerusalem, then will you delight in
right sacrifices . . .] [The kneeling signifies the broken heart.]"

David speaks in Psalms. David established an agreement that showed God accepted David s penitence. He found the answer in Psalms.

LEVITICUS RABBAH X:VII.

1. A. "[And David put his hand in his bag and took out a stone and slung it and struck the Philistine on his forehead; the stone sank into his forehead], and he fell on his face to the ground" (1 Sam. 17:49).

B. Why was it on his face?

C. In the first place, you may explain that it was so that that righteous man, [David], should not have to take the trouble to walk [the length of the body], six cubits and a span.

2. W. They further objected, "And it came to pass that David was successful in all his ways, and the Lord was with him" (1 Sam. 18:14).

X. He said to them, "This too does not signify good fortune. For on that account: And Saul eyed David from that day onward " (1 Sam. 18:9).

Y. They further objected, "And it came to pass that the king dwelt in his palace, and the Lord gave him rest round about" (2 Sam. 7:1).

Z. He said to them, "This too does not signify good fortune. On that very day, Nathan the prophet came to him and said, You will not build the house " (1 Kgs. 8:19).

AA. They said to him, "We have given our [objections]. Now give your [proofs about good fortune]."

BB. He said to them, " And it shall come to pass on that day that a man will keep alive a young cow and two sheep, [and because of the abundance of milk which they give, he will eat curds] [Is. 7:21]. And it shall come to pass in that day that living waters shall go out of Jerusalem [Zech. 14:8]. And it shall come to pass that he will be like a tree planted on streams of water [Ps. 1:3]. And it shall come to pass that he will be like a tree planted by water [Jer. 17:8]. And it shall come to pass that the remnant of Jacob shall be in the midst of many peoples [as dew from the Lord, as showers upon the grass] [Mic. 5:6]. [All of these usages signify good fortune.]"

Here we find a series of exegeses of narratives on David drawn from Scripture, the first ambitious exegesis of the scriptural narrative on David. But there is no coherent and programmed message, only a series of free-standing glosses of verses of Scripture.

LEVITICUS RABBAH XX:I.

4. A. "As to the good man, so is the sinner [and he who swears is as he who shuns an oath]" (Qoh. 9:2).

B. "As to the good man" refers to David: "And he sent and brought him, and he was ruddy, with a lovely face, and good appearance" (1 Sam. 16:12).

C.   Said R. Isaac, " He was of good appearance in knowledge of the law, for whoever looked upon him would remember what he had learned."

D.   "So is the sinner" refers to Nebuchadnezzar: "Break off your sin through righteousness" (Dan. 4:24).

E.   This one [David] built the house of the sanctuary and ruled for forty years, while that one destroyed it and ruled for forty-five years.

F.   Is it not the case of a single fate[s affecting them both]?

5. A.   ["And he who swears is as he who shuns an oath" (Qoh. 9:2).] "He who swears" refers to Zedekiah: "And he also rebelled against King Nebuchadnezzar" (2 Chron. 36:13).

B.   "As he who shuns an oath" (Qoh. 9:3) refers to Samson: "And Samson said to them, You take an oath to me " (Jud. 15:12).

C.   This one died with his eyes having been put out, and that one died with his eyes having been put out.

D.   Is it not the case of a single fate s affecting them both?

A verse of Scripture is applied to David in a conventional composition. Of greater interest: we have a sizable systematic exposition of a narrative of David. The exegetical approach is subordinate and the systematic one is paramount. The encounter with Goliath defines the program and continues to.

LEVITICUS RABBAH XXI:II.

1. A.   R. Samuel b. R. Nahman interpreted [the intersecting verse to speak of] the Philistines:

B.   " When evildoers drew near me [Ps. 27:2] refers to Goliath: And the Philistine drew near morning and night [1 Sam. 17:16].

C.   "And it is written, And the Philistine came on and drew near to David [1 Sam. 17:41].

D.   " To eat my flesh [Ps. 27:2]: The Philistine said to David, "Come to me, and I will give your flesh to the birds of the air and to the beasts of the field" " (1 Sam. 17:44).

2. A.   R. Abba b. R. Kahana said, "[Goliath had to tell David to come to him because] the earth held him fast."

B.   R. Tanhuma said, "I shall give scriptural proof for that proposition. And I shall come to you is not what is written here, rather: Come to me. That teaches that the earth held him fast."

C.   R. Yannai in the name of R. Simeon b. R. Yannai: "The Holy One, blessed be he, put two hundred forty-eight locks on his two hundred forty-eight limbs."

D.   At that moment David said, " Do not, O Lord, grant the desires of the wicked [Ps. 140:8]. Do not grant him his lust.

E.   " Do not let loose his bit [Ps. 140:8]. Do not unloose it.

F.   " May they be high, <u>sela (ib.)</u>. Strengthen his bond [so that he cannot get loose]. "

G. R. Yudan said, "[Goliath] wanted David, because he had lovely eyes and was handsome. Thereupon David said, Do not, O Lord, grant the desires of the wicked [Ps. 140:8] — his lust. But he will give the desire of the righteous " (Prov. 10:24).

H. And rabbis say, "He smote him with leprosy, as you find in Scripture: He said, This day will the Lord shut you up through my hand [1 Sam. 17:46]. And the words shut up refers only to leprosy, as you find in the verse: And the priest will shut up one afflicted by a leprosy sign " (Lev. 13:4).

3. A. [Samuel b. R. Nahman continues:] " My adversaries and foes, they stumbled and fell [Ps. 27:2]: And the stone sank into his forehead, and he fell [1 Sam. 17:49].

B. "From that point on, it is David who said [the remainder of the Psalm] before the Holy One, blessed be he:

C. " Though a host encamp against me [Ps. 27:3]: the camp of the Philistines.

D. " My heart shall not fear [Ps. 27:3].

E. " Though war arise against me [Ps. 27:3]: war against the Philistines.

F. " In this will I trust " (Ps. 27:3).

G. "In this" (Ps. 27:3):

H. Said R. Levi, " In the Scripture [farewell blessing] which Moses wrote in the scroll of the Torah for my forefathers: "And this is what he said of Judah: [Hear, O Lord, the voice of Judah and bring him in to his people. With your hands contend for him and be a help against his adversaries]" " (Deut. 33:7).

LEVITICUS RABBAH XXI:III.

1. A. R. Joshua b. Levi interpreted [the intersecting verse to speak] of the Amalekites:

B. " When evildoers come near me [Ps. 27:2] refers to the Amalekites: And the Amalekites made a raid on the Negeb and on Ziklag [1 Sam. 30:1].

C. " To eat my flesh [Ps. 27:2]: David s two wives also had been taken captive [1 Sam. 30:5].

D. " My adversaries and foes: And David smote them from twilight until the evening of the next day " (1 Sam. 30:17).

2. A. What is the meaning of "of the next day?"

B. Said R. Joshua b. Levi, "Two nights and one day.

C. "Who provided light for him during the nights?

D. "The Holy One, blessed be he, provided light for him during the nights, through comets and lightning.

E. "It is to this that David speaks: For you illumine my lamp " (Ps. 18:29).

3. A. (Joshua b. Levi continues:) "From that point [in the Psalm,] it is David who speaks.

B. " Though a host encamp against me — the camp of the Amalekites.

C. " My heart shall not fear.

D. " Though war arise against me: the war of the Amalekites."

E. "In this I shall trust" (Ps. 27:3).

F. Said R. Levi, "In the Scripture [farewell blessing] which Moses wrote in the scroll of the Torah for my forefathers: And this is what he said of Judah " (Deut. 33:7).

LEVITICUS RABBAH XXI:III

1. A. R. Joshua b. Levi interpreted [the intersecting verse to speak] of the Amalekites:

   B. " When evildoers come near me [Ps. 27:2] refers to the Amalekites: And the Amalekites made a raid on the Negeb and on Ziklag [1 Sam. 30:1].

   C. " To eat my flesh [Ps. 27:2]: David s two wives also had been taken captive [1 Sam. 30:5].

   D. " My adversaries and foes: And David smote them from twilight until the evening of the next day " (1 Sam. 30:17).

2. A. What is the meaning of "of the next day?"

   B. Said R. Joshua b. Levi, "Two nights and one day.

   C. "Who provided light for him during the nights?

   D. "The Holy One, blessed be he, provided light for him during the nights, through comets and lightning.

   E. "It is to this that David speaks: For you illumine my lamp " (Ps. 18:29).

3. A. (Joshua b. Levi continues:) "From that point [in the Psalm,] it is David who speaks.

   B. " Though a host encamp against me — the camp of the Amalekites.

   C. " My heart shall not fear.

   D. " Though war arise against me: the war of the Amalekites."

   E. "In this I shall trust" (Ps. 27:3).

   F. Said R. Levi, "In the Scripture [farewell blessing] which Moses wrote in the scroll of the Torah for my forefathers: And this is what he said of Judah " (Deut. 33:7).

At last we have come to a powerful confrontation between the narrative of David and the Psalms read as records of David s life. Involved is the encounter with Goliath or the encounter with the Amalekites. Details of the encounter are addressed systematically. What the exegesis contributes is clarity of detail. But the context dews not focus on the Rabbi David at all. Divine favor defines the motif, and no effort is invested in linking David to the study of the Torah or in the supernatural favor accorded to David. The Rabbinic canon does not contain a great many systematic ad protracted expositions of chapters of David s life

LEVITICUS RABBAH XXIII:XI.

1. A. Said R. Yosé, "There are three who were overwhelmed by sexual desire, but who made an oath [to resist]: Joseph, David, and Boaz.

B. "How do we know it in the case of Joseph?

C. " How shall I do such a great wickedness and sin against God " (Gen 39:9).

D. R. Huna in the name of R. Idi: "This verse of Scripture does not say, And sin against the Lord, but rather, . . . against God. [The meaning is that] he imposed an oath on his passion, By God! I shall not sin and I shall not do this evil thing! "

2. A. [Yosé continues:] "How do we know it in the case of David? But David said to Abishai, . . . As the Lord lives, the Lord will smite him . . . [1 Sam. 26:9-10]."

3. A. To whom did he take the oath?

B. R. Yohanan and R. Simeon b. Laqish:

C. R. Yohanan said, "He took the oath to his passion."

D. R. Simeon b. Laqish said, "He took the oath to Abishai:

E. " As the Lord lives! If you touch him, I shall mix your blood with his.

F. "That is in line with the following verse of Scripture: But David said to Abishai, Do not destroy him, [for who can put forth his hand against the Lord s anointed and be guiltless?]" (1 Sam. 26:9).

3. A. [Yosé continues:] "How do we know it in the case of Boaz?

B. " As the Lord lives! Lie down until the morning " (Ruth 3:13).

4. A. R. Yudan and R. Honia:

B. R. Yudan said, "For that entire night, his passion kept him in distress and enticed him with arguments, saying to him, You are unmarried, and she is unmarried, you are looking for a wife, and she is looking for a husband. Go and have sexual relations with her, and let her be acquired for you as a wife through an act of sexual relations.

C. "He took an oath to his passion: As the Lord lives!

D. "And to the woman he said, Lie down until the morning. "

E. Said R. Honia, " A wise man is strong (BWZ) [Prov. 24:5]: A wise man was Boaz (BWZ).

F. " A man of knowledge increases strength [Prov. 24:5]: for he overcame his passion through an oath."

Joseph, David, and Boaz form a set of models: how virile men are expected to restrain themselves. A pattern governs the composition: how do we know it? All three men took an oath to resist passion.

Leviticus Rabbah XXIV:II.

2. A. R. Huna in the name of R. Aha produces the following verse: " A Psalm of David. I will sing of mercy and of justice, to you, O Lord, will I sing [Ps. 101:1].

B. "Said David before the Holy One, blessed be he, Lord of the world, if you act mercifully with me, I shall sing, if you impose justice on me, I shall sing. One way or the other: To you, O Lord, shall I sing."

3. A.   Said R. Tanhum b. R. Yudan, "It is written, In God, whose word I praise, in the Lord, whose word I praise [Ps. 56:11].

B.   "If it is with the attribute of justice that he comes to deal with me: In God, whose word I praise.

C.   "If it is with the attribute of mercy that he comes to deal with me: In the Lord, whose word I praise.

D.   "One way or the other: In the Lord, whose word I praise. "

4. A.   And rabbis say, " I suffered distress and anguish. Then I called on the name of the Lord [Ps. 116:3-4]. I will lift up the cup of salvation and call on the name of the Lord [Ps. 116:13].

B.   "One way or the other: Then I called on the name of the Lord. "

6. A.   Said R. Yudan, "It is written, You, O Lord, are on high forever more [Ps. 92:9].

B.   "You give high status in your world. You gave the priesthood to Aaron forever: It is an everlasting covenant of salt [Num. 18:19].

C.   "You gave the monarchy to David forever: Should you not know that the Lord, God of Israel, gave the monarchy [over Israel to David for ever] [2 Chron. 13:5].

D.   "You gave holiness to Israel forever: Speak to all the congregation of the people of Israel, You shall be holy " (Lev. 19:2).

Ps. 101:1 is attributed to David and read as a statement of his. Then the pattern established in the first instance is amplified with reference to other verses of Psalms, Ps. 101:1, Ps. 56:11, Ps. 116:13, Ps. 92:9 . Ps. 101:1, Ps. 56:11, Ps. 116:13, Ps. 92:9.The exegesis is not a systematic reading of a sequence of verses of Psalms but is spelled out through a guiding proposition.

LEVITICUS RABBAH XXVI:II.

1. A.   R. Yosé of Malehayya and R. Joshua of Sikhnin, in the name of R. Levi: "Children in David s time, before they had tasted the taste of sin [reached sexual maturity], were able to expound the Torah in forty-nine different ways to reach a decision on uncleanness, and in forty-nine different ways to reach a decision on cleanness.

B.   "And David prayed for them: You, O Lord, protect them [Ps. 12:7].

C.   "Preserve their learning in their heart.

D.   " Protect them forever from this generation " (Ps. 12:7).

E.   "From the generation that deserves destruction."

2. A.   After all this glory, [that generation of disciples] went out to war and fell.

B.   It was because there were renegades among them.

C.   That is in line with what David says, "My soul is in the midst of lions. I lie down among them that are aflame, sons of men whose teeth are spears and arrows, their tongues sharp swords" (Ps. 57:4).

D.   "My soul is in the midst of lions" refers to Abner and Amasa, who were lions in the Torah.

E.   "I lie down among them that are aflame" refers to Doeg and Ahitophel, who were burning with gossip.

F. "Sons of men whose teeth are spears and arrows" refers to the men of Keilah: "Will the men of Keilah hand me over?" (1 Sam. 32:11).

G. "Their tongues are sharp swords" refers to the Ziphites: "When the Ziphites came and said to Saul, Does David not hide himself with us? " (1 Sam. 23:19).

H. At that moment said David, "Now what is the Presence of God doing in the world? Be exalted, O God, above the heavens [Ps. 57:5]. Remove your Presence from their midst!"

I. But the generation of Ahab was made up of idolaters. But because there were no renegades among them, they would go out to war and win.

J. That is in line with what Obadiah said to Elijah: "Has it not been told my lord what I did when Jezebel killed the prophets of the Lord, how I hid a hundred men of the Lord s prophets by fifties in a cave and fed them with bread and water?" (1 Kgs. 18:13).

K. If bread, why water? But this teaches that it was harder to bring the water than the bread.

L. Elijah proclaimed on Mount Carmel, saying, "And I alone remain as a prophet to the Lord" (1 Kgs. 18:22).

M. Now the entire people were well informed [that there were other prophets who had survived], but they did not reveal it to the king.

Ps. 12:7 expresses David s prayer for the Israelite children. Ps. 57:4-5 explains the situation in David s words.

LEVITICUS RABBAH 2.

A. R. Yosé b. R. Yudan in the name of R. Yosé b. R. Nehorai says, "It is always the case that the Holy One, blessed be he, demands an accounting for the blood of those who have been pursued from the hand of the pursuer.

B. "Abel was pursued by Cain, and God sought [an accounting for] the pursued: And the Lord looked [favorably] upon Abel and his meal offering [Gen. 4:4].

C. "Noah was pursued by his generation, and God sought [an accounting for] the pursued: You and all your household shall come into the ark [Gen. 7:1]. And it says, For this is like the days of Noah to me, as I swore [that the waters of Noah should no more go over the earth] [Is. 54:9].

D. "Abraham was pursued by Nimrod, and God seeks what has been driven away : You are the Lord, the God who chose Abram and brought him out of Ur [Neh. 9:7].

E. "Isaac was pursued by Ishmael, and God seeks what has been driven away : For through Isaac will seed be called for you [Gen. 21:12].

F. "Jacob was pursued by Esau, and God seeks what has been driven away : For the Lord has chosen Jacob, Israel for his prized possession [Ps. 135:4].

G. "Moses was pursued by Pharaoh, and God seeks what has been driven away : Had not Moses His chosen stood in the breach before Him [Ps. 106:23].

H. "David was pursued by Saul, and God seeks what has been driven away : And he chose David, his servant [Ps. 78:70].

I. "Israel was pursued by the nations, and God seeks what has been driven away : And you has the Lord chosen to be a people to him [Deut. 14:2].

J. "And the rule applies also to the matter of offerings. A bull is pursued by a lion, a sheep is pursued by a wolf, a goat is pursued by a leopard.

K. "Therefore the Holy One, blessed be he, has said, Do not make offerings before me from those animals that pursue, but from those that are pursued: When a bull, a sheep, or a goat is born " (Lev. 22:27).

LEVITICUS RABBAH XXIX:XII

1. A. "In the seventh month" (Lev. 23:24).

B. Under all circumstances the seventh is preferred.

H. Among kings the seventh is preferred: Saul, Ishbosheth, David, Solomon, Rehoboam, Abijah, and Asa: "And Asa called to the Lord his God" (2 Chron. 14:10).

I. Among sons the seventh is preferred: "Usam, the sixth, and David, the seventh" (1 Chron. 2:15).

David is on long lists: cases in which God favors the pursued over the pursuer, cases in which the seventh is preferred

LEVITICUS RABBAH XXX:II

1. A. "You show me the path of life, [in your presence] there is fullness of joy" (Ps. 16:11).

B. Said David before the Holy One, blessed be he, "Show me the open gateway to the life of the world to come."

2. A. R. Yudan said, "David said before the Holy One, blessed be he, Lord of the ages, "Show me the path of life."

B. "Said the Holy One, blessed be he, to David, If you seek life, look for fear, as it is said, "The fear of the Lord prolongs life" " (Prov. 10:27).

C. R. Azariah said, "The Holy One, blessed be he, said to David, David, if you seek life, look for suffering (YYSWRYN), as it is said, "The reproofs of discipline (MWSR) are the way of life" " (Prov. 6:23).

D. Rabbis say, "The Holy One, blessed be he, said to David, David, if you seek life, look for Torah, as it is said, It is a tree of life to those that hold fast to it " (Prov. 3:18).

E. R. Abba said, "David said before the Holy One, blessed be he, Lord of the ages, "Show me the path of life.""

    F.   "Said to him the Holy One, blessed be he, Start fighting and exert yourself! Why are you puzzled? Work and eat: "Keep my commandments and live" " (Prov. 4:4).

Ps. 16:11 is interpreted as a statement of David to God. This is amplified.

LEVITICUS RABBAH XXX:III

1. A.   "He will regard the prayer of the destitute [and will not despise their supplication]" (Ps. 102:17).
   B.   Said R. Abin, "We are unable to make sense of David s character. Sometimes he calls himself king, and sometimes he calls himself destitute.
   C.   "How so? When he foresaw that righteous men were going to come from him, such as Asa, Jehoshaphat, Hezekiah, and Josiah, he would call himself king as it is said, Give the king your judgments, O God [Ps. 72:1].
   D.   "When he foresaw that wicked men would come forth from him, for example, Ahaz, Manasseh, and Amon, he would call himself destitute, as it is said, A prayer of one afflicted, when he is faint [and pours out his complaint before the Lord] [Ps. 102:1].
2. A.   R. Alexandri interpreted the cited verse (Ps. 102:1) to speak of a worker. [The one afflicted is the worker. The word for faint, TP, bears the meaning, cloak oneself, hence in prayer. The worker then has delayed his prayer, waiting for the overseer to leave, at which point he can stop and say his prayer. So he postpones his prayer.] [So Alexandri says], "Just as a worker sits and watches all day long for when the overseer will leave for a bit, so he is late when he says [his prayer], [so David speaks at Ps. 102:1: Hear my prayer, O Lord; let my cry come to you]."
   B.   "That [interpretation of the word TP] is in line with the use in the following verse: And those that were born late belonged to Laban " (Gen. 30:42).
   C.   What is the meaning of "those that were born late"?
   D.   R. Isaac bar Haqolah said, "The ones that tarried."
3. A.   Another interpretation: "He will regard the prayer of the destitute individual [and will not despise their supplication]" (Ps. 102:17):
   B.   Said R. Simeon b. Laqish, "As to this verse, the first half of it is not consistent with the second half, and vice versa.
   C.   "If it is to be, He will regard the prayer of the destitute [individual], he should then have said, And will not despise his supplication.
   D.   "But if it is to be, He will not despise their supplication, then he should have said, He will regard the prayer of those who are destitute.
   E.   "But [when David wrote,] He will regard the prayer of the individual destitute, this [referred to] the prayer of Manasseh, king of Judah.

F.   "And [when David wrote,] He will not despise their supplication, this [referred to] his prayer and the prayer of his fathers.

G.   "That is in line with the following verse of Scripture: And he prayed to him, and he was entreated (YTR) of him " (2 Chron. 33:13).

Ps. 102:17 is read as David's statement to God. We see that Leviticus Rabbah chooses verses of Psalms that are read in the context of David s life.

LEVITICUS RABBAH XXXIV:XVI.
1. A.   "And your ancient ruins shall be rebuilt" (Is. 58:12).

B.   R. Tarfon gave to R. Aqiba six silver centenarii, saying to him, "Go, buy us a piece of land, so we can get a living from it and labor in the study of Torah together."

C.   He took the money and handed it out to scribes, Mishnah teachers, and those who study Torah.

D.   After some time R. Tarfon met him and said to him, "Did you buy the land that I mentioned to you?"

E.   He said to him, "Yes."

F.   He said to him, "Is it any good?"

G.   He said to him, "Yes."

H.   He said to him, "And do you not want to show it to me?"

I.   He took him and showed him the scribes, Mishnah teachers, and people who were studying Torah, and the Torah that they had acquired. He said to him, "Is there anyone who works for nothing? Where is the deed covering the field?"

J.   He said to him, "It is with King David, concerning whom it is written, He has scattered, he has given to the poor, his righteousness endures for ever " (Ps. 112:9).

David is the object of a statement of Ps. 112:9.

LEVITICUS RABBAH XXXV:I
1. A.   "When I think of your ways, I turn my feet to your testimonies" (Ps. 119:59).-

B.   Said David before the Holy One, blessed be he, "Lord of the ages, everyday I take thought and say, To such and such a place, I am going to walk, To such and such a house I am going to walk, but my feet always bring me to synagogues and study houses.

C.   "That is in line with the following verse of Scripture: I turn my feet to your testimonies " (Ps. 119:59).

Ps. 119:59 is spoken by David.

[1] IS DAVID AN ACTIVE PLAYER OR A ROUTINE AND SCARCELY ANIMATE ONE? In a number of important cases the book of Psalms is read as a statement of David in the

context of David s life. This yields a fresh reading f Scripture, but it does not point to a Rabbinic program that governed the reading of the David narratives.

[2] WHAT COMPONENTS OF THE COLLECTION MAKE ROUTINE GLOSSES OF THE RECEIVED SCRIPTURES and which ones provide more than minor glosses of the tradition? The component that imposes a fresh perspective of David is supplied by the reading pf Psalms as autobiographical.

[3] CAN WE IDENTIFY A PRONOUNCED BIAS OR A POLEMIC in the utilization of David? David is represented as a model of piety. He is a heroic figures by reason of virtue., The particular traits of Rabbis play only a limited role.

[4] HOW IS DAVID COMPARABLE TO OTHER SAGES IN THIS DOCUMENT? David is more than a learned sage, he expresses an intense relationship with the Almighty.

The earlier compilations contained relatively brief discussions of random verses. In Leviticus Rabbah we find protracted analytical expositions and extended expositions of facts of Scripture that prove an abstract proposition. The example is LEVITICUS RABBAH 2. A. R. Yosé b. R. Yudan in the name of R. Yosé b. R. Nehorai says, "It is always the case that the Holy One, blessed be he, demands an accounting for the blood of those who have been pursued from the hand of the pursuer..." The figure of David matches numerous models all making the same point. In the Talmud the extended expositions of narratives or expositions of David's convictions take an important position for the first time.

9

David in Pesiqta Derab Kahana

Pesiqta deRab Kahana follows the pattern in form and program of Leviticus Rabbah, and some of its composites reproduce those of Leviticus Rabbah. As in Leviticus Rabbah so in its match here David appears as a striking individual, in a set of protracted expositions unlike compositions that stand out from the David-materials in the earlier compilations.

PESIQTA DERAB KAHANA II:I.

1. A. *O Lord, how many are my foes! Many are rising against me; many are saying of me, there is no help for him in God. Sela* (Ps. 3:2-3):

B. R. Samuel bar Immi and Rabbis:

C. R. Samuel bar Immi interpreted the verse to speak of Doeg and Ahitophel:

D. *"...many are saying of me,* refers to Doeg and Ahitophel. Why does he refer to them as 'many'?

E. "For they formed a majority in Torah-study.

F. *"...many are saying of me, –* They say to David, 'A man who has seized a ewe-lamb, killed the shepherd, and made Israelites fall by the sword – will he have salvation? *There is no help for him in God.'*

G. "Said David, 'And you, O Lord, have concurred with them, writing in your Torah, saying, *The adulterer and the adulteress will surely die* (Lev. 20:10).

H. *"'But you, O Lord, are a shield about me* (Ps. 3:4): For you have formed a protection for me through the merit attained by my ancestors.

I. *"' My glory* (Ps. 3:4): For you restored me to the throne.

J. *"' And the lifter of my head* (Ps. 3:4): While I was liable to you to have my head removed, you raised my head through the prophet,

Nathan, when he said to me, *Also the Lord has removed your sin and you will not die* (2 Sam. 12:13).' "

K. And rabbis interpreted the verse to refer to the nations of the world:

L. *"Many* – these are the nations of the world.

M. "Why does he call them many? For it is written, *Ah the uproar of many peoples* (Is. 17:12).

N. *"...many are saying of me:* this refers to Israel.

O. "' A nation that heard from the mouth of its God at Mount Sinai, *You shall have no other gods before me* (Ex. 20:3), and yet after forty days said to the calf, *This is your god, O Israel* (Ex. 32:4) – will such a nation have salvation?

P. "'...*there is no help for him in God. Sela.*' [so said the nations of the world].

Q. "The Israelites said, 'And you, O Lord, have concurred with them, writing in your Torah, ' *And you shall say, one who sacrifices to other gods will be utterly exterminated* (Ex. 22:19).'

R. "' *But you, O Lord, are a shield about me* (Ps. 3:4): For you have afforded protection for us on account of the merit accrued by our ancestors.'

S. "' *My glory* (Ps. 3:4): For you have brought your Presence to come to rest among us.

T. "' *And the lifter of my head* (Ps. 3:4): While I was liable to you to have my head removed, you raised my head through Moses: *When you lift up the head [RSV: take the census] of the people of Israel, then each shall give a ransom for himself to the Lord when you number them, that there be no plague among them when you number them* (Ex. 30:12)."

David is a The Rabbinic sage, and embodies the Rabbinic system. That involves Torah-study. The theological issue is raised in the setting of David's sin. David expresses verses of Psalms in the context of his own life. The contrary view has the nations at issue. The exposition of Ps. 3:2-4 in terms of Davids life yields a protracted composition and generates an alternative in the nations of the world,

PESIQTA DERAB KAHANA III:XVI

1. A. *[And Moses built an altar and called the name of it, The Lord is my banner,] saying, 'A hand upon the throne of the Lord. The Lord will have war with Amalek from generation to generation'* (Ex. 17:15-16):

B. It was taught in the name of R. Ilai: "The Holy One, blessed be He, took an oath: ' By my right hand, by my right hand, by my throne, by my throne, if proselytes come from any of the nations of the world, I shall accept them, but if they come from the seed of Amalek I shall never accept them.'

C. "And so was the case with David: *And David said to the youth who told him [that Saul and Jonathan had died], Where do you*

come from? And he said, I am the son of an Amalekite convert (2
Sam. 1:13)."

D.   Said R. Isaac, "He was Doeg the Edomite."

E.   [Continuing C:] "*And David said to him, Your blood be upon your
own head* (2 Sam. 1:16)."

F.   Said R. Isaac, "What is written is, *your bloods*, meaning, he said
to him, ' You [Doeg] have shed much blood in Nob, city of the
priests.'"

David carries forward the curse of the Amalekites.

PESIQTA DERAB KAHANA IV:I.I

3. A.   R. Yosé of Malehayya and R. Joshua of Sikhnin in the name of R.
Levi: "Children in David's time, before they had tasted the taste of
sin [reaching sexual maturity] were able to expound the Torah in
forty-nine different ways to reach a decision on uncleanness and
in forty-nine different ways to reach a decision on cleanness.

B.   "And David prayed for them: *You O Lord protect them* (Ps. 122:7).
Preserve their learning in their heart.

C.   *"Protect them forever from this generation* (Ps. 12:7). From the
generation that deserves destruction."

4. A.   And after all this praise [for their achievements, and David's prayer
for them], that generation of disciples went out to war and fell.

B.   It was because there were renegades among them.

C.   That is in line with what David says, *My soul is in the midst of
lions, I lie down among them that are aflame, sons of men whose
teeth are spears and arrows, their tongues sharp swords* (Ps. 57:4).

D.   *My soul is in the midst of lions* refers to Abner and Amasa, who
were lions in the Torah.

E.   *I lie down among them that are aflame* refers to Doeg and
Ahitophel, who were burning up with gossip.

F.   *Sons of men whose teeth are spears and arrows* refers to the men
of Keilah: *Will the men of Keilah hand me over* (1 Sam. 32:11).

G   *Their tongues are sharp swords* refers to the Ziphites: *When the
Ziphites came and said to Saul, Does David not hide himself with
us* (1 Sam. 23:19).

H.   At that moment said David, "Now what is the presence of God
doing in the world? *Be exalted, O God, above the heavens* (Ps.
57:5).

David speaks through Ps. 122:7. Ps. 57:4-5 clarifies an incident in David's
life.

PESIQTA DERAB KAHANA V:III.

1. A.   *Hope deferred makes the heart sick, [but a desire fulfilled is a tree
of life. He who despises the word brings destruction on himself,*

> *but he who respects the commandments will be rewarded. The teaching of the wise is a fountain of life, that one may avoid the snares of death]* (Prov. 13:12-14):

2. A.   Another interpretation: *"Hope deferred makes the heart sick* – this refers to David, who was anointed and then ruled only after two years had passed.

B.   *"...but a desire fulfilled is a tree of life* – this refers to Saul, who was anointed and then ruled right away.

C.   On account of what merit [did Saul have that good fortune]?

D.   On account of the merit accruing for the good deeds which were to his credit, for he was humble and modest.

E.   For he ate his ordinary food [not deriving from his share of an animal sacrificed in the Temple, for example] in a state of cultic cleanness [as if he were eating holy food deriving from his share of an offering made in the Temple].

F.   And, further, he would spend his own funds so as to protect the funds of Israel.

G.   And he treated as equal the honor owing to his servant with the honor owing to himself.

H.   Judah bar Nahman in the name of R. Simeon b. Laqish: "For he was one who was subject to study of the Torah: *By me [the Torah speaks] princes rule* (Prov. 18:16). *By me kings rule* [and Saul ruled through his study of the Torah] (Prov. 8:15)."

13. A.   And rabbis say, "In the septennate in which the son of David comes, in the first of the seven year spell, *I shall cause it to rain on one town and not on another* (Amos 4:7).

R.   Said R. Levi, "If you see one generation after another blaspheming, look for the footsteps of the messiah-king.

S.   "What verse of Scripture indicates it? *Remember Lord the taunts hurled at your servant, how I have borne in my heart the calumnies of the nations; so have your enemies taunted us, O Lord, taunted the successors of your anointed king* (Ps. 89:51).

T.   "What follows? *Blessed is the Lord for ever, amen, amen* (Ps. 89:52)."

Saul observed the Rabbinic interpretation of purity laws and studied the Torah. The advent of the son of David or the Messiah is scheduled.. I do not reproduce the greater part of the exposition, since it has no bearing on the picture of David himself.

Pesiqta deRab Kahana VII:1

1. A.   R. Tanhum of Jaffa in the name of R. Nunayya of Caesarea opened discourse by citing the following verse: *"But when I thought how to understand this, it seemed to me a wearisome task* (Ps. 73:16).

B.   "Said David, ' No one can reckon the exact moment of midnight except for the Holy One, blessed be He, but, as for me, *But when*

I thought how to understand this, it seemed to me a wearisome task.

C.   "For no creature can reckon the exact moment except for him, for it is said: *And it came to pass at midnight [that the Lord smote all the firstborn in the land of Egypt, from the firstborn of Pharaoh who sat on his throne to the firstborn of the handmaiden behind the millstones, and all the firstborn of the cattle. And Pharaoh rose up in the night, he and all his servants and all the Egyptians, and there was a great cry in Egypt, for there was not a house where one was not dead. And he summoned Moses and Aaron by night and said, "Rise up, go forth from among my people, both you and the people of Israel, and go, serve the Lord as you have said. Take your flocks and your herds, as you have said, and be gone; and bless me also!]* (Ex. 12:29-32)."

David speaks at Ps. 74:16.

PESIQTA DERAB KAHANA VII:IV

1. A.   *At midnight I rise to give you thanks for the justice of your decrees. I keep company with all who fear you, with all who follow your precepts. The earth is full of your never-failing love; O Lord, teach me your statutes* (Ps. 119:62-64):

   B.   R. Phineas in the name of R. Eleazar bar Menahem: "What would David do?

   C.   "He would take a psaltery and a harp and put them at his pillow and get up at midnight and play on them.

   D.   "And the sages of Israel would hear the sound and say, ' Now if King David is occupied with Torah-study, how much the more so should we!'

   E.   "It came about that all of Israel would occupy themselves in the study of Torah."

2. A.   Said R. Levi, "There was a window by the bed of David, open to the north, and the harp was suspended at it, and as the north went blew at midnight, it would rush through the harp, and the harp would give forth sound on its own, in line with this verse: *When the instrument played* (2 Kgs. 3:5).

   B.   "What it says is not, 'when David played...,' but, *When the instrument played.*

   C.   "This indicates that the harp would give forth sound on its own."

   D.   "And the sages of Israel would hear the sound and say, ' Now if King David is occupied with Torah-study, how much the more so should we!'

   E.   "It came about that all of Israel would occupy themselves in the study of Torah."

David invokes Ps, 119:62-64, which speaks of David in the context of Torah-study. David is the model for all Israel for Torah-study. Nature conveyed the meaning of midnight study. David is the m0odel of the Rabbinic sage who studies the Torah intensively.

Pesiqta deRab Kahana XI:XIV

1. A. *To David: To you, O Lord my God, I lift up my heart, [in you I trust, do not put me to shame, let not my enemies exult over me]* (Ps. 25:1-2):

 B. The word for *lift up* is so written that it may be read, *bend low.*.

 C. Said David before the Holy One, blessed be He, "Lord of the ages, my soul is bent low because of those who are destined to give up their lives in the sanctification of God' s name."

 D. "And who is this? It is the entire generation of the persecution [of Hadrian, following Bar Kokhba' s war].

 E. Said the Holy One, blessed be He, to him, "And did they lose on that account? Is their share not in [eternal] life? *Their share is in eternal life. That which is laid up for you will fill their belly* (Ps. 17:14).

 F. Said David before the Holy One, blessed be He, "Lord of the ages, do I have my share with them?"

 G He said to him, "What is written is not *that which is laid up for them will fill their belly,* but rather, *That which is laid up for you will fill their belly* (Ps. 17:14) – what is yours and what is theirs.

 H. Said David before the Holy One, blessed be He, "Lord of the ages, these and those come about on account of the power accruing for studying the Torah and doing good deeds, but, as for me, *Only through righteousness may I see your face* (Ps. 17:15)."

 I. Said R. Hiyya bar Ba, "If someone should say to you, ' Give your life for the sanctification of God' s name,' say to him, ' I shall give it up, on condition that they cut off my head right away.'

 J. "But let it not be done as was done in the generation of the persecution, when they would put fiery iron balls in their armpits and sharpened reeds under their fingernails.:"

Ps 25.1-12, 17:14 speaks for David.

Pesiqta deRab Kahana XII:XII

1. A. *In the third month after Israel [had left Egypt, they came to the wilderness of Sinai. They set out from Rephidim and entered the wilderness of Sinai, where they encamped, pitching their tent opposite the Mountain. Moses went up the mountain of God, and the Lord called to him from the mountain and said, 'Speak thus to the house of Jacob and tell this to the sons of Israel: You have seen with your own eyes what I did to Egypt and how I have carried you on eagles 'wings and brought you here to me. If only you will now listen to me and keep my covenant, then out of all peoples you shall become my special possession; for the whole earth is mine.*

You shall be my kingdom of priests, my holy nation'] (Exodus 19:1-6).

B. This is in line with the following verse of Scripture: *Have I not written for you three-fold sayings full of knowledge and wise counsel [to show you what is right and true, that you may give a true answer to those who sent you?]* (Prov. 22:20-21).

C. If you wish to take counsel from the Torah, take it.

D. Said David, "When I wanted to take counsel in the Torah, I would look into the Scripture and take counsel."

E. So it is said, *I will meditate on your precepts and fix my eyes on your ways, [I will delight in your statutes and I will not forget your word]* (Ps. 119:15-16).

The theme of David's speaking through Psalms continues, now at Ps, 119 :15.

PESIQTA DERAB KAHANA XV:XI

5. A. That is in line with what David said, *That they may be delivered for the sake of your beloved or redeem them for your right hand's sake, answer me* (Ps. 60:7):

B. Said David before the Holy One, blessed be He, "So long as Israel continues to enjoy merit, do it for them *for the sake of your beloved,* Abraham, Isaac, and Jacob.

C. "But when Israel no longer continues to enjoy merit, do it *for your right hand's sake:*

D. ...*for your right hand's sake, answer me* (Ps. 60:7).

6. A. [...*for your right hand's sake, answer me* (Ps. 60:7):] Said David before the Holy One, blessed be He, "Lord of the ages, why is it the case that whoever loves you wanders? Let them rest, as you have said, *Deliver us.*

B. On this basis, the sages have included in the Sabbath liturgy the prayer that begins with the word, *Deliver us.*

David speaks through Ps. 60:7.

PESIQTA DERAB KAHANA XVIII:I

1. A. *O sons of a man, how long shall my honor suffer shame? [How long will you love vain words and seek after lies? But know that the Lord has set apart the faithful for himself; the Lord hears when I call to him]* (Ps. 4:2-3):

2. A. ...*how long shall my honor suffer shame? [How long will you love vain words and seek after lies?]* (Ps. 4:3):

B. Said David, "How long will you bring shame on my honor and call me merely, ' Son of Jesse:' *Why has the son of Jesse not come* (1 Sam. 20:27). *I saw the son of Jesse* (1 Sam. 16:18). *Will the son of Jesse give everyone of you [fields]* (1 Sam. 22:7). Do I not have a name?' "

3. A.   *...how long will you love vain words and seek after lies?]* (Ps.
            4:3):

   B.   ...pursuing after words of vanity: "[The Lord] has abandoned him,
            forgotten him, the kingdom will never again return to him."

4. A.   *...and seek after lies?* (Ps. 4:3):

   B.   "What are you thinking? Is it that because my kingdom has been
            taken away from me for a while, that it is forever?"

5. A.   *But know that the Lord has set apart the godly for himself; [the
            Lord hears when I call to him]:*

   B.   "He has already sent word to me through the prophet Nathan and
            said to me, *The Lord will indeed remove your sin and you will not
            die* (2 Sam. 13:14)."

Ps. 4:3 is interpreted in the setting of David's life.

PESIQTA DERAB KAHANA XXIII:X

3. A.   *In the seventh month* (Lev. 23:24):

   B.   Under all circumstances the seventh is preferred.

   H.   Among the sons, the seventy is preferred: Eliab, Abinadab,
            Shemael, Nethanel, Raddai, Ozem, and David was *the seventh* (1
            Chron. 2:15).

   I.   Among kings the seventh is preferred: Saul, Ishbosheth, David,
            Solomon, Rehoboam, Abijah, and Asa: *And Asa called to the Lord
            his God* (2 Chron. 14:10).

   J.   Among years of the sabbatical cycle the seventh is preferred: *And
            in the seventh there will be a year of rest* (Ex. 23:11).

   K.   Among days the seventh is preferred: *And God blessed the seventh
            day* (Gen. 2:3).

   L.   Among months the seventh is preferred: *In the seventh month on
            the first day of the month* (Lev. 23:24).

David is merely an item on a list.

PESIQTA DERAB KAHANA XXIV:II

3. A.   *...far-off seas:*

   H.   That view accords with what R. Yosé bar Halapta said, "There are
            particular times for prayer:

   I.   "David came along and spelled them out: *But as for me, may my
            prayer be for you, O Lord, at a propitious time* (Ps. 69:14):

   J.   "Said David before the Holy One, blessed be He, ' Lord of the
            ages, when I pray before you, may it be a propitious time.' "

   K.   *God, in the abundance of your mercy, answer me with your true
            salvation* (Ps. 69:14):

David invokes Ps. 69:14

Pesiqta deRab Kahana XXIV:V

1. A. *The sacrifices of God are a broken spirit, a wounded heart, [O
God, you will not despise. Let it be your pleasure to do good to
Zion, to build a new the walls of Jerusalem. Then only shall you
delight in the appointed sacrifices, then shall young bulls be offered
on your altar]* (Ps. 51:17-19):

   B. Zabedee bar Levi and R. Yosé bar Paitres and rabbis:

   C. One said, "Said David before the Holy One, blessed be He, ' Lord
of the ages, If you accept me as a penitent, I know that my son,
Solomon, is going to go and build the sanctuary and offer on it all
of the required offerings.'

   D. "It is in accord with this verse of Scripture: *The sacrifices of God
are a broken spirit, a wounded heart, [O God, you will not despise.
Let it be your pleasure to do good to Zion, to build a new the walls
of Jerusalem. Then only shall you delight in the appointed
sacrifices, then shall young bulls be offered on your altar]* (Ps.
51:17-19).

   E. "' And I know that you will *do good to Zion, to build a new the
walls of Jerusalem.*

   F. "' *Then only shall you delight in the appointed sacrifices, then
shall young bulls be offered on your altar]* (Ps. 51:17-19).' "

   G Another said, "How do we know of one who carries out penitence
that the Holy One, blessed be He, regards it as though he had gone
up to Jerusalem, built the house of the sanctuary, built the altar,
and offered on it all required offerings?

   H. "It is in accord with this verse of Scripture: *The sacrifices of God
are a broken spirit, a wounded heart, O God, you will not despise.*

   I. "And it is further written: *Let it be your pleasure to do good to
Zion, to build a new the walls of Jerusalem. Then only shall you
delight in the appointed sacrifices, [then shall young bulls be
offered on your altar]* (Ps. 51:17-19)."

David speaks through Ps, 51:17-19. He formulates a theology of
repentance.

Pesiqta deRab Kahana XXV:II

2. A. R. Huna in the name of R. Abbahu, "It is as if, while forgetfulness
is not a trait of his, for the sake of Israel he turns forgetful.

   B. *"Who is a god like you? You take away guilt, you pass over the sin
[of the remnant of your own people, you do not let your anger
rage for ever but delight in love that will not change]* (Mic. 7:18).

   C. "And so said David: You have borne the transgression of your
people, you have covered over all their sin. Sela (Ps. 85:3)."

David speaks through Ps. 85:3.

Pesiqta deRab Kahana XXVI:1

1. A. R. Simeon b. R. Abin opened [discourse by citing the following verse of Scripture]: *"Since one fate comes to all, to the righteous and the wicked, [to the good and the evil, to the clean and the unclean, to him who sacrifices and him who does not sacrifice]* (Qoh. 9:2). **4. A.** *As to the good man, so is the sinner and he who swears is as he who shuns an oath* (Qoh. 9:2):] *As to the good man* refers to David: *And he sent and brought him, and he was ruddy, with a lovely face, and good appearance]* (1 Sam. 16:12).

   B. *So the sinner* refers to Nebuchadnezzar: *Break off your sin through righteousness* (Dan. 4:24).

   C. This one [David] built the house of the sanctuary and ruled for forty years, while that one destroyed it and ruled for forty-five years.

   D. Is it not the case of *a single fate affecting them both?*

One fate meets everyone; David exemplifies that commonplace along with Nebuchadnezzar.

Pesiqta deRab Kahana XXVII:III

1. A. *He will regard the prayer of the destitute [and will not despise their supplication]* (Ps. 102:17):

   B. Said R. Reuben, "We are unable to make sense of David's character. Sometimes he calls himself king, and sometimes he calls himself destitute.

   C. "How so? When he foresaw that righteous men were going to come from him, such as Asa, Jehoshaphat, Hezekiah, and Josiah, he would call himself king as it is said, *Give the king your judgments, O God* (Ps. 72:1).

   D. "When he foresaw that wicked men would come forth from him, for example, Ahaz, Manasseh, and Amon, he would call himself destitute, as it is said, *A prayer of one afflicted, when he is faint [and pours out his complaint before the Lord]* (Ps. 102:1)."

3. A. [Another interpretation: *He will regard the prayer of the destitute [and will not despise their supplication]* (Ps. 102:17):] Said R. Simeon b. Laqish, "As to this verse, the first half of it is not consistent with the second half, and vice versa.

   B. "If it is to be, ' *He will regard the prayer of the destitute* [individual],' he should then have said, ' And will not despise *his* supplication.'

   C. "But if it is to be, ' *He will not despise their supplication,* ' then he should have said, ' He will regard the prayer of *those* who are destitute.'

   D. "But [when David wrote,] *He will regard the prayer of the individual destitute*, this [referred to] the prayer of Manasseh, king of Judah.

F. "And [when David wrote,] *He will not despise* their *supplication*, this [referred to] his prayer and the prayer of his fathers.

G. "That is in line with the following verse of Scripture: *And he prayed to him, and he was entreated of him* (2 Chron. 33:13)."

4. A. R. Isaac interpreted the verse *He will regard the prayer of the destitute [and will not despise their supplication]* (Ps. 102:17) to speak of these generations which have neither king nor prophet, neither priest nor Urim and Thummim, but who have only this prayer alone.

B. "Said David before the Holy One, blessed be He, ' Lord of the ages, "Do not despise their prayer. *Let this be recorded for a generation to come* ' (Ps. 102:19).

C. "On the basis of that statement, [we know that] the Holy One, blessed be He, accepts penitents.

D. *"So that a people yet unborn may praise the Lord* (Ps. 102:19).

E. "For the Holy One, blessed be He, will create them as a new act of creation."

David delivers various messages through Ps. 102:17.

PESIQTA DERAB KAHANA XXVIII:I

1. A. *On the eighth day you shall have a solemn assembly. [You shall do no laborious work, but you shall offer a burnt-offering, an offering by fire, a pleasing odor to the Lord...These you shall offer to the Lord at your appointed feasts in addition to your votive-offerings and your freewill-offerings, for your burnt-offerings and for your cereal-offerings and for your drink-offerings and for your peace-offerings]* (Numbers 29:35-9):

B. *But you have increased the nation, O Lord, you have increased the nation; [you are glorified; you have enlarged all the borders of the land]* (Is. 17:25):

C. You gave security to the wicked Pharaoh. Did he then call you "Lord"? Was it not with blasphemies and curses that he said, *Who is the Lord, that I should listen to his voice* (Ex. 5:2)!

D. You gave security to the wicked Sennacherib. Did he then call you "Lord"? Was it not with blasphemies and curses that he said, *Who is there among all the gods of the lands...* (2 Kgs. 18:35).

E. You gave security to the wicked Nebuchadnezzar. Did he then call you "Lord"? Was it not with blasphemies and curses that he said, *And who is God to save you from my power* (Dan. 3:15).

F. *...you have increased the nation; you are glorified:*

G. You gave security to David and so he blessed you: *David blessed the Lord before all the congregation* (1 Chr. 29:10).

H. You gave security to his son, Solomon, and so he blessed you: *Blessed is the Lord who has given rest to his people Israel* (1 Kgs. 8:56).

I.   You gave security to Daniel and so he blessed you: *Daniel answered and said, Blessed be the name of God* (Dan. 2:20)

The pattern is blatant: you gave security to...did he call you Lord? Not at all. That is the pattern for the gentiles, The Israelites' pattern differs. You gave security and so he blessed you, David is not a particular player; he submits to a common pattern.

[1] IS DAVID AN ACTIVE PLAYER OR A ROUTINE AND SCARCELY ANIMATE ONE? David cites and glosses Psalms, which is treated as a collection of David's reflections on himself and his condition. Whenever David cites Psalms he proceeds to express a personal conviction. He is an active player throughout the compositions that emerge in Psalms,

[2] WHAT COMPONENTS OF THE COLLECTION MAKE ROUTINE GLOSSES OF THE RECEIVED SCRIPTURES and which ones provide more than minor glosses of the tradition? The pattern is that David speaks through Psalms, and all other verses of Scripture form a miscellaneous composite of this and that.

[3] CAN WE IDENTIFY A PRONOUNCED BIAS OR A POLEMIC in the utilization of David? David emerges in the voice of Psalms as repentant and righteous.

[4] HOW IS DAVID COMPARABLE TO OTHER SAGES IN THIS DOCUMENT? David is unlike any other sages in this collection. He is not shaped in the model of the sage, on the contrary, he calls to mind the prophets in his speaking through Psalms. He is a monarch and progenitor of the Messiah — these are givens. But an effort is made to turn him into a rabbi by establishing him as a disciple of Torah-study.

10

David in Esther Rabbah I

Esther Rabbah I supplies exegetical observations. He figures on lists.

ESTHER RABBAH I IV:1

1. A.   R. Isaac commenced by citing the verse, "'When the righteous are increased, the people rejoice, but when the wicked rule, the people sigh' (Prov. 29:2).

   B.   "When the righteous achieve great power, there is joy and happiness in the world, and wow! wow! for the world.

   C.   "'And king David' (1 Kgs. 1:10): [since the word for 'and' yields the Hebrew wah, translated wow, the sense is] 'wow that David is king.'

   D.   "'And king Solomon' (1 Kgs. 11:1): [since the word for 'and' yields the Hebrew wah, translated wow, the sense is] 'wow that Solomon is king.'

   E.   "'And king Asa' (1 Kgs. 15:22): [since the word for 'and' yields the Hebrew wah, translated wow, the sense is] 'wow that Asa is king.'

   F.   "That is thus the case for the kings of Israel.

   G.   "How do we know that the same rule applies to the kings of the nations of the world?

David provides an example of the phenomenon to which the sages make reference.

ESTHER RABBAH I VIII:1

1. A.   R. Berekhiah commenced by citing the verse, "'Who has wrought and done it? He who called the generations from the beginning' (Is. 41:4):

B.   "From the beginning of the creation of the world, the Holy One blessed be he designated for every one what was suitable.

C.   "Adam was first of all creatures,

D.   "Cain was first of murderers,

E.   "Abel was first of all victims,

F.   "Noah the first of all those who would be saved from disaster,

G.   "Abraham was the first of all the circumcised,

H.   "Isaac the first of all those who were bound for sacrifice,

I.   "Jacob the first of all those who were without blemish,

J.   "Judah the first of the tribes,

K.   "Joseph the first of the pious,

L.   "Aaron the first of the priests,

M.   "Moses the first of the prophets,

N.   "Joshua the first of the conquerors,

O.   "Othniel the first of those who divide the spoils,

P.   "Samuel the first of those who anoint,

Q.   "Saul the first of those who are anointed,

R.   "David the first of the singers,

S.   "Solomon the first of the builders,

T.   "Nebuchadnezzar the first of the destroyers,

U.   "Ahasuerus the first of those who sell [people at a price],

V.   "Haman the first of those who buy [people at a price]."

David provides an example of the phenomenon to which the sages make reference.

ESTHER RABBAH I XVIII:v

3. A.   [Another explanation of the verse, "From men by your hand, O Lord, from men] whose portion in life is of the world. [May their belly be filled with what you have stored up for them; may their children have more than enough; may they leave something over to their babes" (Ps. 17:14)]:

B.   Said David before the Holy One, blessed be he, "Lord of the world, Is it possible that I have a portion with them in this world?"

C.   Said to him the Holy One, blessed be he, "David, no, what is written here is not, 'what they have stored up will fill your belly' but rather, 'May their belly be filled with what you have stored up for them.'

D.   "The meaning is, everyone is going to eat of the surplus of your wealth. [Simon, p. 51, n. 2: will enjoy the hereafter for your sake.]"

E.   David was therefore informed that he has a portion in the world to come.

F.   And he further said, "Lord of the world, these come by reason of the power of the Torah, religious obligations, and good deeds, that they have accrued. But as for me: 'I shall behold your face through charity' (Ps. 17:15) for ever." [David will merit the world to come by reason of philanthropy.]

David is promised a portion in the world to come.

ESTHER RABBAH I XXXVIII:

I 4. A. "And rehearse it in the ears of Joshua" (Ex. 17:14):
   B. this is one of four instances in which a hint was given to a righteous man.
   C. Two took it and two did not.
   D. Moses was given a hint and did not take it.
   E. Jacob was given a hint and did not take it.
   F. David and Mordecai were given hints and took them.
7. A. David and Mordecai took the hints that were given to them.
   B. David said, "Your servant smote both the lion and the bear" (1 Sam. 17:36).
   C. David reflected, "What sort of unusual person am I, that I can smite these dangerous animals?
   D. "It must mean that some calamity is going to befall the Israelites, and through me they will be delivered."

Moses, Jacob, Mordecai and David form a list for the stated purpose.

[1] IS DAVID AN ACTIVE PLAYER OR A ROUTINE AND SCARCELY ANIMATE ONE? Psalms does not occur in David's name and David is not an active player in any of the narratives. He figures as an item on a list.

[2] WHAT COMPONENTS OF THE COLLECTION MAKE ROUTINE GLOSSES OF THE RECEIVED SCRIPTURES and which ones provide more than minor glosses of the tradition? David is an item on a list, as we have observed, and not as an active player

[3] CAN WE IDENTIFY A PRONOUNCED BIAS OR A POLEMIC in the utilization of David? I see nothing that takes up a fresh perspective. David supplies a number of routine facts for lists.

[4] HOW IS DAVID COMPARABLE TO OTHER SAGES IN THIS DOCUMENT? David is established in the model of others on lists.

11

David in Song of Songs Rabbah

Song of Songs Rabbah provides a sequence of interpretations of the Song of Songs verse by verse, with emphasis on those intersecting with Psalms.

SONG OF SONGS RABBAH XLVIII:1

1. A. "Your neck is like the tower of David:"
   B. This is how David extolled you in his book.
   C. And how did David extol you in his book? "To him who divided the Red Sea in two...and made Israel pass through the midst" (Ps. 136:13-14).
2. A. "built for an arsenal:"
   B. What is the sense of "arsenal?"
   C. It is a book that was said by many mouths [the words for mouths and arsenal use the same consonants].
3. A. Ten men said the book of Psalms:
   B. the first Man, Abraham, Moses, David, Solomon, thus five.
   C. As to these five none differs.
   D. Who were the other five?
   E. Rab and R. Yohanan:
   F. Rab said, "Asaph, Heman, Jeduthun, the three sons of Korach, and Ezra.
   G. R. Yohanan said, "Asaph, Heman, Jeduthun are one; the three sons of Korach and Ezra."
   H. In the view of Rab Asaph is not covered by the sons of Korach, and in the view of R. Yohanan, the Asaph here is the same as the Asaph there [the Asaph mentioned in Psalms is the one in 1 Chr. 25:2].

I.   But because he was a master of the Torah, he had the merit of reciting a Psalm with his brothers, and he had the merit also to recite a Psalm entirely on his own.

J.   In the opinion of Rab, it was another Asaph: "Under the hand of Asaph, who prophesied according to the direction of the king" (1 Chr. 25:2).

5. A.   [Reverting to No. 3:] R. Huna in the name of R. Aha: "Even though ten men wrote the book of Psalms, among them all, the only one of them in whose name the Psalms are said is David, king of Israel.

B.   "The matter may be compared to the case of a group of men who wanted to recite a hymn to the king. Said the king to them, 'All of you sing pleasantly, all of you are pious, all of you are praiseworthy to say a hymn before me. But Mr. So-and-so is the one who will say it in behalf of all of you.

C.   "'Why so? Because his voice is sweet.

D.   "Thus when the ten righteous men proposed to say the book of Psalms, said the Holy One, blessed be He, to them, all of you are praiseworthy to say a hymn before me. But Mr. So-and-so is the one who will say it in behalf of all of you.

E.   "'Why so? Because his voice is sweet.

F.   "So when the ten righteous men proposed to recite the book of Psalms, said the Holy One, blessed be He, to them, 'All of you are praiseworthy to say a hymn before me. But David is the one who will say it in behalf of all of you.

G.   "'Why so? Because his voice is sweet.'

H.   "That is in line with the following verse of Scripture: 'The sweet one of the songs of Israel' (2 Sam. 23:1)."

6. A.   [Supply: "The sweet one of the songs of Israel" (2 Sam. 23:1)"]

B.   R. Huna in the name of R. Aha said, "It is the one who sweetens the songs of Israel, namely, David son of Jesse."

7. A.   "whereon hang a thousand bucklers:"

B.   All those thousands and myriads who stood at the Sea and whom I protected, I protected only on account of the merit of that one who will come in a thousand generations. [Simon, p. 181, n. 4: Moses, who came to give the Torah, "commanded to a thousand generations" (Ps. 105:8).]

8. A.   "all of them shields of warriors:"

B.   This encompasses the one who stands and rules over his inclination to do evil and overcomes his inclination to do evil,

C.   for instance, Moses in his time,

D.   David in his time,

E.   Ezra in his time.

F.   The entire generation depends on him [the words for shield and depend use the same consonants].

G.   And through whom is the Red Sea opened up for you? It is through your two breasts, Moses and Aaron.

The segments of Psalms through which David speaks are differentiated from the segments that were written by others. Psalm 136:13-14 forms the initial reading, XLVIII.3 spells out matters. David has the sweetest voice of all of them.

SONG OF SONGS RABBAH XLVIII:IX

3. A. Another explanation of the verse, "'Before I was aware, my fancy set me in a chariot beside my prince:'"
   B. Scripture speaks of David.
   C. Yesterday he was escaping from Saul.
   D. Today: "David was king" (2 Sam. 8:15).
   E. So in his own regard he recited the verse, "Before I was aware, my fancy set me in a chariot beside my prince."
5. A. For said R. Meir, "The Holy One, blessed be He, took an oath that he would take the kingdom of the house of David out of his hand: 'As I live, says the Lord, though Coniah son of Jehoiakim king of Judah were the signet upon my right hand, yet I would pluck you hence' (Jer. 22:24)."
   B. Said R. Hanina b. R. Isaac, "'From there I should take away the dominion of the house of David.'"

The House of David is denied dominion.

[1] IS DAVID AN ACTIVE PLAYER OR A ROUTINE AND SCARCELY ANIMATE ONE? David presents a commentary to the book of Psalms. He is one of ten such participants, including the first Man, Abraham, Moses, David, Solomon.

[2] WHAT COMPONENTS OF THE COLLECTION MAKE ROUTINE GLOSSES OF THE RECEIVED SCRIPTURES and which ones provide more than minor glosses of the tradition? The bulk of the comments on Song of Songs are routine glosses.

[3] CAN WE IDENTIFY A PRONOUNCED BIAS OR A POLEMIC in the utilization of David? Even though ten men wrote the book of Psalms, among them all, the only one of them in whose name the Psalms are said is David, king of Israel. David is a unique figure,

[4] HOW IS DAVID COMPARABLE TO OTHER SAGES IN THIS DOCUMENT? David is distinguished by a sweet voice. He studies the Torah like a sage.

12

David in Ruth Rabbah

David figures at the center of Ruth Rabbah. But the reading of Ruth Rabbah tells the story of Ruth and Boaz, not of David and the coming of the Messiah.

RUTH RABBAH XXI:I

11. A. "Tell me, O Lord, what my term is, what is the measure of my days; I would know how fleeting my life is. [You have made my life just handbreadths long; its span is as nothing in your sight; no man endures longer than a breath. Man walks about as a mere shadow; mere futility is his hustle and bustle, amassing and not knowing who will gather in]" (Ps. 39:5-7):

B. Said David before the Holy One, blessed be He, "Lord of the world, tell me when I shall die."

C. He said to him, "It is a secret that is not to be revealed to a mortal, and it is not possible for me to tell you."

D. He said to him, "...what is the measure of my days."

E. He said to him, "Seventy years."

F. He said to him, "'I would know how fleeting my life is.' Tell me on what day I am going to die."

G. He said to him, "On the Sabbath."

H. He said to him, "Take off one day [not on the Sabbath, since on that day the body cannot be tended]?

I. He said to him, "No."

J. He said to him, "Why?"

K. He said to him, "More precious to me is a single prayer that you stand and recite to me than a thousand whole-offerings that your son, Solomon, is going to offer before me: 'A thousand burnt-offerings did Solomon offer on that altar' (1 Kgs. 3:4)."

L. He said to him, "Add one day for me."

M   He said to him, "No."

N.   He said to him, "Why?"

O.   He said to him, "The term of your son is at hand."

P.   For R. Simeon b. Abba said in the name of R. Yohanan, "Terms of office are defined in advance, and one does not overlap the other even to the extent of a hair's breadth."

12. A.   He died on a Pentecost that coincided with the Sabbath.

B.   The Sanhedrin went in to greet Solomon.

C.   He said to them, "Move him from one place to another."

D.   They said to him, "And is it not a statement of the Mishnah: One may anoint and wash the corpse, so long as it is not moved [M. Shab. 23:5]?"

E.   He said to them, "The dogs of father's house are hungry."

F.   They said to him, "And is it not a statement of the Mishnah: They may cut up pumpkins on the Sabbath for an animal and a carcass for dogs [M. Shab. 24:4]?"

G.   What did he then do?

H.   He took a spread and spread it over the body, so that the sun should not beat down on him.

I.   Some say, he called the eagles and they spread their wings over him, so that the sun should not beat down on him.

David states his message through Ps. 39:5-7: tell me when I shall die. He died on a Pentecost that coincided with the Sabbath.

RUTH RABBAH XXXV:I

1. A.   "He was with David at Pas-dammim, and there the Philistines were gathered together to battle, where there was a plot of ground full of barley...but they...defended it" (1 Chr. 11:13-14):
"Let your eyes be upon the field which they are reaping and go after them. Have I not charged the young men not to molest you? And when you are thirsty, go to the vessels and drink what the young men have drawn" (Ruth 2:9)

B.   "...your eyes": this is the Sanhedrin.

2. A.   There are two hundred forty eight limbs in a human being, but people follow only their eyes:

B.   "Let your eyes be upon the field which they are reaping and go after them."

3. A.   "Have I not charged the young men not to molest you":

B.   That they not distance you [from being a Jew].

4. A.   "And when you are thirsty, go to the vessels":

B.   These are the righteous, who are called vessels:

C.   "How are the mighty fallen and the vessels of war perished" (2 Sam. 1:27).

5. A.   "...and drink what the young men have drawn":

B.   this refers to the Festival of Drawing the Water.

C.   Why is it called "drawing the water"?

D. Because from there they drew the Holy Spirit:

E. "Therefore with joy you shall draw water out of the wells of salvation" (Is. 12:3).

6. A. "So three warriors got through the Philistine camp":

B. Why were they three?

C. For the law is fully clarified only by three.

7. A. "...and drew water from the cistern which is by the gate of Bethlehem, and they carried it back. But when they brought it to David, he would not drink it":

B. He did not want the law to be decided in their name [which would portray the decision as schismatic].

C. He made it anonymous, and so established it as decided law for all generations to come:

D. A king may break through a field so as to make a highway, and none may prevent him from doing so.

8. A. Bar Qappara said, "It was the Festival [of Tabernacles], and it was the occasion of the libation of water, during the age in which high places were permitted.

B. "'So three warriors got through the Philistine camp':

C. "Why three?

D. "One to kill, one to clear away the dead, and the third to bring the jug in a condition of cultic purity [unaffected by corpse-uncleanness]."

9. A. R. Hunia in the name of R. Joseph said, "He required rulings on the laws governing kidnapped women."

10. A. R. Simeon b. Rabbi said, "He sought to build the house of the sanctuary."

When David makes a Halakhic ruling his authority is accepted.

Ruth Rabbah XXVII:I

1. A. "Now Naomi had a moda [kinsman] of her husband's, a man of wealth, of the family of Elimelech, whose name was Boaz (Ruth 2:1)":

B. The word *moda* means kinsman.

2. A. ["A man of wealth" translates what is literally "a mighty man of valor, so:] said R. Abbahu, "If a giant marries a giantess? What do they produce? Mighty men of valor.

B. "Boaz married Ruth, and whom did they produce? David: 'Skillful in playing, and a mighty man of valor, and a man of war, prudent in affairs, good-looking, and the Lord is with him' (1 Sam. 16:18)."

3. A. [Supply: "Skillful in playing, and a mighty man of war, prudent in affairs, good-looking, and the Lord is with him" (1 Sam. 16:18)":]

B. "Skillful in playing": in Scripture.

C. "...and a mighty man of valor": in Mishnah.

D. "...a man of war": who knows the give and take of the war of the Torah.

F. "'...and dip your morsel in vinegar': this speaks of his sufferings: 'O Lord, do not rebuke me in your anger' (Ps. 6:2).

G. "'So she sat beside the reapers': for the throne was taken from him for a time."

H. As R. Huna said, "The entire six months that David fled from Absalom are not counted in his reign, for he atoned for his sins with a she-goat, like an ordinary person [rather than with a he-goat, as does the king]."

I. [Resuming from G:] "'and he passed to her parched grain': he was restored to the throne: 'Now I know that the Lord saves his anointed' (Ps. 20:7).

J. "'...and she ate and was satisfied and left some over': this indicates that he would eat in this world, in the days of the messiah, and in the age to come.

2. A. "The second interpretation refers to Solomon: 'Come here': means, to the throne.

B. "'...and eat some bread': this is the bread of the throne: "And Solomon's provision for one day was thirty measures of fine flour and three score measures of meal' (1 Kgs. 5:2).

C. "'...and dip your morsel in vinegar': this refers to the dirty of the deeds [that he did].

D. "'So she sat beside the reapers': for the throne was taken from him for a time."

E. For R. Yohai b. R. Hanina said, "An angel came down in the form of Solomon and sat on the throne, but he made the rounds of the doors throughout Israel and said, 'I, Qohelet, have been king over Israel in Jerusalem' (Qoh. 1:12).

F. "What did one of them do? She set before him a plate of pounded beans and hit him on the head with a stick, saying, 'Doesn't Solomon sit on the throne? How can you say, "' am Solomon, king of Israel"?'"

G. [Reverting to D:] "'and he passed to her parched grain': for he was restored to the throne.

H. "'...and she ate and was satisfied and left some over': this indicates that he would eat in this world, in the days of the messiah, and in the age to come.
Is it not on the authority of Doeg? He is a sectarian, and he will not leave this world whole. But it is not possible to send you away bare.

K. "'All the honor of the king's daughter is [remaining] within the palace' (Ps. 45:14): it is incumbent on a woman not to go out and provide [food], it is incumbent on a man to do so.

L. "'And because they hired Balaam against you' (Dt. 23:5): a man does the hiring, and a woman does not."

The cited verse is interpreted in the setting of the lives of David and Solomon.

Ruth Rabbah LIX:1

1. A. "At midnight I will rise to give thanks to you because of your righteous judgments" (Ps. 119:62):

   B. [In the version of Lamentations Rabbah LXXV:i.4:] R. Phineas in the name of R. Eleazar b. Menahem said, "There was a harp placed under his pillow, and he would get up and play it at night."

   C. R. Levi said, "There was a harp suspended above David's bed, and when midnight came, the north wind would blow upon it, and it made a melody on its own

   D. "'When the instrument played' (2 Kgs. 3:15): what is written is not 'when he played on the instrument' but 'when the instrument played' on its own.

   E. "Now when David would hear the sound, he would get up and study the Torah.

   F. "When the Israelites heard that David was studying the Torah, they would say, 'If David, King of Israel, is studying the Torah, how much more should we!' They immediately got up and studied the Torah."

2. A. "[At midnight I will rise to give thanks to you] because of your righteous judgments" (Ps. 119:62):

   B. The judgments that you brought on Pharaoh: "And the Lord plagued Pharaoh and his house with great plagues" (Gen. 12:17).

   C. And the righteous judgments that you carried out with Abraham and Sarah.

4. A. Another interpretation of the verse, "[At midnight I will rise to give thanks to you] because of your righteous judgments" (Ps. 119:62):

   B. The judgments that you carried out upon the Egyptians, and the acts of righteousness that you did for our ancestors in Egypt.

   C. For they had in hand no religious deeds to carry out so that they might be redeemed, but you gave them two religious deeds to carry out so that they would be saved.

   D. And what were they? The blood of the Passover offering and the blood of circumcision.

   E. Said R. Levi, "On that night the blood of the Passover offering and the blood of circumcision were mingled: 'And when I passed by you and saw you wallowing in your blood, I said to you, In your blood, live, yes, I said to you, in your blood, live' (Ez. 16:6)."

5. A. Another interpretation of the verse, "[At midnight I will rise to give thanks to you] because of your righteous judgments" (Ps. 119:62):

   B. [David speaks,] "The acts of judgment that you brought upon the Ammonites and Moabites.

   C. "And the righteous deeds that you carried out for my grandfather and my grandmother [Boaz, Ruth, of whom David speaks here].

   D. "For had he hastily cursed her but once, where should I have come from?

E.   "But you put in his heart the will to bless her: 'And he said, "May
     you be blessed by the Lord."'"

David as an embodiment of the disciple of sages is presented in detail
here

RUTH RABBAH LXIV:I

4. A.   [Supply: "So she held it, and he measured out six measures of
        barley and laid it upon her":]

B.   Said R. Judah b. R. Simon, "It is on the merit of 'and he measured
     out six measures of barley and laid it upon her' that six righteous
     persons came forth from him, and each one of them had six virtues.

C.   "[These are] David, Hezekiah, Josiah, Hananiah, Mishael, Azariah,
     Daniel, and the royal Messiah:

D.   "David: 'Skillful in playing and a mighty man of valor, and a man
     of war, prudent in affairs, and a comely person, and the Lord is
     with him' (1 Sam. 16:18).

E.   "Hezekiah: 'That the government may be increased and of peace
     there be no end, upon the throne of David and upon his kingdom,
     to establish it and to uphold it, through justice and through
     righteousness' (Is. 9:6). 'And his name is called wonderful,
     counselor, mighty, strong, everlasting father, prince of peace' (Is.
     9:5)."

F.   Some say, "'Be increased' is written with a closed M." ["God
     intended Hezekiah to be the Messiah, but the closed M teaches
     that he was shut up from that honor because he had not sung God's
     praises."]

G.   [Reverting to E:] "Josiah: 'For he shall be as a tree planted by
     waters, that spreads out its roots by the river' (Jer. 17:8).

H.   "Hananiah, Mishael, and Azariah: 'Youths in whom there was no
     blemish but fair to look on, and skilful in all wisdom, and skilful
     in knowledge, and discerning in thought, and such as had ability'
     (Dan. 1:4).

I.   "Daniel: 'A surpassing spirit, and knowledge and understanding,
     interpreting of dreams and declaring of riddles and loosing of knots
     were found in the same Daniel' (Dan. 5:12).

J.   "...and the royal Messiah: 'And the spirit of the Lord shall rest
     upon him, the spirit of wisdom and understanding' (Is. 11:2)."

Ps. 119:62 marks David as a disciple of Torah-study. He possessed the
virtues of the sages and is a model for the disciple of the sage.

RUTH RABBAH LXXXV:I

1. A.   ["Now these are the descendants of Perez: Perez was the father of
        Hezron":]

B.   R. Abba b. Kahana commenced by citing the following verse: "'Rage and do not sin; [commune with your own heart upon your bed and shut up]' (Ps. 4:5).

C.   "Said David before the Holy One, blessed be He, 'How long will they rage against me and say, "Is his family not invalid [for marriage into Israel]? Is he not descended from Ruth the Moabitess?"'

D.   "'...commune with your own heart upon your bed': [David continues,] 'You too have you not descended from two sisters?

E.   "'You look at your own origins "and shut up."

F.   "'So Tamar who married your ancestor Judah – is she not of an invalid family?

G.   "'But she was only a descendant of Shem, son of Noah. So do you come from such impressive genealogy?'"

2. A. [Supply: "Rage and do not sin; [commune with your own heart upon your bed and shut up":]

B.   R. Jacob b. R. Abijah said, "Fight against your inclination to do evil and do not sin."

C.   Rabbis say, "Anger your inclination to do evil and do not sin."

3. A. "Now these are the descendants of Perez: Perez was the father of Hezron": [Gen. R. XII:III cites what follows in connection with this verse "These are the generations of the heaven" (Gen. 2:4)]:

B.   Said R. Abbahu, "In every passage in which the word 'these' occurs, the effect of the usage is to cast a blemish on what has gone before. But where it says, 'And these,' the effect is to add to what has gone before.

C.   [Lacking in Ruth Rabbah:] "In the present context, it is said, 'These...,' and the effect is to disqualify what has gone before. And what has been disqualified [and so rejected]? The unformedness and void."

David stands in chains of tradition.

Ruth Rabbah LXXXIX:I

1. A. R. Isaac commenced discourse by citing this verse: "Then I said, Lo, I have come [in the roll of the book it is written of me]' (Ps. 40:8).

B.   "[David says,] 'Then I had to recite a song when I came, for the word "then" refers only to a song, as it is said, "Then sang Moses" (Ex. 15:1).

C.   "'I was covered by the verse, "An Ammonite and a Moabite shall not come into the assembly of the Lord" (Dt. 23:4), but I have come "in the roll of the book it is written of me" (Ps. 40:8).

D.   "'"...in the roll": this refers to the verse, [David continues], "concerning whom you commanded that they should not enter into your congregation" (Lam. 1:10).

E.   "'"...of the book it is written of me": "An Ammonite and a Moabite shall not enter into the assembly of the Lord" (Dt. 23:4).

F.   "'It is not enough that I have come, but in the roll and the book it is written concerning me:

G.   """...in the roll": Perez, Hezron, Ram, Amminadab, Nahshon, Salmon, Boaz, Obed, Jesse, David.

H.   """...in the book": "And the Lord said, Arise, anoint him, for this is he"' (1 Sam. 16:12)."

2. A.   R. Huna says, "It is written, 'For God has appointed me another seed' (Gen. 4:25) – seed from another place, meaning the Messiah."

3. A.   [Following the version at Genesis Rabbah XXXIX:X.1]: R. Berekhiah b. R. Simon in the name of R. Nehemiah: "The matter may be compared to the case of a king who was traveling from place to place, and a pearl fell out of his crown. The king stopped there and held up his retinue there, collected sand in heaps and brought sieves. He had the first pile sifted and did not find the pearl. So he did with the second and did not find it. But in the third heap he found it. People said, 'The king has found his pearl.'

B.   "So said the Holy One, blessed be He, to Abraham, 'Why did I have to spell out the descent of Shem, Arpachshad, Shelah, Eber, Peleg, Reu, Serug, Nahor, and Terah (1 Chr. 1:24)? Was it not entirely for you?' 'Abram, the same is Abraham' (1 Chr. 1:24).

C.   "'And he found his heart faithful before you' (Neh. 9:8). [Freedman, p. 319, n. 2: He was the pearl that God found.]

D.   "So said the Holy One, blessed be He, to David, 'Why did I have to spell out the descent of Perez, Hezron, Ram, Aminadab, Nachshon, Salmon, Boaz, Obed, and Jesse? Was it not entirely for you?'

E.   "Thus: 'I have found David my servant, with my holy oil have I anointed him' (Ps. 89:21)."

Ps. 40:8 explains the sequence of authorities in the process of descent to David.

RUTH RABBAH LXXXV:I

1. A.   ["Now these are the descendants of Perez: Perez was the father of Hezron" (Ruth 4;18):]

B.   R. Abba b. Kahana commenced by citing the following verse: "'Rage and do not sin; [commune with your own heart upon your bed and shut up]' (Ps. 4:5).

C.   "Said David before the Holy One, blessed be He, 'How long will they rage against me and say, "Is his family not invalid [for marriage into Israel]? Is he not descended from Ruth the Moabitess?"'

D.   "'...commune with your own heart upon your bed': [David continues,] 'You too have you not descended from two sisters?

E.   "'You look at your own origins "and shut up."

F.   "'So Tamar who married your ancestor Judah – is she not of an invalid family?

G.   "'But she was only a descendant of Shem, son of Noah. So do you come from such impressive genealogy?'"

2. A. [Supply: "Rage and do not sin; [commune with your own heart upon your bed and shut up":]

B. R. Jacob b. R. Abijah said, "Fight against your inclination to do evil and do not sin."

C. Rabbis say, "Anger your inclination to do evil and do not sin."

3. A. "Now these are the descendants of Perez: Perez was the father of Hezron": [Gen. R. XII:III cites what follows in connection with this verse": These are the generations of the heaven" (Gen. 2:4)]:

B. Said R. Abbahu, "In every passage in which the word 'these' occurs, the effect of the usage is to cast a blemish on what has gone before. But where it says, 'And these,' the effect is to add to what has gone before.

C. [Lacking in Ruth Rabbah:] "In the present context, it is said, 'These...,' and the effect is to disqualify what has gone before. And what has been disqualified [and so rejected]? The unformedness and void."

In the path of Ps. 4:5 David's connection through Ruth is spelled out.

RUTH RABBAH LXXXIX:I

1. A. R. Isaac commenced discourse by citing this verse: "Then I said, Lo, I have come [in the roll of the book it is written of me]' (Ps. 40:8).

B. "[David says,] 'Then I had to recite a song when I came, for the word "then" refers only to a song, as it is said, "Then sang Moses" (Ex. 15:1).

C. "'I was covered by the verse, "An Ammonite and a Moabite shall not come into the assembly of the Lord" (Dt. 23:4), but I have come "in the roll of the book it is written of me" (Ps. 40:8).

D. "''...in the roll": this refers to the verse, [David continues], "concerning whom you commanded that they should not enter into your congregation" (Lam. 1:10).

E. "''...of the book it is written of me": "An Ammonite and a Moabite shall not enter into the assembly of the Lord" (Dt. 23:4).

F. "'It is not enough that I have come, but in the roll and the book it is written concerning me:

G. "''...in the roll": Perez, Hezron, Ram, Amminadab, Nahshon, Salmon, Boaz, Obed, Jesse, David.

H. "''...in the book": "And the Lord said, Arise, anoint him, for this is he"' (1 Sam. 16:12)."

2. A. R. Huna says, "It is written, 'For God has appointed me another seed' (Gen. 4:25) – seed from another place, meaning the Messiah."

3. A. [Following the version at Genesis Rabbah XXXIX:X.1]: R. Berekhiah b. R. Simon in the name of R. Nehemiah: "The matter may be compared to the case of a king who was traveling from place to place, and a pearl fell out of his crown. The king stopped there and held up his retinue there, collected sand in heaps and

brought sieves. He had the first pile sifted and did not find the pearl. So he did with the second and did not find it. But in the third heap he found it. People said, 'The king has found his pearl.'

B. "So said the Holy One, blessed be He, to Abraham, 'Why did I have to spell out the descent of Shem, Arpachshad, Shelah, Eber, Peleg, Reu, Serug, Nahor, and Terah (1 Chr. 1:24)? Was it not entirely for you?' 'Abram, the same is Abraham' (1 Chr. 1:24).

C. "'And he found his heart faithful before you' (Neh. 9:8). [Freedman, p. 319, n. 2: He was the pearl that God found.]

D. "So said the Holy One, blessed be He, to David, 'Why did I have to spell out the descent of Perez, Hezron, Ram, Aminadab, Nachshon, Salmon, Boaz, Obed, and Jesse? Was it not entirely for you?'

E. "Thus: 'I have found David my servant, with my holy oil have I anointed him' (Ps. 89:21)."

Affixed to a number of lists is the one of holy men,

RUTH RABBAH LXXXV:I

1. A. ["Now these are the descendants of Perez: Perez was the father of Hezron":]

B. R. Abba b. Kahana commenced by citing the following verse: "'Rage and do not sin; [commune with your own heart upon your bed and shut up]' (Ps. 4:5).

C. "Said David before the Holy One, blessed be He, 'How long will they rage against me and say, "Is his family not invalid [for marriage into Israel]? Is he not descended from Ruth the Moabitess?"'

D. "'...commune with your own heart upon your bed': [David continues,] 'You too have you not descended from two sisters?

E. "'You look at your own origins "and shut up."

F. "'So Tamar who married your ancestor Judah – is she not of an invalid family?

G. "'But she was only a descendant of Shem, son of Noah. So do you come from such impressive genealogy?'"

2. A. [Supply: "Rage and do not sin; [commune with your own heart upon your bed and shut up":]

B. R. Jacob b. R. Abijah said, "Fight against your inclination to do evil and do not sin."

C. Rabbis say, "Anger your inclination to do evil and do not sin."

3. A. "Now these are the descendants of Perez: Perez was the father of Hezron": [Gen. R. XII:III cites what follows in connection with this verse": These are the generations of the heaven" (Gen. 2:4)]:

B. Said R. Abbahu, "In every passage in which the word 'these' occurs, the effect of the usage is to cast a blemish on what has gone before. But where it says, 'And these,' the effect is to add to what has gone before.

C. [Lacking in Ruth Rabbah:] "In the present context, it is said, 'These...,' and the effect is to disqualify what has gone before. And what has been disqualified [and so rejected]? The unformedness and void."

Ps. 4:5 accounts for the position of David on the specified lists of holy men.

RUTH RABBAH LXXXIX:1

1. A. R. Isaac commenced discourse by citing this verse: "Then I said, Lo, I have come [in the roll of the book it is written of me]' (Ps. 40:8).
   B. "[David says,] 'Then I had to recite a song when I came, for the word "then" refers only to a song, as it is said, "Then sang Moses" (Ex. 15:1).
   C. "'I was covered by the verse, "An Ammonite and a Moabite shall not come into the assembly of the Lord" (Dt. 23:4), but I have come "in the roll of the book it is written of me" (Ps. 40:8).
   D. ""...in the roll": this refers to the verse, [David continues], "concerning whom you commanded that they should not enter into your congregation" (Lam. 1:10).
   E. ""...of the book it is written of me": "An Ammonite and a Moabite shall not enter into the assembly of the Lord" (Dt. 23:4).
   F. "'It is not enough that I have come, but in the roll and the book it is written concerning me:
   G. ""...in the roll": Perez, Hezron, Ram, Amminadab, Nahshon, Salmon, Boaz, Obed, Jesse, David.
   H. ""...in the book": "And the Lord said, Arise, anoint him, for this is he"' (1 Sam. 16:12)."
2. A. R. Huna says, "It is written, 'For God has appointed me another seed' (Gen. 4:25) – seed from another place, meaning the Messiah."

RUTH RABBAH LXXXIX:1

1. A. R. Isaac commenced discourse by citing this verse: "Then I said, Lo, I have come [in the roll of the book it is written of me]' (Ps. 40:8).
   B. "[David says,] 'Then I had to recite a song when I came, for the word "then" refers only to a song, as it is said, "Then sang Moses" (Ex. 15:1).
   C. "'I was covered by the verse, "An Ammonite and a Moabite shall not come into the assembly of the Lord" (Dt. 23:4), but I have come "in the roll of the book it is written of me" (Ps. 40:8).
   D. ""...in the roll": this refers to the verse, [David continues], "concerning whom you commanded that they should not enter into your congregation" (Lam. 1:10).
   E. ""...of the book it is written of me": "An Ammonite and a Moabite shall not enter into the assembly of the Lord" (Dt. 23:4).

F. "'It is not enough that I have come, but in the roll and the book it is written concerning me:

G. ""'...in the roll": Perez, Hezron, Ram, Amminadab, Nahshon, Salmon, Boaz, Obed, Jesse, David.

H. ""'...in the book": "And the Lord said, Arise, anoint him, for this is he"' (1 Sam. 16:12).'"

2. A. R. Huna says, "It is written, 'For God has appointed me another seed' (Gen. 4:25) – seed from another place, meaning the Messiah."

3. A. [Following the version at Genesis Rabbah XXXIX:X.1]: R. Berekhiah b. R. Simon in the name of R. Nehemiah: "The matter may be compared to the case of a king who was traveling from place to place, and a pearl fell out of his crown. The king stopped there and held up his retinue there, collected sand in heaps and brought sieves. He had the first pile sifted and did not find the pearl. So he did with the second and did not find it. But in the third heap he found it. People said, 'The king has found his pearl.'

B. "So said the Holy One, blessed be He, to Abraham, 'Why did I have to spell out the descent of Shem, Arpachshad, Shelah, Eber, Peleg, Reu, Serug, Nahor, and Terah (1 Chr. 1:24)? Was it not entirely for you?' 'Abram, the same is Abraham' (1 Chr. 1:24).

C. "'And he found his heart faithful before you' (Neh. 9:8). [Freedman, p. 319, n. 2: He was the pearl that God found.]

D. "So said the Holy One, blessed be He, to David, 'Why did I have to spell out the descent of Perez, Hezron, Ram, Aminadab, Nachshon, Salmon, Boaz, Obed, and Jesse? Was it not entirely for you?'

E. "Thus: 'I have found David my servant, with my holy oil have I anointed him' (Ps. 89:21)."

Ps, 89:21 accounts for the descent of David.

RUTH RABBAH LXXXV:I

1. A. ["Now these are the descendants of Perez: Perez was the father of Hezron" (Ruth 4:18):]

B. R. Abba b. Kahana commenced by citing the following verse: "'Rage and do not sin; [commune with your own heart upon your bed and shut up]' (Ps. 4:5).

C. "Said David before the Holy One, blessed be He, 'How long will they rage against me and say, "Is his family not invalid [for marriage into Israel]? Is he not descended from Ruth the Moabitess?"'

D. "'...commune with your own heart upon your bed': [David continues,] 'You too have you not descended from two sisters?

E. "'You look at your own origins "and shut up."

F. "'So Tamar who married your ancestor Judah – is she not of an invalid family?

G. "'But she was only a descendant of Shem, son of Noah. So do you come from such impressive genealogy?'"

2. A.   [Supply: "Rage and do not sin; [commune with your own heart upon your bed and shut up":]

   B.   R. Jacob b. R. Abijah said, "Fight against your inclination to do evil and do not sin."

   C.   Rabbis say, "Anger your inclination to do evil and do not sin."

3. A.   "Now these are the descendants of Perez: Perez was the father of Hezron": [Gen. R. XII:III cites what follows in connection with this verse": These are the generations of the heaven" (Gen. 2:4)]:

   B.   Said R. Abbahu, "In every passage in which the word 'these' occurs, the effect of the usage is to cast a blemish on what has gone before. But where it says, 'And these,' the effect is to add to what has gone before.

   C.   [Lacking in Ruth Rabbah:] "In the present context, it is said, 'These...,' and the effect is to disqualify what has gone before. And what has been disqualified [and so rejected]? The unformedness and void."

The descendant of Ruth is identified.

[1] Is David an active player or a routine and scarcely animate one? David is an active participant in the declarations of the propositions involving him. These involve Psalms above all.

[2] What components of the collection make routine glosses of the received Scriptures and which ones provide more than minor glosses of the tradition? David's descent is a principal motif.

[3] Can we identify a pronounced bias or a polemic in the utilization of David? David descends from dubious lineage yet is the progenitor of the Messiah.

[4] How is David comparable to other sages in this document? The motif of David is an heir of the Messiah competes with the motif of David as descended from Ruth.

13

David in Lamentations Rabbah

Lamentations Rabbah does not address issues of David.

LAMENTATIONS RABBAH XXI.I.

2. A.   Said R. Yosé b. Halapta, "Whoever knows how many years the Israelites worshipped idolatry knows also when the son of David will come."

B.   "And we have three verses of Scripture that support this position.

C.   "'And I will visit upon her the days of the Baalim, wherein she offered to them ' (Hos. 2:15).

D.   "The second: 'And it came to pass that, as he called and they would not hear, so they shall call and I will not hear ' (Zech. 7:13).

E.   "The third: 'And when they ask, Because of what did the Lord our God do all these things? you shall answer them, Because you forsook me and served alien gods on your own land, you will have to serve foreigners in a land not your own ' (Jer. 5:19)."

The son of David, the Messiah, will come at the specified time.

LAMENTATIONS RABBI XXX.I.

1. A.   Zabedee b. Levi commenced [by citing the following verse of Scripture]: "'The kings of the earth did not believe, or any of the inhabitants of the world, that foe or enemy could enter the gates of Jerusalem. [This was for the sins of her prophets and the iniquities of her priests, who shed in the midst of her the blood of the righteous. They wandered, blind, through the streets, so defiled with blood that none could touch their garments] ' (Lam. 4:12-13).

B. "There were four kings, each of whom asked for this but not that, and these are they: David, Asa, Jehoshaphat, and Hezekiah.

C. "David said, 'Let me pursue my enemies and overtake them ' (Ps. 18:38).

D. "Said to him the Holy One, blessed be He, 'I shall do it. "And David smote them from the twilight even to the evening of the next day ' (1 Sam. 30:17)."

Ps. 18:38 is interpreted by David.

[1] Is DAVID AN ACTIVE PLAYER OR A ROUTINE AND SCARCELY ANIMATE ONE? David signals the coming of the Messiah. But the representation of David in the document is sparse.

[2] WHAT COMPONENTS OF THE COLLECTION MAKE ROUTINE GLOSSES OF THE RECEIVED SCRIPTURES and which ones provide more than minor glosses of the tradition? The glosses are routine,

[3] CAN WE IDENTIFY A PRONOUNCED BIAS OR A POLEMIC in the utilization of David? The segment is insufficient for answering this question,

[4] How IS DAVID COMPARABLE TO OTHER SAGES IN THIS DOCUMENT?

The same answer applies to all the classes: the data are too sparse to make a difference.

14

David in The Fathers
According to Rabbi Nathan

The Fathers according to R. Nathan text A contains two statements of David, one an expansion of Ps. 139:21-22, the other an allusion fo a narrative of David.

THE FATHERS ACCORDING TO RABBI NATHAN XVI:VI.

1. A. **and hatred for people**: how so?

   B. This teaches that a person should not have the plan of say, "Love sages and hate disciples," "love disciples and hate common folk," but rather, "Love them all, and hate heretics, apostates and informers."

   C So did David say, *Do I not hate those, Lord, that hate you? And do I not strive with those who rise up against you? I hate them with utmost hatred, I regard them as my enemies* (Ps. 139:21-22)."

   D. But does Scripture not say, *You shall love your neighbor as yourself, I am the Lord* (Lev 19:18)?

   E. Why so? Because I have created him, and if he does a proper deed with you [Goldin: if he acts as thy people do, thou shalt love him], you should love him too, but if not, you should not love him.

David speaks through Ps. 139:21-22.

THE FATHERS ACCORDING TO RABBI NATHAN XL:XVIII:I.

1. A. [In] any loving relationship which depends upon something, [when] that thing is gone, the love is gone. But any which does not depend upon something will never come to an end.

B.   What is a loving relationship which depends upon something?
      That is the love of Amnon and Tamar [II Sam. 13:15]. And one
      which does not depend upon something: That is the love of David
      and Jonathan

David exemplifies the teaching on a loving relationship that does not
depend upon something. The participation of David in ARNA is limited.

15

David in Yerushalmi Berakhot and Zeraim

The two Talmuds contain substantial narratives and scriptural amplifications of David's scriptural statements. We pay special attention to the protracted expositions of David's life and teaching, We have come across only a very small collection of sustained exegesis and narrative, The narrative is precipitated by s Ps. 57:8].

YERUSHALMI BERAKHOT

YERUSHALMI BERAKHOT [I:12]

[L] When David dined at the royal dinner, he would rise at midnight. And when he dined at his own [private] dinner, he would rise [at the time about which it says] "My eyes awake before the watches of the night."

[M] In either case, at dawn one would not find David asleep. As David said, "Awake, my glory! Awake, O harp and lyre! I will awake before dawn [Ps. 57:8]."

[N] [One should interpret the verse as follows:] In glory I awaken to recite my words. My glory is as naught until I recite my words [of praise for you].

[O] "I will awake the dawn" [means] *I will awaken before the dawn. The dawn will not awaken me.*

[P] But his [evil] impulse tried to seduce him [to sin]. And it would say to him, "David. It is the custom of kings that the dawn awakens them. And you say, 'I will awake the dawn.' It is the custom of kings that they sleep until the third hour [of the day]. And you say,

'At midnight I rise,'" And [David] used to say [in reply], "[I rise early,] 'Because of thy righteous ordinances' [Ps. 119:62]."

[Q]   And what would David do? R. Pinhas in the name of R. Eleazar b. R. Menahem, "He used to take a harp and lyre and set them as his bedside. And he would rise at midnight and play them so that the associates of Torah should hear. And what would the associates of Torah say? 'If King David involves himself with Torah, how much more so should we.'" [S adds: We find that all of Israel was engaged in Torah study on account of David.]

[R]   Said R. Levi, "A lyre was suspended at David's window. And the north wind would blow at night, set it swinging around, and it would play by itself [and wake him]. Similarly [Scripture says concerning Elisha], 'And when the minstrel [lit.: the instrument] played [kngn hmngn] [2 Kings 3:15]. It does not say, 'When he played on the instrument [kngn bmngn]' but rather when the instrument played [kngn hmngn]. The lyre would play by itself."

Ps. 57:8 speaks for David and the narrative overall sets David up as an exemplary Rabbinic sage, This is a good example of the Rabbinization of the Davidic collection,

YERUSHALMI BERAKHOT 2:3

[II:3A]   *Now R. Yohanan required that [his students] attribute his teachings to him [whenever they repeated them].*

[B]   Accordingly, even King David [implied that a person who repeats his words attribute them to him]. He asked [God] for mercy, "Let me dwell in thy tent for ever!" [Ps. 61:4].

[C]   [How should one interpret this verse?] R. Pinhas, R. Jeremiah in the name of R. Yohanan, "Did it ever cross David's mind that he would live forever? Rather so said David, 'Let me merit that my words be spoken in my name in the synagogues and in the study halls.'"

Ps. 61:4 has David aspire to the attainments of the Rabbinic sage.

YERUSHALMI BERAKHOT 9:2

[III:5 A]   R. Huna, Simeon Qamatraya in the name of R. Samuel bar Nahman, "'And Jonathan the son of Gershom, son of Menasseh [alt. reading in Judges: Moses], and his sons were priests to the tribe of the Danites until the day of captivity of the Land' (Judges 18:30). The letter nun [in the name mnsh] is suspended [above the other letters]. [This teaches that] if he was worthy, [they called him] Son of Moses [msh, without the nun]. But if not, [they called him] Son of Menasseh [who was evil, cf. II Kings 21]."

[B]   *The associates posed the following question to R. Samuel bar Nahman,* "If he [Jonathan] was a priest to a foreign god, why was he granted longevity? [The verse says, "His sons were priests …until the day of the captivity of the Land. So they set up Micah's graven image which he made, as long as the house of God was at Shiloh" (Judges 18:30-31).]

[C] He said to them, "[He was granted longevity] because he acted maliciously toward his idol."

[D] How did he act maliciously toward his idol? *A person would come to him to make an offering to the idol of a bull, a goat, or a ram, and would say to him "May this be recompense for me."*

[E] He [Jonathan] would say to the person, "What good will this do for you? [This idol] neither sees, nor hears, nor eats, nor drinks, nor does good, nor does evil, nor speaks."

[F] The person would say to him, "By your life! *Then what shall I do [instead]?"*

[G] *And Jonathan would say to him, "Go, make and bring to me container of fine flour, and prepare with it ten eggs, and bring it to me. And he [the idol] shall eat from all that you bring, and I shall seek recompense for you from him." As soon as the person [brought all this and] left, Jonathan ate the food.*

[H] *One time a scoundrel came before him [to offer a sacrifice to the idol], and Jonathan told him the same thing ["What good will this do for you, etc."]. He said to Jonathan, "If it is of no use [to offer a sacrifice to the idol] then what are you doing here [serving as its priest]?" He said to him, "This is my livelihood."*

[I] When David became king, he sent for and brought [Jonathan] before him. He said to him, "You are the grandson of that righteous man [Moses]. How can you worship a foreign god?"

[J] He said to him, "I have received this tradition from my grandfather's house. 'It is better to sell yourself into service of a foreign god than to go begging for sustenance.'"

[K] [David] said to him, "God forbid. He [your grandfather] never said such a thing! [You have corrupted the tradition and erred.] Rather he said, 'It is better to sell yourself into service that is foreign to you ['bwdh shy' zrh lk and not 'bwdh zrh,] than to go begging.'"

[L] Since David saw how much [Jonathan] loved money, what did he do? He made him his treasurer.

[M] In this regard [the verse says], "And Shebuel the son of Gershom, son of Moses, was chief officer in charge of the treasuries" (I Chron. 26:24). [Jonathan was called] Shebuel because he returned [sb] to serve God ['l] with all his heart and with all his might. "He was the chief officer in charge of the treasuries," that is, David appointed him [Jonathan] to be his treasurer.

[N] *They raised an objection to R. Samuel bar Nahman,* "Lo, it is written, '[Jonathan] and his sons were priests to the tribe of the Danites until the day of the captivity of the Land' (Judges 18:30). [How can you say that David appointed him treasurer?]"

[O] He said to them, "When David died, Solomon succeeded him, and replaced his officers. And [Jonathan] went back to his old corrupt ways [and served as a priest of idolatry for the Danites].

[P] In this regard [the verse says, 'Now there dwelt an old prophet in Bethel' (I Kings 13:11). They say that [idolater in Jeroboam's kingdom] was him, [Jonathan the Danite]."

The narrative of Jonathan the Danite is expanded and completed. David plays major role.

YERUSHALMI BERAKHOT 9:5

[I:1.C] R. Huna in the name of R. Aha, "'A Psalm of David. I will sing of loving kindness and justice; to the, O Lord, I will sing' (Ps 101:1). David said to the Holy One, blessed be He, 'If you act towards me out of loving kindness, I will sing, and if you act towards me out of justice, I will sing. Either way, to thee O Lord, I will sing.'"

[D] Said R. Tanhuma b. Judah, "'In God, whose word I praise, in the Lord, whose word I praise' (Ps. 56:10). For both [God's] attribute of justice, and the [Lord's] attribute of mercy, I praise."

[E] And sages say, "'I will lift up the cup of salvation and call on the name of the Lord' (Ps. 116:13). 'I suffered distress and anguish. Then I called on the name of the Lord' (Ps. 116:3-4). For both [salvation and distress] he, 'Called on the name of the Lord.'"

[F] Said R. Yudan b. Pilah, "Thus Job said, 'The Lord gave and the Lord has taken away; blessed be the name of the Lord' (Job 1:21). Just as he gave with mercy, so he took with mercy. Moreover, when he gave, he consulted with no one. But when he took, he consulted with his court."

Ps 56:10, 101:1 and Ps, 116:3-4 form the foundations for this account. This is a fine example of the transformation of Psalms into chapters im the life of David.

YERUSHALMI PEAH

YERUSHALMI PEAH 1:1

[IX:13] A. Said R. Abba bar Kahana, "The generation of David was made up entirely of righteous persons. But because of informers in their midst, they went to war and died. This is what David said, 'I lie down among man-eating lions whose teeth are spears and arrows, whose tongue is a sharp sword' (Ps. 57:5).

B. "'I lie down among … lions:' this speaks of Abner and Amasa, who were lions but who were killed [2 Sam. 3:27, 20:10];

C. "'man-eating lions:' this speaks of Doeg and Ahitofel, who were eaten alive by gossip [2 Sam. 22:20-23]

D. "'whose teeth are spears and arrows:' this speaks of Keilah, as it is written, 'will the men of Keilah deliver me into his hands? Will Saul come down as your servant heard' (1 Sam. 23:11);

E. " 'whose tongue is a sharp sword:' this speaks of the Ziphites: 'when the Ziphites came and told Saul, Know, David is hiding among us' (Ps. 54:2)."

Ps. 57:5 forms the center of the narrative.

YERUSHALMI PEAH 1:1

[IX:15] A. Why is gossip called the three pronged weapon? Because it kills three, the one who spreads it, the one who listens to it, and the one about whom it is spread.

B. In the time of Saul four were killed, Doeg, who spread the gossip, Saul, who listened to it, Ahimelech, about whom it was told, and Abner.

C. Why was Abner killed?

D. R. Joshua b. Levi, R. Simeon b. Laqish, and rabbis:

E. R. Joshua b. Levi: "Because when he set up Saul's son Ishbosheth as king over the Northern Kingdom, he treated the blood of young men lightly: 'Abler said to Joab, Let the young men come forward and sport before us. Yes let them, Joab replied' (2 Sam. 2:14)."

F. R. Simeon b. Laqish: "Because he put his own name before the name of King David: 'Abner immediately sent messengers to David, saying, To whom shall the land belong' (2 Sam. 3:12). He wrote, 'From Abner to David.'"

G. and rabbis: "Because he did not allow Saul to be appeased by David: 'Please, sir, take a close look at the corner of your cloak in my hand, for when I cut off the corner of your cloak, I did not kill you. You must see plainly that I have done nothing evil or rebellious, and I have never wronged you. Yet your are aiming at taking my life (Sam. 24:12).

H. [Abner] said to him, Why do you pay attention to his murmurings. Your cloak was caught in a thorn bush. But when they came to the encampment, Saul said, Did you not, Abner, explain about the edge of the robe, saying, Your cloak was caught in a thorn bush? Will you also claim that the spear and cruse of oil were caught in a thorn bush?'"

I. Some say, "Because he had a chance to warn Nov the city of the priests but didn't do so."

[IX:14] A. At that moment David said to the Holy One, blessed be he, "Lord of the world! Will your presence descend upon the earth? May your presence rise up from among them!"

B. That is in line with Scripture: "Exalt yourself over the heavens, God, let your glory be over all the earth" (Ps. 57:6).

C. [By contrast to David's generation,] Ahab's generation was made up entirely of idolaters. Yet because there were no informers in their midst, when they went down to battle they were victorious.

D. That is in line with what Obadiah said to Elijah, "My lord has surely been told what I did when Jezebel was killing the prophets of the Lord, how I hid a hundred prophets of the Lord, fifty men to a cave, and provided them with food and drink" (1 Kgs. 18:13).

E. [with food and drink]: if bread is mentioned, why mention water, and if water is mention, by mention bread? Both are requires to teach you that water was more difficult to provide than bread.

F. "Then Elijah said to the people on Mount Carmel, 'I am the only prophet of the Lord left'" (1 Kgs. 18:22).

G. *All the people knew that the prophets were alive but did not inform the king.*

The narrative reaches its climax at Ps. 57:6.

[1] IS DAVID AN ACTIVE PLAYER OR A ROUTINE AND SCARCELY ANIMATE ONE? The story of Ps. 57:8 about David's rising at midnight shows him as an active disciple of Torah-study. Ps. 119:62 animates David's exemplary conduct.

[2] WHAT COMPONENTS OF THE COLLECTION MAKE ROUTINE GLOSSES OF THE RECEIVED SCRIPTURES and which ones provide more than minor glosses of the tradition? The importance of Psalms as records of David's inner life is paramount.

[3] CAN WE IDENTIFY A PRONOUNCED BIAS OR A POLEMIC in the utilization of David? David as sage is the key motif throughout.

[4] HOW IS DAVID COMPARABLE TO OTHER SAGES IN THIS DOCUMENT? David is nothing other than a sage.

16

David in Yerushalmi Moed

YERUSHALMI YOMA

YERUSHALMI YOMA 6:3

[I: H] the story about a priest in Sepphoris, who grabbed his share and the share of his fellow, and they called him "Son of the Bean," to this day.

[I] This is the meaning of what David said, "Rescue me, O my God, from the hand of the wicked, from the grasp of the unjust and cruel man" (Ps. 71:4) .

David's statement at Ps, 71:4 is clarified in a story.

YERUSHALMI YOMA 7:3

[IV:2 A] Now two questions may not be presented at the same time.

[B] But if two questions have been presented [to the Urim and Thummim] at the same time —

[C] *there is a Tannaite authority who teaches,* "One receives an answer to the first question but not to the second one."

[D] *And there is a Tannaite authority who teaches,* "One receives an answer to the second question but does not receive an answer to the first question."

[E] *And there is a Tannaite authority who teaches,* "One does not receive an answer either to the first question or to the second question."

[F] *He who says,* "One receives an answer to the first question but not to the second one," *adduces in evidence the following verse:* "Then said David, 'O Lord, the God of Israel, thy servant has surely heard that Saul seeks to come to Keilah, to destroy the city on my account.

103

Will the men of Keilah surrender me into his hand? Will Saul come down, as thy servant has heard? O Lord, the God of Israel, I beseech thee, tell thy servant.' And the Lord said, 'He will come down'"(1 Sam. 23:10-11).

[G] David did not ask properly. It was necessary to ask in this way: "Will Saul come down...," and if he comes down, "Will the men of Keilah surrender me into his hand?"

[H] *The one who says,* "One receives an answer to the second question but does not receive an answer to the first question," *adduces in evidence the following verse:* "Will the men of Keilah surrender me into his hand?"

[I] *The one who says,* "One does not receive an answer either to the first question or to the second question," adduces in evidence the following verse: "And David inquired of the Lord, 'Shall I pursue after this band? Shall I overtake them?' He answered him, 'Pursue; for you shall surely overtake and shall surely rescue'"(I Sam. 30:8).

[J] David sought mercy: "Will the men of Keilah surrender me into his hand? Will Saul come down, as thy servant has heard? O Lord, the God of Israel, I beseech thee, tell thy servant" (I Sam. 23:11).

[K] Note that he asked two questions but got three answers.

[L] "And David inquired of the Lord, 'Shall I pursue after this band? Shall I overtake them?' He answered him, 'Pursue; for you shall surely overtake and shall surely rescue'"(I Sam. 30:8).

The narrative concerns the proper mode of asking and answering questions of God: he asked two questions but got three answers.

YERUSHALMI TAANIT

YERUSHALMI TAANIT 2:9

[I:2. A] Was it not appropriate to list David and Solomon, and only afterward, Elijah and Jonah [who came after their time]?

[B] It was to conclude the entire prayer with, ". . . who has mercy on the land."

[I:4. A] *There is no problem as to Solomon* [who said a prayer concerning Jerusalem], for it is written, "I have built thee an exalted house, a place for thee to dwell in forever" (I Kings 8:13).

[B] But why David? Because he sought to conduct a census [but, in the end, stayed the plague that ensued by entreating in behalf of the land (2 Sam. 24:25)].

[C] Said R. Abbahu, "It is written, 'Answer me when I call, O God of my right! Thou has given me room when I was in distress' (Ps. 4:1)

[D] "Said David before the Holy One, blessed be he, 'Lord of the ages! Whenever I came into a tight spot you broadened it for me. I got into a tight spot with Bathsheba, and you gave me Solomon. I got into a tight spot in [counting] Israel, and you gave me the holy house.'"

David's statement at Ps. 4:1 is expounded,. The sample is too small to permit finding answers to the governing questions.

17

David in Yerushalmi Nashim

YERUSHALMI SOTAH

YERUSHALMI SOTAH 1:7

[III:1.A] **And since he stole three hearts — his father's, the court's, and the Israelite's — since it is said, And Absalom stole the heart of the men of Israel (II Sam. 15:6) — therefore three darts were thrust into him, since it is said, And he took three darts in his hand and thrust them through the heart of Absalom (II Sam. 18:14).**

[B] **His father's,** as it is written, "And at the end of forty years [Absalom said to the king, 'Pray let me go and pay my vow, which I have vowed to the lord, in Hebron]'" (2 Sam. 15:7).

[C] "The whole reign of David was only forty years, and here it says this! But when the Israelites sought a king: " For your servant vowed a vow [while I dwelt at Geshur in Aram, saying, 'If the Lord will indeed bring me back to Jerusalem, then I will offer worship to the Lord]'" (2 Sam. 15:8).

[D] [David] said to [Absalom], " What do you want here?"

[E] He said, " Write out an order that two men whom I will take may come with me."

[F] He said to him, " Tell me whom you wish to take, and I shall write the order."

[G] He said to him, " Write it out blank, and I'll choose whomever I want."

[H] He wrote the order with blank spaces.

[I] He went and chose his men, two by two, until he reached two hundred men. That is in line with what is written: " With Absalom went two hundred men from Jerusalem who were invited guests, and they went in their simplicity and knew nothing. And while Absalom was offering the sacrifices, he sent for Ahithophel" (2 Sam. 15:11).

[J] "Invited" by David.

[K] "Going in their simplicity" because of Absalom.

[L] "And they knew nothing" of the conspiracy of Ahithophel.

[M] Huna in the name of R. Aha: " And all of them were heads of sanhedrins."

[N] When they saw things going opposite to the will of the king, they said, " Lord of all ages, let us fall into the hand of David, and let David not fall into our hand. For if we fall into David's hand, lo, he will have mercy on us. But if, God forbid, David should fall into our hand, we shall not have mercy on him."

[O] That is in line with what David said: " He will deliver my soul in safety from the battle that I wage, for many are arrayed against me" (Ps. 55:19).

[P] **And the heart of the court:** " Absalom said moreover, 'O that I were a judge in the land!'" (2 Sam. 15:4).

[Q] "Thus Absalom did [to all of Israel who came to the king for judgment]" (2 Sam. 15:6).

[R] **And the heart of all Israelites:** " So Absalom stole the hearts of the men of Israel" (2 Sam. 15:6).

David is secondary in this exposition. The statement of Ps. 55:19 is clarified.

YERUSHALMI SOTAH 8:10

[I:4. A] Abraham made the impulse to do evil into good.

[B] What is the Scriptural basis for that statement?

[C] " And thou didst find his heart faithful before thee, [and didst make with him the covenant to give to his descendants the land of the Canaanite, the Hittite, the Amorite, the Perizzite, the Jebusite, and the Girgashite]" (Neh. 9:8).

[D] Said R. Aha, " He made an agreement with it: '[And thou didst find his heart faithful before thee,] and didst make with him the covenant [to give to his descendants the land of the Canaanite, the Hittite, the Amorite, the Perizzite, the Jebusite, and the Girgashite]' (Neh. 9:8)."

[E] But David was unable to overcome it, so he had to kill it in his heart.

[F] What is the Scriptural basis for that statement?

[G] "[For I am poor and needy,] and my heart is stricken within me" (Ps. 109.22).

Ps. 109.22 supports the proposition about David.

[1] IS DAVID AN ACTIVE PLAYER OR A ROUTINE AND SCARCELY ANIMATE ONE? David's role is an active one,

[2] WHAT COMPONENTS OF THE COLLECTION MAKE ROUTINE GLOSSES OF THE RECEIVED SCRIPTURES and which ones provide more than minor glosses of the tradition? David's conflict with Absalom does more than supply minor glosses.

[3] CAN WE IDENTIFY A PRONOUNCED BIAS OR A POLEMIC in the utilization of David? The scriptural narrative favors David and the glosses follow suit.

[4] HOW IS DAVID COMPARABLE TO OTHER SAGES IN THIS DOCUMENT? David is not portrayed as a sage. To that characterization of the heroes of Israel he plays no role

18

David in Yerushalmi Neziqin

Yerushalmi Horayot

Yerushalmi Horayot II:

[1. A] Who is the anointed priest? It is the one who is anointed with the anointing oil, not the one who is dedicated by many garments [M. 3:2G]:

[B] Said R. Huna, "For all those six months during which David was on the run from Absalom, it was through a she-goat that he would attain atonement for himself, like any ordinary person."

Before David was anointed as king, he was in the status of an ordinary Israelite.

Yerushlami Sanhedrin

Y. Sanhedrin 2:3

[A] The king does not judge, and [others] do not judge him;

[B] does not give testimony, and [others] do not give testimony about him;

[C] does not perform the rite of removing the shoe, and others do not perform the rite of removing the shoe with his wife;

[D] does not enter into levirate marriage, nor [does his brother] enter levirate marriage with his wife.

[H] R. Judah says, "A king may marry the widow of a king.

[I] "For so we find in the case of David, that he married the widow of Saul,

[J]   "For it is said, 'And I gave you your master's house and your
      master's wives into your embrace ' (II Sam. 12:8)."

[I:1.A]   **[The king] does not judge [M. San. 2:3].** And has it not been
          written: "[So David reigned over all Israel;] and David administered
          justice and equity to all his people" (2 Sam. 8:15).

[B]   And yet do you say [that the king does not judge]?

[C]   [From this verse of Scripture, we draw the following picture:] He
      would indeed judge a case, declaring the innocent party to be
      innocent, the guilty party to be guilty. But if the guilty party was
      poor, he would give him [the funds needed for his penalty] out of
      his own property. Thus he turned out doing justice for this one
      [who won the case] and doing charity for that one [who had lost
      it].

[D]   Rabbi says, "[If] a judge judged a case, declaring the innocent
      party to be innocent, and the guilty party to be guilty, [the cited
      verse of Scripture indicates that] the Omnipresent credits it to him
      as if he had done an act of charity with the guilty party, for he has
      taken out of the possession of the guilty party that which he has
      stolen."

[II:1.A]   **And [others] do not judge him [M. San. 2:3A].** This is in line
           with the verse [in the Psalm of David], "From thee [alone] let my
           vindication come!" (Ps. 17:2).

[B]   R. Isaac in the name of Rabbi: "King and people are judged before
      Him every day, as it is said, '...and may he do justice for his servant
      and justice for his people Israel, as each day requires' (1 King
      8:59)."

[IV:1.A]   **Others do not marry the widow [M. San. 2:3G] or the woman
           divorced by a king.**

[B]   This is by reason of that which is said: "So [David's concubines]
      were shut up until the day of their death, living as if in widowhood"
      (2 Sam. 20:3).

[C]   R. Yudah bar Pazzi in the name of R. Pazzi in the name of R.
      Yohanan: "This teaches that David [treating them as forbidden
      though in law they were not] would have them dressed and adorned
      and brought before him every day, and he would say to his libido,
      'Do you lust after something forbidden to you? 'By your life! I
      shall now make you lust for something which is permitted to you."

[D]   Rabbis of Caesarea say, "They were in fact forbidden [20b] to him
      [and it was not merely that he treated the women whom Absalom
      had raped as forbidden to him, but the law deemed them prohibited].

[E]   "For if a utensil belonging to an ordinary man used by an ordinary
      man is prohibited for use of a king, a utensil belonging to a king
      which was used by an ordinary man — is it not an argument *a
      fortiori* that the king should be forbidden to make use of it?"

[V:1. A]   **R. Judah says, "The king may marry the widow of a king. For
           we find in the case of David that he married widows of Saul,
           for it is said, 'And I gave you your master's house and your**

master's wives into your embrace ' (2 Sam. 12:8)" [M. San. 2:3H-N].

[B] This refers to Rispah, Abigail, and Bath Sheba (1 Sam. 25:3), for he came from Kelubai.

[V:3. A] "David heard in the wilderness that Nabal was shearing [his sheep. So David sent ten young men; and David said to the young men, 'Go up to Carmel, and go to Nabal, and greet him in my name]. And thus shall you salute the living one: 'Peace be to you, [and peace be to your house, and peace be to all that you have '" (1 Sam. 25:46).

[B] Said R. Yusta bar Shunam, "They became a whole camp."

[C] "And Nabal answered David's servants, ['Who is David? ']" (1 Sam.. 25:10).

[D] How do we know that in **capital cases they begin from the side [the youngest members of the court] [M. San. 4:2]**?

[E] Samuel the Elder taught before R. Aha: "" And David said to his men, [Gird every man his sword, and every man girded on his sword, and David also girded on his sword ' (1 Sam. 25:13)." [David thus is the last to express his opinion.]

[F] "'And he railed at them ' (1 Sam. 25:14) — what is the meaning of 'And he railed at them '?

[G] "He incited them with words."

[H] "Now therefore know this and consider what you should do; [for evil is determined against our master and against all his house, and he is so ill-natured that one cannot speak to him" (1 Sam. 25:17).

[I] "And as she rode on the ass... behold, David and his men came down toward her;] and she met them" (1 Sam. 25:20).

[J] She showed her thigh, and they followed out of desire for her.

[K] ""... she met them ' — all of them had [involuntary] ejaculations."

[L] "Now David said, 'Surely in vain have I guarded [all that this fellow has in the wilderness... and he has returned me evil for good. God do so to the enemies of David... if by morning I leave so much as] one who pisses against the wall of all who belong to him '" (I Sam. 25:21-22).

[M] [This reference to one who pisses on a wall is to a dog.] Now what place is there for referring to a dog, who pisses on the wall? The meaning is that even a dog will get no pity.

[N] "When Abigail saw David, she made haste, and alighted from the ass, and fell before David on her face, and bowed to the ground]" (1 Sam. 25:23).

[O] She said to him, "My lord, David, as to me, what have I done? And my children — what have they done? My cattle — what have they done?"

[P] He said to her, "It is because [Nabal] has cursed the kingdom of David."

[Q] He said to him, "And are you [now] a king?"

[R] He said to her, "And has not Samuel anointed me as king?"

[S] She said to him, "Our lord Saul's coinage still is in circulation."

[T] "But I your handmaid..." (I Sam. 25:25) — this teaches that he demanded to have sexual relations with her.

[U] Forthwith she removed her stained [sanitary napkin] and showed it to him [indicating that she was in her menses and forbidden to have sexual relations on that account].

[V] He said to her, "Can one examine stains at night?"

[W] They said to him, "And let your ears hear what your mouth speaks. They do not examine sanitary napkins by night — and do they judge capital cases by night [as David was judging Nabal]!"

[X] He said to her, "The trial concerning him was complete while it was still day."

[Y] She said to him, ""[And when the Lord has done to my lord according to all the good that he has spoken concerning you my lord shall have no causes of grief, [for pangs of conscience, for having shed blood without cause].'"

[Z] Said R. Eliezer, "There were indeed doubts [riddles] there."

[AA] R. Levi was reviewing this pericope. R. Zeira told the associates, "Go and listen to R. Zeira, for it is not possible that he will lay out the pericope without saying something fresh about

[BB] Someone went in and told them that that was not so.

[CC] R. Zeira heard and said, "Even in matters of biblical stories there is the possibility of saying something fresh:

[DD] "" . . . have no doubts... ' — that is, there were indeed causes [riddles] there."

[EE] [Continuing Abigail's speech to David:] "When word of your cause of grief goes forth, people will say about you, 'You are a murderer (1 Sam. 25:31), and you are destined to fall *(ibid.)* into sin, specifically to err through the wife of a man. It is better that there should be but one such case, and not two.

[FF] "A much greater sin is going to come against you than this one. Do not bring this one along with the one which is coming."

[GG] "For having shed blood" (1 Sam. 25:31) — "You are going to rule over all Israel, and people will say about you, 'He was a murderer. '

[HH] "And that which you say, 'Whoever curses the dominion of the house of David is subject to the death penalty, '

[II] "but you still have no throne."

[JJ] "[And when the Lord has dealt well with my lord], then remember your handmaid" (1 Sam. 25:31).

[KK] This indicates that she treated herself as available [to David by referring to herself as his handmaid], and since she treated herself as available, Scripture itself treated her as diminished.

[LL] For in every other passage you read, "Abigail," but in this one: "And David said to Avigal" (1 Sam. 25:32).

[MM] "And David said..., 'Blessed be your discretion, and blessed be you, who have kept me this day from blood-guilt '" (1 Sam. 25:33) — in two senses, in the sense of the blood of menstruation, and in the sense of bloodshed [for she kept him from both kinds of blood-guilt].

The story about David highlights his virtue. This is a sizable exposition. Ps. 61:4, Ps. 17:2 are interpreted.

YERUSHALMI SANHEDRIN 2:4

[A] **[If] [the king] suffers a death in his family, he does not leave the gate of his palace.**

[B] **R. Judah says, "If he wants to go out after the bier, he goes out,**

[C] **"for thus we find in the case of David, that he went out after the bier of Abner,**

[D] **"since it is said, 'And King David followed the bier ' (2 Sam. 3:31)."**

[E] **They said to him, "This action was only to appease the people."**

[F] **And when they provide him with the funeral meal, all the people sit on the ground, while he sits on a couch.**

YERUSHALMI SANHEDRIN 2:4

[I:2. A] *There is a Tannaite authority who teaches that* the women go first [in the mourning procession], and the men after them.

[B] *And there is a Tannaite authority who teaches that* the men go first, and the women afterward.

[C] *The one who said that* the women go first invokes as the reason that they caused death to come into the world.

[D] *The one who said that* men go first invokes the reason that it is to preserve the honor of Israelite women, so that people should not stare at them.

[E] Now is it not written **"And King David followed the bier"** (7 **Sam. 3:31). They said to him, "This action was only to appease the people"** [M. San.2:4D-E].

[F] *Once he appeased the women, he went and appeased the men [in the view of A].*

[G] *Or: Once he appeased the men, he went and appeased the women [in the view of B].*

[I:3. A] "And David returned [to bless his household. But Michal the daughter of Saul came out to meet David, and said, 'How the king of Israel honored himself today, uncovering himself today before the eyes of his servants' maids, as one of the vulgar fellows shamelessly uncovers himself! ']" (2 Sam. 6:20).

[B] What is the meaning of "one of the vulgar fellows"?

{C] Said R. Ba bar Kahana, "The most vulgar of them all — this is a dancer!"

[D] She said to him, "Today the glory of father's house was revealed."

[E] They said about Saul's house that [they were so modest] that their heel and their toe never saw [their privy parts].

[F] *This is in line with that which is written,* "And he came to the sheepfolds [by the way, where there was a cave; and Saul went in to relieve himself]" (1 Sam. 24:3).

[G] R. Bun bar R. Eleazar: "It was a sheepfold within yet another sheepfold."

[H] "And Saul went in to relieve himself" ["cover his feet"]: [David] saw him lower his garments slightly and excrete slightly [as needed].

[I] [David] said, "Cursed be anyone who lays a hand on such modesty."

[J] *This is in line with that which he said to him,* "Lo, this day your eyes have seen [how the Lord gave you today into my hand in the cave; and some bade me kill you, but it spared you]" (1 Sam. 24:10).

[K] It is not written, "I spared you," but "It spared you" — that is, "Your own modesty is what spared you."

[L] And David said to Michal, "But by the maids of whom you have spoken, by them I shall be held in honor" (2 Sam. 6:22).

[M] For they are not handmaidens ('amahot), but mothers ('immahot).

[N] And how was Michal punished? "And Michal the daughter of Saul had no child to the day of her death" (2 Sam. 6:23).

[O] And is it now not written, ". . . and the sixth was Ithream of Eglah, David's wife" (2 Sam. 3:5)?

[P] She lowed like a cow (Eglah) and expired [giving birth on the day of her death].

[Q] You have no Israelite who so lowered himself in order to do religious deeds more than did David.

[R] On what account did he lower himself for the sake of religious deeds?

[S] For the people were staring at the ark and dying, as it is written, "And he slew some of the men of Beth Shemesh, [because they looked into the ark of the Lord; he slew seventy men, and fifty thousand men, of them, and the people mourned because the Lord had made a great slaughter among the people]" (1 Sam. 6:19).

[T] R. Haninah and R. Mana: one said, "" And he smote of the people seventy men ' — this refers to the Sanhedrin.

[U] ""And fifty thousand men ' — for they were comparable in worth to fifty thousand men."

[V] And one of them said, "" He smote of the people seventy men ' — this is the Sanhedrin.

[W] "" And fifty thousand ' — the ordinary people as well."

[X] It is written, "A song of ascents of David: O Lord, my heart is not lifted up" (Ps. 131:1)"when Samuel anointed me."

[Y} "My eyes are not raised too high" (Ps. 131:1) — "when I slew Goliath."

[Z] "And I do not occupy myself with things too great [or too marvelous for me]" (Ps. 131:1)" — when I brought the ark up."

[AA] "Or too wondrous for me" — "when they put me back on my throne."

[BB] "But I have calmed and quieted my soul, like a child quieted at its mother's breast" (Ps. 131:2)" — "Like a child which gives up goes down from its mother's belly, so my soul is humbled for me."

Ps. 131:2 speaks for David. Here we have a formidable exposition of David's conduct.

YERUSHALMI SANHEDRIN 2:5

[A] **[The king] calls out [the army to wage] a war fought by choice on the instructions of a court of seventy-one.**

[B] **He [may exercise the right to] open a road for himself, and [others] may not stop him.**

[C] **The royal road has no required measure.**

[D] **All the people plunder and lay before him [what they have grabbed], and he takes the first portion.**

YERUSHALMI SANHEDRIN 2:5

[II:2.A] "He was with David at Pas-dammim, [when the Philistines were gathered there for battle. There was a plot of ground full of barley, and the men fled from the Philistines. But he took his stand in the midst of the plot and defended it, and slew the Philistines; and the Lord saved them by a great victory]" (1 Chron. 11:13-14). [Note also 2 Sam. 23:11f.: "And next to him was Shammah, the son of Agee the Hararite. The Philistines gathered together at Lehi, where there was a plot of ground full of lentils; and the men fled from the Philistines. But he took his stand in the midst of the plot and defended it, and slew the Philistines; and the Lord wrought a great victory."]

[B] R. Yohanan said, "It was a field as red as blood [so the place-name is taken literally]."

[C] And R. Samuel said, "[It was so called] for from that place the penalties ceased [as will be explained below]."

[D] "When the Philistines were gathered [there for battle, there was a plot of ground full of barley." R. Jacob of Kepar Hanan said, "They were lentils, but their buds were as fine as those of barley [which accounts for the divergence between 1 Chron. 11:12 and 2 Sam. 23:11]."

[E] Said R. Levi, "This refers to the Philistines, who came standing up straight like barley, but retreated bent over like lentils."

[F] One Scripture says, "There was a plot of ground full of barley" (1 Chron. 11:13), and it is written, ". . . full of lentils" (2 Sam. 23:11).

[G] [20c] R. Samuel bar Nahman said, "The event took place in a single year, and there were two fields there, one of barley, the other of lentils."

[H] [To understand the following, we must refer to 2 Sam. 23:15 16: "And David longed and said, 'O that someone would give me water

to drink from the well of Bethlehem which is by the gate! ' And
the three mighty men broke through the host of the Philistines and
drew water out of the well of Bethlehem that was by the gate."
Now "water" here is understood to mean "learning," "gate" the
rabbinical court, and David is thus understood to require instruction.
At issue is the battlefield in which the Philistines had hidden
themselves, that is, as at Pasdammim. What troubled David now is
at issue.] David found it quite obvious that he might destroy the
field of grain and pay its cost (DMYM).

[I]   *Could it be obvious to him that* he might destroy the field and not
        pay its cost [to its Israelite owners]? [It is not permissible to rescue
        oneself by destroying someone else's property, unless one pays
        compensation. So that cannot be at issue at all.]

[J]   [If he did have to pay, as he realized, then what he wanted to know
        "at the gate" was] which of them to destroy, and for which of the
        two to pay compensation [since he did not wish to destroy both
        fields such as, at G, Samuel posits were there].

[K]   [These are then the choices] between the one of lentils and the one
        of barley.

[L]   The one of lentils is food for man, and the one of barley is food for
        beast. The one of lentils is not liable, when turned into flour, for a
        dough offering, and the one of barley is liable, when turned into
        flour, for dough offering. As to lentils, the *omer* is not taken
        therefrom; as to barley the *omer* is taken therefrom. [So these are
        the three choices before David, and since there were two fields, he
        wanted to know which to burn and for which to pay compensation.]

[M]   [This entire picture of the character of the battlefield is rejected by
        rabbis,] for rabbis say, "There was one field, but the incident took
        place [twice, in a period of] two years [and hence, in one year, it
        was planted with one crop, in the other year, the other].

[N]   "David then should have learned from the rule prevailing in the
        preceding year. But they do not derive a rule from one year to the
        next."

[O]   One verse states, "They took their stand in the midst of the plot
        and defended it" (1 Chron. 11:14).

[P]   And the other Scripture states, ". . . and he defended it" (2 Sam.
        23:12).

[Q]   What this teaches is that he restored the field to its owner, and it
        was as precious to him as a field planted with saffron.

[II:3.A] It is written, "And David said longingly, 'O that some one would
        give me water to drink from the well of Bethlehem [which is by
        the gate ']" (1 Chron. 11:17).

[B]   R. Hiyya bar Ba said, "He required a teaching of law."

[C]   "Then the three mighty men broke through [the camp of the
        Philistines]" (1 Chron. 11:18).

[D]   Why three? Because the law is not decisively laid down by fewer
        than three.

[E] "But David would not drink of it; [he poured it out to the Lord. and said, 'Far be it from me before my God that I should do this. Shall I drink the lifeblood of these men? For at the risk of their lives they brought it ']" (1 Chron. 11:18-19).

[F] David did not want the law to be laid down in his own name.

[G] "He poured it out to the Lord" — establishing [the decision] as [an unattributed] teaching for the generations [so that the law should be authoritative and so be cited anonymously].

[H] [Delete:] **He may exercise the right of eminent domain in order to open a road for himself and others may not stop him.**

[I] Bar Qappara said, "It was the festival of Sukkot, and the occasion was the water offering on the altar, and it was a time in which high places were permitted [before the centralization of the cult in Jerusalem]. [So the view that David required a legal teaching is not accepted; it was literally water which David wanted and got.]"

[J] "And three mighty men broke through..." — Why three? One was to kill [the Philistines]; the second was to clear away the bodies; and the third [avoiding the corpse-uncleanness] was to bring the flask for water in a state of cultic cleanness.

[K] One version of the story states, "... He poured it out to the Lord..." (1 Chron. 11:18).

[L] And the other version of the story states, "He spilled it..." (2 Sam. 23:16).

[M] The one which states "spilled" supports the view of R. Hiyya bar Ba [who treats the story as figurative], and the one which stated, "poured it out to the Lord" supports the picture of Bar Qappara [who treats it as a literal account].

[N] Huna in the name of R. Yosé, "David required information on the laws covering captives."

[O] R. Simeon b. Rabbi says, "What he thirsted after was the building of the house for the sanctuary [the Temple]."

The interpretation of Scripture transforms the narrative of Scripture into an account of Torah study.

YERUSHALMI SANHEDRIN 2:6

[II:1.A] He should not multiply horses to himself" (Dt. 17:16) — only enough for his chariot (M. San. 2:6F]:

[B] This is in line with the following: "And David hamstrung all the chariot horses, but left enough for a hundred chariots" (2 Sam. 8:4).

The law of Deuteronomy on the king is illustrated through David.

YERUSHALMI SANHEDRIN 10:1

[V:1.A] Doeg was a great man in learning of Torah.

[B] The Israelites came and asked David, "In regard to the showbread, what is the law as to its overriding the restrictions of the Sabbath?"

[C] He said to them, "Arranging it overrides the restrictions of the Sabbath, but kneading the dough and cutting it out do not override the restrictions of the Sabbath."

[D] Now Doeg was there, and he said, "Who is this one who comes to teach in my presence?"

[E] They told him, "It is David, son of Jesse."

[F] Forthwith, he went and gave advice to Saul, king of Israel, to kill Nob, the city of the priests.

[G] *This is in line with the following statement of Scripture:* "And the king said to the guard who stood about him, 'Turn and kill the priests of the Lord; because their hand is also with David, [and they knew that he had fled, and did not disclose it to me]. ' [But the servants of the king would not put forth their hand to fall upon the priests of the Lord]" (1 Sam. 22:17). Who were they.

[H] Said R. Samuel bar R. Isaac, "They were Abner and Amasa."

[I] *They said to him, "Now do you have any claim against us except for this belt and this cloak? Lo, they are thrown down before you!"*

[J] "[And the king said to the guard who stood about him, 'Turn and kill the priests of the Lord; because their hand is also with David, and they knew that he had fled, and did not disclose it to me. '] But the servants of the king would not put forth their hands to fall upon the priests of the Lord" (1 Sam. 22:17).

[K] "And the king said to Doeg…"

[L] Said R. Judah bar Pazzi, "It is written, 'to Du-eg ' (DWYYG)."

[M] He said to him, "You are trapped like a fish, you have done a great thing.

[N] "[Then the king said to Doeg], 'You turn and fall upon the priests. ' And Doeg the Edomite turned and fell upon the priests, [and he killed that day eighty-five persons who wore the linen ephod]" (1 Sam. 22:18).

[O] *Now did not R. Hiyya teach,* "They do not appoint two high priests at the same time"? [How could there be many?]

[P] But this teaches that all of them were worthy of the high priests.

[Q] How was he [shown to be ultimately] set apart?

[R] R. Haninah and R. Joshua b. Levi —

[S] One of them said, "Fire burst forth from the house of the Holy of Holies and licked round about him."

[T] And the other one said, "His old students got together with him, and they were studying, but he forgot [his learning].

[U] "[This fulfills the verse which says, 'He swallows down riches and vomits them up again; God casts them out of his belly' (Job 20:25). [That was a sign of his excommunication; and the students killed him.]"

[VI:1. A] Ahithophel was a man mighty in Torah learning.

[B] It is written, "David again gathered all the chosen men of Israel, thirty thousand. [And David arose and went with all the people who were with him... to bring up from there the ark of the Lord]" (2 Sam. 6:1-2).

[C] R. Berekiah in the name of R. Abba bar Kahana: "Ninety thousand elders did David appoint on a single day, but he did not appoint Ahithophel among them."

[D] *This is in line with that which is written in Scripture:* "David again gathered all the chosen men of Israel, thirty thousand...." *That is, "And he added" means "thirty." And "again" means "thirty." The Scripture explicitly speaks of thirty. Lo, there are then ninety in all.*

[E] You find that when David came to bear the ark of the covenant of the Lord, he did not bear it in accord with the Torah:

[F] "And they carried the Ark of God on a new cart, [and brought it out of the house of Abinadab which was on the hill; and Uzzah and Ahio, the sons of Abinadab, were driving the new cart]" (2 Sam. 6:3). [That is, the Torah requires that the priests carry it, but they carried it in a cart instead.]

[G] *Now the ark carried the priests on high, but let them fall down; the ark carried the priests on high, but let them fall down to the ground.*

[H] *David sent and brought Ahithophel. He said to him, "Will you not tell me what is with this ark, which raises the priests up high and casts them down to the ground, raises the priests on high and casts them down to the ground?"*

[I] *He said to him, "Send and ask those wise men whom you appointed!"*

[J] *Said David, "One who knows how to make the ark stop and does not do so in the end is going to be put to death through strangulation."*

[K] *He said to him, "Make a sacrifice before [the ark], and it will stop."*

[L] *This is in line with the following verse which is written in Scripture:* "And when those who bore the ark of the Lord had gone six paces, he sacrificed an ox and a fatling" (2 Sam. 6:13).

[M] R. Haninah and R. Mana —

[N] One of them said, "At every step an ox and a fatling, and at the end, seven oxen and seven rams."

[O] And the other said, "At every step seven oxen and seven rams, and at the end, an ox and a fatling."

[P] Said the Holy One, blessed be he, to Ahithophel, *"A teaching which children say every day in the school you did not report to him!*

[Q] *"*" But to the sons of Kohath he gave none, because they were charged with the care of the holy things which had to he carried on the shoulder ' (Num. 7:9).

[R] *"And this [to sacrifice] you told him!"*

[S] And so you find that when David came to dig the foundations of the Temple, *he dug fifteen hundred cubits and did not reach the nethermost void. In the end he found one clay pot, and he wanted to remove it.*

[T] *It said to him, "You cannot do so."*

[U] *He said to it, "Why not?"*

[V] *It said to him, "For here I am the cover over the great deep."*

[W] *He said to it, "And how long have you been here?"*

[X] *It said to him, "From the time that I heard the voice of the All-Merciful at Sinai:* 'I am the Lord your God, [who brought you out of the land of Egypt, out of the house of bondage] ' (Ex. 20:2), the earth shook and trembled.

[Y] *"And I am set here to seal the great deep."*

[Z] *Even so, [David] did not listen to it.*

[AA] *When he removed the clay pot, the great deep surged upward to flood the world.*

[BB] *And Ahithophel was standing there. He said, "Thus will David be strangled [in the flood] and I shall become king."*

[CC] *Said David, "He who is a sage, knowing how to stop up the matter, and does not stop it, will in the end be put to death through strangulation."*

[DD] *[Ahithophel] said what he said and stopped up [the flood]..*

[EE] David began to say a Psalm, "A song of ascents. [In my distress I cry to the Lord, that he may answer me]" (Ps. 120:1).

[FF] "A song of ascents" (ma 'alot) is a song for a hundred (meah) ascents (olot).

[GG] At every hundred cubits he would say a psalm.

[HH] Even so, in the end [Ahithophel] was strangled to death.

[II] *Said R. Yosé, "This is in line with what the proverb says: A person has to scruple about a curse of a great master, even if it was fo nought."*

[JJ] R. Jeremiah in the name of R. Samuel bar Isaac, "A scroll which Samuel handed over to David did Ahithophel recite by means of the Holy Spirit."

[KK] *What did Ahithophel do?*

[LL] *When someone came to him for advice, he would say to him, "Go and do thus and so, and if you don 't believe me, then go and ask the Urim and Thummim."*

[MM] *And the man would go and ask and find out that indeed that was how matters were.*

[NN] *This is in line with that which is written in Scripture:* "Now in those days the counsel which Ahithophel gave was as if one consulted [the oracle of God; so was the counsel of Ahithophel esteemed, both by David and by Absalom]" (2 Sam. 16:23).

[OO] You read "Man"; it is not written thus, for the Scripture could not call him a [mere] man.

[PP] How was he set apart?

[QQ] "When Ahithophel saw that his counsel was not followed, he saddled his ass [and went off home to his own city]. [And he set his house in order, and hanged himself; and he died, and was buried in the tomb of his father]" (2 Sam. 17:23).

[RR] Three things did Ahithophel command his sons, saying to them:

[SS] "Do not rebel against the royal house of David, *for we shall find that the Holy One, blessed be he, shows favor to them even in public.*

[TT] "And do not have business [29b] dealings with someone on whom the hour smiles.

[UU] "And if the day of Pentecost is bright, sow the best quality of wheat."

[VV] *But they did not know whether it meant "bright" in dew or "bright" in dry heat.*

Before he was anointed as king, he is an ordinary Israelite. Yerushalmi Sanhedrin presents a massive exposition of the law of the monarchy with important allusions to David. This is an unprecedented development.

[1] IS DAVID AN ACTIVE PLAYER OR A ROUTINE AND SCARCELY ANIMATE ONE? Only upon ordination is David recognized as a principal actor.

[2] WHAT COMPONENTS OF THE COLLECTION MAKE ROUTINE GLOSSES OF THE RECEIVED SCRIPTURES and which ones provide more than minor glosses of the tradition? The exposition of M. San. 2:2-3 extend the treatment of David beyond all previous boundaries.

[3] CAN WE IDENTIFY A PRONOUNCED BIAS OR A POLEMIC in the utilization of David? David is a model for the monarch and enjoyed the loyalty of his troops. He modestly was last to express his opinion.

[4] HOW IS DAVID COMPARABLE TO OTHER SAGES IN THIS DOCUMENT? The motif of David as disciple of sages does not predominate. But "O that someone would give me water to drink from the well of Bethlehem which is by the gate!" speaks of thirst for Torah learning.

19

David in Bavli Berakhot

II.8. A. [Reverting to the statement that David got up at midnight:, "At midnight I rise to give thanks to you because of your righteous ordinances" (Ps. 119:62),] *Did David get up at midnight? He got up at dusk of the evening.*

B. For it is written, "I got up with the neshef and cried" (Ps. 119:147).

C. *And this word neshef speaks of the evening, for it is written, "In the neshef, in the evening of the day, in the blackness of the night and the darkness" (Prov. 7:9).*

D. *Said R. Oshaiah said R. Aha, "This is the sense of the passage:* 'Half the night never passed for me in sleep' [and that is the meaning of Ps. 119:162]."

E. R. Zira said, "Up to midnight he would doze like a horse, from that point he would regain full energy like a lion.

F. R. Ashi said, "Up to midnight he would deal with teachings of Torah. From that point he would engage in songs and praises."

G. *But does the word neshef refer to dusk? Surely the word refers to the morning light, for it is written, "And David slew them from the neshef to the evening of the next day" (1 Sam. 30:17), with the sense "from the morning to evening."*

H. *No, that is not the sense. Rather, it is from dusk, to dusk on the next day.*

I. *If that were the case, the passage should read, "From dusk to dusk" or "from evening to evening."*

J. *Rather, said Raba, "The word neshef has two meanings. One refers to the dawn of day, when the evening disappears and the morning comes, and the other to when the day disappears and the evening comes [and neshef in this instance refers to dusk]."*

II.9. A. *Did David really know exactly when it was midnight? Now Moses,*
our master, did not know, for it is written, "At about midnight I
will go out into the midst of Egypt" (Ex. 11:4). What is the sense
of "at about midnight" cited in the preceding verse? If I should
say that that is language which the Holy One, blessed be he, said
to him, that is, "At about midnight," is it possible that before
Heaven there is such a doubt [as to the exact time of night? That is
impossible.] Rather, [God] said to him, "At midnight," but Moses
is the one who came along and said, "At about midnight." It follows
that he was in doubt as to exactly when it was midnight. Could
David then have known exactly when it was?

   B. *David had a device for telling when it was.*

   C. For R. Aha bar Bizna said R. Simeon the Pious said, "David had a
harp suspended over his bed, and when midnight came, the north
wind would come and blow on the strings, and the harp would
play on its own. David immediately got up and undertook Torah-
study until dawn.

   D. "When it was dawn, the sages of Israel came into him. They said
to him, 'Our lord, O king, your people Israel needs sustenance.'

   E. "He said to them, 'Let them go and make a living from one another.'

   F. "They said to him, 'A handful [of food] cannot satisfy a lion, and
a hole in the ground cannot be filled up from its own clods.'

   G. "He said to them, 'Go and organize marauders.'

   H. "They forthwith took counsel with Ahitophel and sought the advice
of the sanhedrin and addressed a question to the Urim and
Thumim."

   I. *Said R. Joseph, "What verse indicates this?* 'And after Ahithofel
was Jehoiada, son of Benaiah, and Abiathar, and the captain of the
king's host was Joab' (1 Chr. 27:34).

   J. "'Ahithofel was counselor,' and so it is said, 'Now the counsel of
Ahithofel, which he counseled in those days, was as if a man
inquired of the word of God' (2 Sam. 16:23).

   K. "[4A] 'Benaiah, son of Jehoiada' refers to the sanhedrin.

   L. "'And Abiathar' refers to the Urim and Thumim. And so it says,
'And Benaiah, son of Jehoiada, was in charge of the Kerethi and
Pelethi' (2 Sam. 20:23).

   M. *"Why were the Urim and Thumim so called? They were called*
'Kerethi' because their words are decisive [korethim], and 'Pelethi'
because they are distinguished (muflaim) through what they say.

   N. "And then comes 'the captain of the king's host, Joab.'"

   O. *Said R. Isaac bar Ada, and some say R. Isaac, son of R. Idid, said,*
"What is the verse of Scripture that makes this point? 'Awake, my
glory, awake, psaltery and harp, I will awake the dawn' (Ps. 57:9)."

   P. *[Reverting to A-B,] R. Zira said, "Moses most certainly knew when*
it was midnight, and so did David.

   Q. *"But since David knew, what did he need a harp for? It was to*
wake him up from his sleep.

R.   *"And since Moses also knew, why did he say,* 'at about midnight'?

S.   "Moses thought that the astrologers of Pharoah might make a mistake and then claim that Moses was a charlatan [should the event not take place exactly when Moses predicted, if he made too close a statement for their powers of calculation]."

T.   For a master has said, "Teach your tongue to say, 'I don't know,' lest you turn out to lie.'"

U.   *R. Ashi said, "[The matter of Ex. 11:4] took place at midnight on the night of the thirteenth toward dawn of the fourteenth. And this is what Moses said to Israel:* 'The Holy One, blessed be he, has said, "Tomorrow at about midnight, at around this time, I shall go forth into the midst of Egypt."'"

II.10. A.   "A prayer of David: Keep my soul, for I am pious" (Ps. 86:1-2).

B.   Levi and R. Isaac.

C.   One of them said, "This is what David said before the Holy One, blessed be he, 'Lord of the world, am I not pious? For all kings, east and west, sleep to the third hour, but as for me: "At midnight, I rise to give thanks to you" (Ps. 119:62).'"

D.   The other said, "This is what David said before the Holy One, blessed be he, 'Lord of the world, am I not pious? For all kings, east and west, sit in all their glory with their retinues, but as for me, my hands are sloppy with menstrual blood and the blood of the fetus and placenta, which I examine so as to declare a woman clean for sexual relations with her husband.

E.   "'And not only so, but, further, in whatever I do, I take counsel with Mephiboshet, my master, and I say to him, "Rabbi Mephiboshet, did I do right in the judgment I gave? Did I do right in acquitting? Did I do right in awarding an advantage? Did I do right in declaring something clean? Did I do right in declaring something unclean?" and in no way have I been ashamed [to depend on his judgment].'"

F.   *Said R. Joshua, son of R. Idi, "What verse of Scripture supports that view of David?* 'And I recite your testimonies before kings and am not ashamed' (Ps. 119:46)."

II.11. A.   *A Tannaite authority stated:* His name was not Mephiboshet but Ishbosheth. But why did he bear that name? Because he shamed David in criticizing his legal decisions. Therefore David gained merit so that Kileab [2 Sam. 3:3] should come forth from him."

B.   And R. Yohanan said, "His name was not Kileab but rather Daniel. Why, then, was he called Kileab? Because he shamed Mephiboshet in criticizing his legal decisions.

C.   "And concerning him said Solomon in his sagacity, 'My son, if your heart is wise, my heart will be glad, even mine' (Prov. 23:15).

D.   "And he further said, 'My son, be wise and make my heart glad, that I may answer him who taunts me' (Prov. 27:11)."

II.12. A.   *Now did David really call himself "pious"?*

B.   And has it not been written, "I am not sure to see the good reward of the Lord in the land of the living" (Ps. 27:13). [How could David have been unsure, if he knew he was pious?]

C.   *A Tannaite authority taught in this connection in the name of R. Yosé, "Why are there dots over the word for 'not sure'?*

D.   "Said David before the Holy One, blessed be he, 'Lord of the world, I am confident you pay a good reward to the righteous in the coming future, but I do not know if I shall have a share among them or not. Perhaps sin will cause [punishment for me instead of reward].'"

E.   *That accords with what R. Jacob bar Idi said, for R. Jacob bar Idi contrasted two verses of Scripture, as follows: "It is written, 'And behold, I am with you and will keep you wherever you go' (Gen. 28:15), and another verse states, 'Then Jacob was greatly afraid' (Gen. 32:8).*

F.   "[Why the contrast between God's promise and Jacob's fear?] [Jacob thought to himself,] 'Sin which I have done may cause [punishment for me instead].'"

G.   *That accords with what has been taught on Tannaite authority:*

H.   "Till your people pass over, O Lord, till your people pass over, that you have acquired" (Ex. 15:16).

I.   "Till your people pass over" refers to the first entry into the land [in Joshua's time].

J.   "Till your people pass over, that you have acquired" refers to the second entry into the land [in the time of Ezra and Nehemiah. Thus a miracle was promised not only on the first occasion, but also on the second. But it did not happen the second time around. Why not?]

K.   On the basis of this statement, sages have said, "The Israelites were worthy of having a miracle performed for them in the time of Ezra also, just as it had been performed for them in the time of Joshua b. Nun, but sin caused [the miracle to be withheld]."

III.1. A.   And sages say, "Until midnight" [M. 1:1D]:

COMPOSITE ON PSALM 145

III.3. A.   Said R. Eleazar bar Abina, "Whoever says the Psalm, 'Praise of David' (Ps. 145) three times a day may be assured that he belongs to the world to come."

B.   *What is the scriptural basis for that view?*

C.   *If you should say that it is because the Psalm follows the order of the alphabet, there also is the Psalm,* "Happy are they that are upright in the way" (Ps. 119) *which goes through the alphabet eight times [and should be a preferred choice on that account]. Rather, it is because, in Ps. 145, there is the sentence,* "You open your hand and satisfy every living thing with favor" (Ps. 145:16).

D.   *If that is the case, then in the Great Hallel (Ps. 136), we find the phrase,* "Who gives food to all flesh" (Ps. 136:25), *which one would do better to recite.*

E. *Rather, it is because [in Ps. 145] there are both considerations [namely, the entire alphabet and the statement that God provides.]*

III.4.A. [Referring to Ps. 145], said R. Yohanan, "On what account is there no verse beginning with an N is Psalm 145?

B. "It is because the N starts the verse referring to the fall of (the enemies of) Israel.

C. "For it is written, 'Fallen (NPLH), no more to rise, is the virgin of Israel' (Amos 5:2)."

D. *In the West [the Land of Israel] the verse at hand is laid out in this way:* "Fallen, and no more to fall, the virgin of Israel will arise."

E. *Said R. Nahman bar Isaac, "Even so, David went and by the Holy Spirit brought together the N with the following letter of the alphabet, S:* 'The Lord upholds (SMK) all those who fall (NPL) (Ps. 145:14)."

III.45. A. And R. Yohanan said in the name of R. Simeon b. Yohai, "Bringing a child up badly is worse in a person's house than the war of Gog and Magog.

B. "For it is said, 'A Psalm of David, when he fled from Absalom, his son' (Ps. 3:1), after which it is written, 'Lord how many are my adversaries become, many are they that rise up against me' (Ps. 3:2).

C. "By contrast, in regard to the war of Gog and Magog it is written, 'Why are the nations in an uproar? And why do the peoples mutter in vain' (Ps. 2:1).

D. "But it is not written in that connection, 'How many are my adversaries become.'"

E. "A Psalm of David, when he fled from Absalom, his son" (Ps. 3:1):

F. "A Psalm of David"? *It should be,* "A lamentation of David"!

G. Said R. Simeon b. Abishalom, "The matter may be compared to the case of a man, against whom an outstanding bond was issued. Before he had paid it, he was sad. After he had paid it, he was glad.

H. "So too with David, when he the Holy One had said to him, 'Behold, I will raise up evil against you out of your own house,' (2 Sam. 2:11), he was sad.

I. "He thought to himself, 'Perhaps it will be a slave or a bastard child, who will not have pity on me.

J. "When he saw that it was Absalom, he was happy. On that account, he said a psalm."

David speaks through Psalms, here Ps. 119:62, 119:147, 145. The outcome is that David studies the Torah through the night.

BAVLI BERAKHOT 1:2

I.6. A. *Since the verse,* "May the words of my mouth be acceptable" (Ps. 19:15) *would serve equally well at the end of the Prayer as much as at the beginning, why did rabbis ordain that it was to be said at*

the end of the Eighteen Blessings [the Prayer]? Why not say it at
the beginning?

B. Said R. Judah, son of R. Simeon b. Pazzi, "Since David said that
verse only at the end of eighteen chapters [of Psalms, namely, at
the end of Psalm 19], rabbis on that account ordained that it should
come at the end of the Eighteen Blessings."

C. *But the eighteen Psalms [to which reference has just been made]
in fact are nineteen!*

D. "Happy is the man" and "Why are the nations in an uproar" (Ps.
1:1, 2:1) *constitute a single chapter.*

E. For R. Judah, son of R. Simeon b. Pazzi said, "David recited 103
Psalms, and he never said 'Halleluiah' until he had witnessed the
downfall of the wicked.

F. "For it has been said, 'Let sinners cease out of the earth, and let
the wicked be no more. Bless the Lord, O my soul. Halleluiah'
(Ps. 104:35)."

G. *These 103 Psalms in fact are 104 Psalms.*

H. *That then yields the inference that* "Happy is the man" and "Why
are the nations in an uproar" (Ps. 1:1, 2:1) *constitute a single
chapter.*

I. For R. Samuel bar Nahmani said R. Yohanan said, "[10A] Every
chapter that was particularly beloved for David did he open by
saying 'Happy' and close by saying 'Happy.'

J. "He began with 'Happy,' as Scriptures states, 'Happy is the man'
(Ps. 1:1) and he closed with 'Happy,' as Scriptures states, 'Happy
are all who trust in him' (Ps. 2:11)."

BAVLI BERAKHOT 4:3-6

I.1. A. *As to the eighteen benedictions, to what do they correspond?*

B. Said R. Hillel, son of R. Samuel bar Nahmani, "They correspond
to the eighteen times that David mentioned God's name in the
psalm, 'Ascribe to the Lord, sons of might' (Ps. 29:1)."

C. R. Joseph said, "They correspond to the eighteen times that God is
mentioned in the recitation of the Shema."

D. Said R. Tanhuma said R. Joshua b. Levi, "They correspond to the
eighteen vertebrae in the backbone."

I.5. A. As to the seven benedictions [of which the Prayer] for the Sabbath
is made up, to what do they correspond?

B. Said R. Halapta b. Saul, "They correspond to the seven voices that
David said [at Psalm 29] were over the waters."

C. As to the nine benedictions [of which the Additional Prayer] for
the New Year is made up, to what do they correspond?

D. Said R. Isaac of Qartigenin, "They correspond to the seven times
that Hannah mentioned the name of God in her prayer."

E. For a master said, "On the New Year were Sarah, Rachel, and
Hannah remembered [and given children]."

F. As to the twenty-four benedictions of the Prayer said on fast days,
to what do they correspond?

G. Said R. Helbo, "They correspond to the twenty-four times that Solomon used the expression, 'prayer' [Simon] when he brought the ark to the house of the holy of holies [1 Kgs. 8:23-53]."

H. *If so, should we not also say them?*

I. *When did Solomon say them? On a day of supplication* [Simon, p. 176, n. 12: because the gates would not open]. *We too say them on a day of supplication [namely, a fast for rain].*

David's recitation of Psalms forms the center of the exposition.

BAVLI SANHEDRIN 5:1

I.1.A. *Whence [in Scripture] do we find evidence for this rule [of M. 5:1A]?*

B. *Said R. Eleazar, "It is in line with the following verse of Scripture: 'And she was in bitterness of soul' (I Sam. 1:10)."*

C. *But how does that verse prove the point? Perhaps the case of Hannah is different, because her heart was unusually bitter.*

D. *Rather, said R. Yosé b. R. Hanina, "It derives from this verse: 'But as for me, in the abundance of your loving kindness will I come into your house, I will bow down toward your holy temple in fear of you' (Ps. 5:8)."*

E. *But how does that verse prove the point? Perhaps the case of David is different, for in praying he troubled himself more than [most people].*

F. *Rather, said R. Joshua b. Levi, "It derives from this verse: 'Worship the Lord in the beauty of holiness' (Ps. 29:2). Do not read the word used for beauty as its vowels indicate, but rather, impose the vowels to give the meaning of 'trembling.'"*

Ps. 5:8, 29:2 yield propositions on David.

BAVLI BERAKHOT 9:1

I.16.A. Said R. Huna, "To a good person a good dream is not shown, and to a bad person, a bad one."

B. *It has been taught along these same lines on Tannaite authority:*

C. In David's entire life he did not see a good dream, and in Ahitophel's entire life he never saw a bad one.

D. But has it not been written, "There shall no evil befall you" (Ps. 91:10)? And in this connection, said R. Hisda said R. Jeremiah bar Abba, "It is that you will not be disturbed either by bad dreams or by bad fantasies."

E. "Neither shall any plague come near to your tent" (Ps. 91:10). [This means that] when you come home from a trip you will never find that your wife may be in doubt as to whether or not she is menstruating.

F.   *[Reverting to the matter of David, the point is that] while he does not see [bad dream about himself], others may see a bad one [about him].*

G.   *And if a person never sees a bad dream about himself, is this a good thing?*

H.   And has not R. Zeira said, "Whoever sleeps for seven successive days without a seeing a dream is called wicked,

I.   "for it is said, 'He shall abide satisfied, he shall not be visited by evil' (Prov. 19:23) — do not read the word as 'satisfied' but rather as 'seven'"?

J.   *But this is the sense of the matter: One may see but he does not [later on] know what he has seen.*

Ps. 91:10 proves David's point.

BAVLI BERAKHOT 9:1

XIX.17 A.   "And he thought to kill you but he spared you" (1 Sam. 24:11):

B.   Rather than saying, "He thought," [since it is David speaking of what he himself did not do], *it should read,* "And I thought..."

C.   "He spared" *likewise should be* "I spared."

D.   Said R. Eleazar, "Said David to Saul, On the basis of the rules of the Torah, you are liable to be put to death, for lo, you are in pursuit of me, and the Torah has said, "If someone comes to kill you, rise and kill him first."

E.   "'But the modesty that you displayed is what brought pity on you.

F.   *"'And what is it? It is in accord with what is written,* "And he came to the fences by the way, where there was a cave, and Saul went in to cover his feet" (1 Sam. 24:4).'"

G.   It was taught on Tannaite authority:

H.   There was a fence inside of a fence, and a cave inside of a cave.

I.   "To cover" (SK): Said R. Eleazar, "This teaches that he covered himself like a sukkah."

XIX.18 A.   "Then David arose and cut off the skirt of Saul's robe privily" (1 Sam. 24:5):

B.   Said R. Yosé bar Hanina, "Whoever treats clothing without care in the end will not get any benefit from it.

C.   "For it is said, 'Now King David was old, stricken in years, and they covered him with clothes, but he could get no heat' (1 Kgs. 1:1)."

XIX.19 A.   "If it be the Lord who has stirred you up against me, let him accept an offering" (1 Sam. 26:19):

B.   Said R. Eleazar, "Said the Holy One, blessed be he, to David, 'Will you then use the language of "stir up" in my regard? Lo, I am going to make you stumble through a matter which even school children know.'

C.   "For it is written, 'When you take the sum of the children of Israel according to their number, then shall they give every man a ransom

for his soul unto the Lord... [that there be no plague among them]'
(Ex. 30:12).

D. "Forthwith: 'Satan stood up against Israel' (1 Chr. 31:1).

E. "And it is further written, 'He stirred up David against them saying,
Go number Israel' (2 Sam. 24:1).

F. *"But when he counted them, he did not take a ransom from them,*
for it is written, 'So the Lord sent a pestilence upon Israel from
morning even to the time appointed' (2 Sam. 24:15)."

G. *What is this "time appointed"?*

H. Said Samuel the elder, son in law of R. Hanina, in the name of R.
Hanina, "It was from the time at which the daily whole offering
was slaughtered until the time that its blood was sprinkled."

I. R. Yohanan said, "It was actually up to mid day."

XIX.20 A. "And he said to the angel that destroyed the people, it is great" (2
Sam. 24:16):

B. Said R. Eleazar, "Said the Holy One, blessed be he, to the angel,
'Take for me the great man among them, from whom may be exacted
the penalty for many sins for [all of] them. At that moment Abishai,
son of Zeruiah, died, who was in himself worth the better part of
the sanhedrin."

David's conduct when Saul was defecating is expounded.

[1] IS DAVID AN ACTIVE PLAYER OR A ROUTINE AND = SCARCELY ANIMATE ONE?
David is a model for the study of the Torah, which he does through the night.

[2] WHAT COMPONENTS OF THE COLLECTION MAKE ROUTINE GLOSSES OF THE
RECEIVED SCRIPTURES and which ones provide more than minor glosses of the
tradition? David speaks in Psalms.

[3] CAN WE IDENTIFY A PRONOUNCED BIAS OR A POLEMIC in the utilization of
David? The Psalms speak of David and express his ideas.

[4] HOW IS DAVID COMPARABLE TO OTHER SAGES IN THIS DOCUMENT? David
studies the Torah like a sage.

20

David in Bavli Moed

BAVLI SHABBAT I.3

I:1. F. Another matter: "Wherefore I praised the dead that are already dead" (Qoh. 4:2) — *that is in line with what R. Judah said Rab said, for said R. Judah said Rab, "What is the meaning of the verse of Scripture,* 'Show me a token for good that those that hate me may see it and be ashamed' (Ps. 86:17)? Said David before the Holy One, blessed be He, He said before him, 'Lord of the world, forgive me for that sin.'

G. "He said to him, 'It is forgiven to you.'

H. "'Then show me a token for good, that they who hate me may see it and be ashamed, because you, Lord, have helped me and comforted me' (Ps. 86:17).

I. "He said to him, 'While you are alive, I shall not reveal [the fact that you are forgiven], but I shall reveal it in the lifetime of your son, Solomon.'

J. "When Solomon had built the house of the sanctuary, he tried to bring the ark into the house of the Holy of Holies. The gates cleaved to one another. He recited twenty-four prayers [Freedman, p. 734, n. 4: in 2 Chr. 6 words for prayer, supplication and hymn occur twenty-four times], but was not answered.

K. "He said, 'Lift up your head, O you gates, and be lifted up, you everlasting doors, and the King of glory shall come in.' *They rushed on him to swallow him up, crying out,* 'Who is this King of glory? The Lord strong and mighty, the Lord mighty in battle' (Ps. 24:7ff.).

L. "And it is further said, 'Lift up your heads, O you gates even lift them up, you everlasting doors, and the king of glory shall come in. Who is this king of glory? The Lord of hosts, he is the king of glory' (Ps. 24:7).

M. "But he was not answered.

N. "When he said, 'Lord God, turn not away the face of your anointed, remember the mercies of David, your servant' (2 Chr. 6:42), forthwith he was answered.

O. "At that moment the faces of David's enemies turned as black as the bottom of a pot, for all Israel knew that the Holy One, blessed be He, had forgiven him for that sin."

P. [Reverting to F:] "So wasn't Solomon right when he said, 'Wherefore I praised the dead that are already dead' (Qoh. 4:2)?"

Q. And so it is written, "On the eighth day he sent the people away, and they blessed the king and went to their tents joyful and glad of heart for all the goodness that the Lord has showed to David his servant and to Israel his people" (1 Kgs. 8:66):

R. "Went to their tents": They found their wives menstrually clean.

S. "Joyful": Because they had the joy of the splendor of the presence of God.

T. "And glad of heart": Because their wives conceived, and everyone of them produced a son.

U. "For all the goodness that the Lord has showed to David his servant": That he had forgiven him for that sin.

V. "And to Israel his people": *For he had forgiven them the sin they had committed on the Day of Atonement [which they treated as a feast day rather than as a fast day, for the fourteen days included the tenth day of the seventh month].*

W. *And as to what Solomon said,* "For a living dog is better than a dead lion" (Qoh. 9:4), *that is to be understood in accord with what R. Judah said Rab said, for said R. Judah said Rab, "What is the meaning of the verse of Scripture,* 'Lord, make me to know my end, and the measure of my days, what it is; let me know how frail I am' (Ps. 89:5)*?*

X. "Said David before the Holy One, blessed be He, 'Lord of the world: Make me to know my end!'

Y. "He said to him, 'It is a decree of mine that mortals are not to be informed of their end.' '...And the measure of my days, what it is!'

Z. "He said to him, 'It is a decree of mine that mortals are not to be informed how long they will live.' '...Let me know how frail I am!'

AA. "'You will die on the Sabbath.'

BB. "'So let me die on Sunday.'

CC. "'The reign of your son, Solomon, already will have become due, and one reign may not overlap another by even a hairbreadth.'

DD. "'Then let me die on Friday afternoon.'

EE. "He said, "'For a day in your courts is better than a thousand" (Ps. 84:11) — I prefer one day on which you will go into session and engage in Torah study more than a thousand burnt-offerings that your son, Solomon, is destined to offer before me on the altar.'

FF. **[30B]** *"Every Sabbath day he would go into session and study the entire day. That day on which his soul was to find rest, the angel of* death stood before him but couldn't prevail against him, because he didn't interrupt repeating his lessons. He said, 'What should I do with him?'

GG. "There was a garden behind his house. The angel of death came and climbed up and stirred the branches. David went out to see; as he was climbing a ladder, it broke under him. At that point, he fell silent [and ceased from repeating his lessons], and his soul found repose.

HH. "Solomon sent word to the house of study: 'Father has died and is lying in the sun; the dogs of my father's household are hungry. What should I do?'

II. "They sent him word, 'Cut off a piece of carrion meat and put it before the dogs, but as to your father, put a loaf of bread or a child on top of him and carry him away [but you can't handle the corpse without some further, legitimate purpose].'"

JJ. [Reverting to F:] "So wasn't Solomon right when he said, 'Wherefore I praised the dead that are already dead' (Qoh. 4:2)? "Now as to the question that I have presented to you: A lamp bears the classification of lamp, and a human soul is in that same classification of lamp. It is better that the lamp of a mortal be put out before the lamp of the Holy One, blessed be He [so where life is endangered, the lamp may certainly be put out (Freedman).]

Ps. 86:17 speaks for David.

BAVLI SHABBAT 5:1

XII.19. A. Said R. Samuel bar Nahmani said R. Jonathan, "Whoever says David sinned errs: 'And David behaved himself wisely in all his ways, and the Lord was with him' (1 Sam. 18:14) — is it possible that even the opportunity to sin came his way and yet the Presence of God was with him?"

B. So how am I to interpret the language, "Wherefore have you despised the word of the Lord, to do that which is evil in his sight?" (2 Sam. 12:9)?

C. That's what he wanted to do, but he didn't do it.

BAVLI SHABBAT 5:1

XII.20. A. Said Rab, "Rabbi, who comes from David, turns matters around to interpret the verse in his behalf. For of the verse, 'Wherefore have you despised the word of the Lord, to do that which is evil in his sight?' Rabbi says, 'This 'evil' was different from all other references to evil in the Torah. For of all other references to evil in the Torah it is written, 'and he did,' but here it is written, 'to do,' in that that's what he wanted to do, but he didn't do it."

BAVLI SHABBAT 5:1

XII.21. A. "You have smitten Uriah the Hittite with the sword" (2 Sam. 12:9) — you should have judged him in the sanhedrin, but you didn't judge him.

XII.22. A.   "And you have taken his wife to be your wife" (2 Sam. 12:9) — you have marriage rights in her.

     B.   For said R. Samuel bar Nahmani said R. Jonathan, "Whoever went out to do battle for the house of David provides a writ of divorce for his wife in advance [to make sure she is free to remarry if he is lost in battle, his body not being recovered], in line with this verse: 'And to your brothers you shall bring greetings and take your pledge' (1 Sam. 17:18)."

     C.   *What is the meaning of* "and take your pledge"?

     D.   *Said R. Joseph as a Tannaite response,* "That refers to things that are pledged between him and her." [Daiches: These you shall take from them by a writ of divorce.]

XII.23. A.   "And you have slain him with the sword of the children of Ammon" (2 Sam. 12:9):

     B.   Just as on account of the sword of the children of Ammon you are not punished, so for Uriah the Hittite's death you are not punishable.

     C.   *How come? He was rebelling against the kingdom, in saying to him,* "And my lord Joab, and the servants of my lord, are encamped in the open field; shall I then go into my house to eat and drink and lie with my wife" (2 Sam. 11:11).

XII.24. A.   *Said Rab, "When you look into the case of David, you find nothing against him except the matter of Uriah, for it is written,* 'except only in the matter of Uriah the Hittite' (1 Kgs. 15:5)."

     B.   *Abbayye the Elder pointed out this contradiction to what Rab said, "To the contrary? Did Rab say any such thing? Didn't Rab say, 'David paid attention to slander'?"*

     C.   *That's a problem.*

XII.25. A.   *Reverting to the body of the foregoing:*

     B.   Rab said, "David paid attention to slander, as it is written, 'And the king said to him, Where is he? And Ziba said to the king, Behold, he is in the house of Machir the son of Ammiel, [but while Mephiboshet makes disloyal accusations against him, David found that] there was nothing to it' (2 Sam. 9:5). And it is written, 'Then David sent and brought him out of the house of Machir the son of Ammiel from "there was nothing to it."'" *When he looked into the matter, he found he was a liar."*

     C.   *"So when he went and slandered him again, how come he paid attention to it? For it is written,* 'And the king said, And where is your master's son? And Ziba said to the king, Behold, he abides at Jerusalem, for he said, Today shall the house of Israel restore me the kingdom of my father' (2 Sam. 16:3). *And how do we know that he accepted the slander from him a second time? As it is written,* 'Then said the king to Ziba, Behold, yours is all that belongs

to Mephiboshet. And Ziba said, I do obeisance, let me find favor
in your sight, my lord, O King' (2 Sam. 16:4).'"

D. But Samuel said, "David never paid attention to slander, *for he
saw obvious things in him himself [to validate what Ziba said,
and that would not constitute accepting slander], for it is written,*
'And Mephiboshet son of Saul came down to meet the king, and
he had neither dressed his feet nor trimmed his beard nor washed
his clothes' (2 Sam. 19:24), and further, 'And it came to pass,
when he had come to Jerusalem to meet the king, the king said to
him, How come you didn't go with me, Mephiboshet? And he
answered, My Lord, O King, my servant deceived me; for your
servant said, I will saddle an ass for myself that I may ride on it
and go with the king, because your servant is lame. [56B]. And he
has slandered your servant to my lord the king; but my lord the
king is as an angel of God; do therefore what is good in your eyes;
for all my father's house were but dead men before my lord the
king; yet you set your servant among them that ate at your own
table. What right therefore do I have yet that I should cry any more
to the king? And the king said to him, Why do you speak any more
of your matters? I say, you and Ziba divide the land. And
Mephiboshet said to the king, Yes, let him take all, for as much as
my lord the king is come in peace unto his own house' (2 Sam.
19:25-30). He said to him, 'I said, when will you come back in
peace? Yet you treat me so! Not against you do I have resentment,
but against Him who restored you in peace.' So it is written, 'And
the son of Jonathan was Meribbaal' (1 Chr. 8:34, 9:40). Now was
his name really Meribbaal? Surely it was Mephiboshet. But because
he brought about a quarrel [meribah] with his master, an echo came
forth and rebuked him: 'You man of strife son of a man of strife!'
Man of strife as we just said. Son of a man of strife: 'And Saul
came to the city of Amalek and strove in the valley' (1 Sam. 15:5)."

E. Said R. Manni, "...concerning the matter of the valley."

BAVLI SHABBAT 5:1

XII.26. A. Said R. Judah said Rab, "At the moment that Rab said to
Mephiboshet, 'you and Ziba divide the land,' an echo came forth
and said to him, 'Rehoboam and Jeroboam shall divide the
kingdom.'"

BAVLI SHABBAT 5:1

XII.27. A. Said R. Judah said Rab, "Had David not accepted slander, the
kingdom of the house of David would not have been divided, and
the Israelites would not have worshipped idols, and we should
never have been exiled from our land."

BAVLI SHABBAT 5:1

XII.28. A. Said R. Samuel bar Nahmani said R. Jonathan, "Whoever says
Solomon sinned errs, for it is said, 'And his heart was not perfect
with the Lord his God as was the heart of David his father' (1 Kgs.

11:4) — *it was like the heart of David his father that it was not the same, but he also never sinned!"*

B. Then how do I read, "For it came to pass, when Solomon was old, that his wives turned away his heart" (1 Kgs. 11:4)?

C. That is to be read in accord with R. Nathan, for R. Nathan contrasted verses as follows: "'For it came to pass, when Solomon was old, that his wives turned away his heart' (1 Kgs. 11:4), as against, 'And his heart was not perfect with the Lord his God as was the heart of David his father' (1 Kgs. 11:4) — *it was like the heart of David his father that it was not the same, but he also never sinned!*

D. *"This is the sense of the matter:* 'For it came to pass, when Solomon was old, that his wives turned away his heart' (1 Kgs. 11:4) to go after other gods, but he didn't go."

E. *But isn't it written,* "Then would Solomon build a high place for Chemosh the abomination of Moab" (1 Kgs. 11:7)?

F. He wanted to build but he didn't build.

G. *What about the following:* "Then Joshua built an altar to the Lord" (Josh. 8:30) — here, too, does it mean he wanted to build but he didn't build? *What it means is that he did build, and here, too, he did build it!*

H. *Rather, it is in accord with that which has been taught on Tannaite authority:* R. Yosé says, "'And the high places that were before Jerusalem, which were on the right hand of the mount of corruption, which Solomon the king of Israel had built for Ashtoreth the abomination of Moab' (2 Kgs. 23:13) — is it possible that Assa came along and didn't destroy them; then came Jehoshaphat and he didn't destroy them, but only Josiah came and destroyed them?! But isn't it the fact that every idol in the Land of Israel Assa and Jehoshaphat destroyed? But the former ones are compared to the latter: Just as the latter didn't do it, but it was ascribed to them to their glory, so the former ones didn't do it, but it is ascribed to them to their shame."

I. But isn't it written, "And Solomon did that which was evil in the sight of the Lord" (1 Kgs. 11:6)?

J. He had the power to stop his wives from doing those things but he didn't stop them, so Scripture regards him as though he personally had sinned."

XII.29. A. Said R. Judah said Samuel, "It would have been better for that righteous man had he served 'something else' but that Scripture should not say of him, 'And Solomon did that which was evil in the sight of the Lord' (1 Kgs. 11:6)."

BAVLI SHABBAT 5:1

XII.30. A. Said R. Judah said Samuel, "When Solomon married the daughter of Pharaoh, she brought to him a thousand kinds of musical instruments and said to him, 'This one they play for this idol, that one for that idol,' but he never stopped her."

BAVLI SHABBAT 5:1

XII.31. A. Said R. Judah said Samuel, "When Solomon married the daughter of Pharaoh, Gabriel came down and stuck a reed in the sea, and a sandbank gathered around it, on which the great city of Rome was built."

B. *In a Tannaite formulation it is repeated:* On the day that Jeroboam brought the two golden calves, one into Beth El and the other into Dan, a hut was built, and that was Greek Italy.

BAVLI SHABBAT 5:1

XII.32. A. Said R. Samuel bar Nahmani said R. Jonathan, "Whoever says that Josiah ever sinned errs, as it is said, 'And he did that which was right in the eyes of the Lord and walked in all the ways of David his father' (2 Kgs. 22:2). Then how do I read, 'and like unto him there was no king before him, who returned to the Lord with all his heart' (2 Kgs. 23:25)? [If he returned to the Lord, it means he had sinned and so had to repent.] It means, ever judgment he made between the age of eight and eighteen he reviewed. [He wanted to see whether he had made any mistakes.] Might you suppose he took from one and gave to another? Scripture says, 'He took from his own might,' meaning, he restored a judgment out of his own property."

B. *This differs from the view of Rab, for* said Rab, "You have no greater figure among penitents than Josiah in his generation, and a certain person in ours."

C. *So who could that be?*

D. *Abba Jeremiah, father of R. Jeremiah bar Abba, and some say, Aha brother of R. Abba father of R. Jeremiah bar Abba.*

E. *For a master has said, "R. Abba and Aha were brothers."*

F. *Said R. Joseph, "I was in session and dozing and saw in a dream that an angel stretched out his hand and accepted him."*

BAVLI SHABBAT 5:1

XII.19. A. Said R. Samuel bar Nahmani said R. Jonathan, "Whoever says David sinned errs: 'And David behaved himself wisely in all his ways, and the Lord was with him' (1 Sam. 18:14) — is it possible that even the opportunity to sin came his way and yet the Presence of God was with him?"

B. So how am I to interpret the language, "Wherefore have you despised the word of the Lord, to do that which is evil in his sight?" (2 Sam. 12:9)?

C. That's what he wanted to do, but he didn't do it.

BAVLI SHABBAT 5:1

XII.20. A. *Said Rab, "Rabbi, who comes from David, turns matters around to interpret the verse in his behalf. For of the verse, 'Wherefore have you despised the word of the Lord, to do that which is evil in his sight?' Rabbi says, 'This 'evil' was different from all other references to evil in the Torah. For of all other references to evil in the Torah it is written, 'and he did,' but here it is written, 'to do,' in that that's what he wanted to do, but he didn't do it.'"*

XII.21. A. "You have smitten Uriah the Hittite with the sword" (2 Sam. 12:9)
— you should have judged him in the sanhedrin, but you didn't
judge him.

XII.22. A. "And you have taken his wife to be your wife" (2 Sam. 12:9) —
you have marriage rights in her.

B. For said R. Samuel bar Nahmani said R. Jonathan, "Whoever went
out to do battle for the house of David provides a writ of divorce
for his wife in advance [to make sure she is free to remarry if he is
lost in battle, his body not being recovered], in line with this verse:
'And to your brothers you shall bring greetings and take your
pledge' (1 Sam. 17:18)."

C. *What is the meaning of* "and take your pledge"?

D. *Said R. Joseph as a Tannaite response,* "That refers to things that
are pledged between him and her." [Daiches: These you shall take
from them by a writ of divorce.]

XII.23. A. "And you have slain him with the sword of the children of Ammon"
(2 Sam. 12:9):

B. Just as on account of the sword of the children of Ammon you are
not punished, so for Uriah the Hittite's death you are not punishable.

C. *How come? He was rebelling against the kingdom, in saying to
him,* "And my lord Joab, and the servants of my lord, are encamped
in the open field; shall I then go into my house to eat and drink and
lie with my wife" (2 Sam. 11:11).

XII.24. A. *Said Rab, "When you look into the case of David, you find nothing
against him except the matter of Uriah, for it is written,* 'except
only in the matter of Uriah the Hittite' (1 Kgs. 15:5)."

B. *Abbayye the Elder pointed out this contradiction to what Rab said,
"To the contrary? Did Rab say any such thing? Didn't Rab say,
'David paid attention to slander'?"*

C. *That's a problem.*

XII.25. A. *Reverting to the body of the foregoing:*

B. Rab said, "David paid attention to slander, as it is written, 'And
the king said to him, Where is he? And Ziba said to the king, Behold,
he is in the house of Machir the son of Ammiel, [but while
Mephiboshet makes disloyal accusations against him, David found
that] there was nothing to it' (2 Sam. 9:5). And it is written, 'Then
David sent and brought him out of the house of Machir the son of
Ammiel from "there was nothing to it."' *When he looked into the
matter, he found he was a liar."*

C. *"So when he went and slandered him again, how come he paid
attention to it? For it is written,* 'And the king said, And where is
your master's son? And Ziba said to the king, Behold, he abides at

Jerusalem, for he said, Today shall the house of Israel restore me the kingdom of my father' (2 Sam. 16:3). *And how do we know that he accepted the slander from him a second time? As it is written,* 'Then said the king to Ziba, Behold, yours is all that belongs to Mephiboshet. And Ziba said, I do obeisance, let me find favor in your sight, my lord, O King' (2 Sam. 16:4)."

D. But Samuel said, "David never paid attention to slander, *for he saw obvious things in him himself [to validate what Ziba said, and that would not constitute accepting slander], for it is written,* 'And Mephiboshet son of Saul came down to meet the king, and he had neither dressed his feet nor trimmed his beard nor washed his clothes' (2 Sam. 19:24), and further, 'And it came to pass, when he had come to Jerusalem to meet the king, the king said to him, How come you didn't go with me, Mephiboshet? And he answered, My Lord, O King, my servant deceived me; for your servant said, I will saddle an ass for myself that I may ride on it and go with the king, because your servant is lame. **[56B]**. And he has slandered your servant to my lord the king; but my lord the king is as an angel of God; do therefore what is good in your eyes; for all my father's house were but dead men before my lord the king; yet you set your servant among them that ate at your own table. What right therefore do I have yet that I should cry any more to the king? And the king said to him, Why do you speak any more of your matters? I say, you and Ziba divide the land. And Mephiboshet said to the king, Yes, let him take all, for as much as my lord the king is come in peace unto his own house' (2 Sam. 19:25-30). He said to him, 'I said, when will you come back in peace? Yet you treat me so! Not against you do I have resentment, but against Him who restored you in peace.' So it is written, 'And the son of Jonathan was Meribbaal' (1 Chr. 8:34, 9:40). Now was his name really Meribbaal? Surely it was Mephiboshet. But because he brought about a quarrel [meribah] with his master, an echo came forth and rebuked him: 'You man of strife son of a man of strife!' Man of strife as we just said. Son of a man of strife: 'And Saul came to the city of Amalek and strove in the valley' (1 Sam. 15:5)."

E. Said R. Manni, "...concerning the matter of the valley."

BAVLI SHABBAT 5:1

XII.26. A. Said R. Judah said Rab, "At the moment that Rab said to Mephiboshet, 'you and Ziba divide the land,' an echo came forth and said to him, 'Rehoboam and Jeroboam shall divide the kingdom.'"

BAVLI SHABBAT 5:1

XII.27. A. Said R. Judah said Rab, "Had David not accepted slander, the kingdom of the house of David would not have been divided, and the Israelites would not have worshipped idols, and we should never have been exiled from our land."

BAVLI SHABBAT 5:1

XII.28. A. Said R. Samuel bar Nahmani said R. Jonathan, "Whoever says Solomon sinned errs, for it is said, 'And his heart was not perfect with the Lord his God as was the heart of David his father' (1 Kgs. 11:4) — *it was like the heart of David his father that it was not the same, but he also never sinned!*"

B. Then how do I read, "For it came to pass, when Solomon was old, that his wives turned away his heart" (1 Kgs. 11:4)?

C. That is to be read in accord with R. Nathan, for R. Nathan contrasted verses as follows: "'For it came to pass, when Solomon was old, that his wives turned away his heart' (1 Kgs. 11:4), as against, 'And his heart was not perfect with the Lord his God as was the heart of David his father' (1 Kgs. 11:4) — *it was like the heart of David his father that it was not the same, but he also never sinned!*

D. *"This is the sense of the matter:* 'For it came to pass, when Solomon was old, that his wives turned away his heart' (1 Kgs. 11:4) to go after other gods, but he didn't go."

E. *But isn't it written,* "Then would Solomon build a high place for Chemosh the abomination of Moab" (1 Kgs. 11:7)?

F. He wanted to build but he didn't build.

G. *What about the following:* "Then Joshua built an altar to the Lord" (Josh. 8:30) — here, too, does it mean he wanted to build but he didn't build? *What it means is that he did build, and here, too, he did build it!*

H. *Rather, it is in accord with that which has been taught on Tannaite authority:* R. Yosé says, "'And the high places that were before Jerusalem, which were on the right hand of the mount of corruption, which Solomon the king of Israel had built for Ashtoreth the abomination of Moab' (2 Kgs. 23:13) — is it possible that Assa came along and didn't destroy them; then came Jehoshaphat and he didn't destroy them, but only Josiah came and destroyed them?! But isn't it the fact that every idol in the Land of Israel Assa and Jehoshaphat destroyed? But the former ones are compared to the latter: Just as the latter didn't do it, but it was ascribed to them to their glory, so the former ones didn't do it, but it is ascribed to them to their shame."

I. But isn't it written, "And Solomon did that which was evil in the sight of the Lord" (1 Kgs. 11:6)?

J. He had the power to stop his wives from doing those things but he didn't stop them, so Scripture regards him as though he personally had sinned."

BAVLI SHABBAT 5:1

XII.29. A. Said R. Judah said Samuel, "It would have been better for that righteous man had he served 'something else' but that Scripture should not say of him, 'And Solomon did that which was evil in the sight of the Lord' (1 Kgs. 11:6)."

BAVLI SHABBAT 5:1

XII.30. A. Said R. Judah said Samuel, "When Solomon married the daughter of Pharaoh, she brought to him a thousand kinds of musical instruments and said to him, 'This one they play for this idol, that one for that idol,' but he never stopped her."

BAVLI SHABBAT 5:1

XII.31. A. Said R. Judah said Samuel, "When Solomon married the daughter of Pharaoh, Gabriel came down and stuck a reed in the sea, and a sandbank gathered around it, on which the great city of Rome was built."

B. *In a Tannaite formulation it is repeated:* On the day that Jeroboam brought the two golden calves, one into Beth El and the other into Dan, a hut was built, and that was Greek Italy.

BAVLI SHABBAT 5:1

XII.32. A. Said R. Samuel bar Nahmani said R. Jonathan, "Whoever says that Josiah ever sinned errs, as it is said, 'And he did that which was right in the eyes of the Lord and walked in all the ways of David his father' (2 Kgs. 22:2). Then how do I read, 'and like unto him there was no king before him, who returned to the Lord with all his heart' (2 Kgs. 23:25)? [If he returned to the Lord, it means he had sinned and so had to repent.] It means, ever judgment he made between the age of eight and eighteen he reviewed. [He wanted to see whether he had made any mistakes.] Might you suppose he took from one and gave to another? Scripture says, 'He took from his own might,' meaning, he restored a judgment out of his own property."

B. *This differs from the view of Rab, for* said Rab, "You have no greater figure among penitents than Josiah in his generation, and a certain person in ours."

C. *So who could that be?*

D. *Abba Jeremiah, father of R. Jeremiah bar Abba, and some say, Aha brother of R. Abba father of R. Jeremiah bar Abba.*

E. *For a master has said, "R. Abba and Aha were brothers."*

F. *Said R. Joseph, "I was in session and dozing and saw in a dream that an angel stretched out his hand and accepted him."*

BAVLI SHABBAT 5

XII.19. A. Said R. Samuel bar Nahmani said R. Jonathan, "Whoever says David sinned errs: 'And David behaved himself wisely in all his ways, and the Lord was with him' (1 Sam. 18:14) — is it possible that even the opportunity to sin came his way and yet the Presence of God was with him?"

B. So how am I to interpret the language, "Wherefore have you despised the word of the Lord, to do that which is evil in his sight?" (2 Sam. 12:9)?

C. That's what he wanted to do, but he didn't do it.

BAVLI SHABBAT 5:1

XII.20. A. *Said Rab, "Rabbi, who comes from David, turns matters around to interpret the verse in his behalf. For of the verse,* 'Wherefore have you despised the word of the Lord, to do that which is evil in his sight?' Rabbi says, 'This 'evil' was different from all other references to evil in the Torah. For of all other references to evil in the Torah it is written, 'and he did,' but here it is written, 'to do,' in that that's what he wanted to do, but he didn't do it."

BAVLI SHABBAT 5:1

XII.21. A. "You have smitten Uriah the Hittite with the sword" (2 Sam. 12:9) — you should have judged him in the sanhedrin, but you didn't judge him.

BAVLI SHABBAT 5:1

XII.22. A. "And you have taken his wife to be your wife" (2 Sam. 12:9) — you have marriage rights in her.

B. For said R. Samuel bar Nahmani said R. Jonathan, "Whoever went out to do battle for the house of David provides a writ of divorce for his wife in advance [to make sure she is free to remarry if he is lost in battle, his body not being recovered], in line with this verse: 'And to your brothers you shall bring greetings and take your pledge' (1 Sam. 17:18)."

C. *What is the meaning of* "and take your pledge"?

D. *Said R. Joseph as a Tannaite response,* "That refers to things that are pledged between him and her." [Daiches: These you shall take from them by a writ of divorce.]

BAVLI SHABBAT 5:1

XII.23. A. "And you have slain him with the sword of the children of Ammon" (2 Sam. 12:9):

B. Just as on account of the sword of the children of Ammon you are not punished, so for Uriah the Hittite's death you are not punishable.

C. *How come? He was rebelling against the kingdom, in saying to him,* "And my lord Joab, and the servants of my lord, are encamped in the open field; shall I then go into my house to eat and drink and lie with my wife" (2 Sam. 11:11).

BAVLI SHABBAT 5:1

XII.24. A. *Said Rab, "When you look into the case of David, you find nothing against him except the matter of Uriah, for it is written,* 'except only in the matter of Uriah the Hittite' (1 Kgs. 15:5)."

B. *Abbayye the Elder pointed out this contradiction to what Rab said, "To the contrary? Did Rab say any such thing? Didn't Rab say, 'David paid attention to slander'?"*

C. *That's a problem.*

BAVLI SHABBAT 5:1

XII.25. A. *Reverting to the body of the foregoing:*

B. Rab said, "David paid attention to slander, as it is written, 'And the king said to him, Where is he? And Ziba said to the king, Behold, he is in the house of Machir the son of Ammiel, [but while Mephiboshet makes disloyal accusations against him, David found that] there was nothing to it' (2 Sam. 9:5). And it is written, 'Then David sent and brought him out of the house of Machir the son of

Ammiel from "there was nothing to it."' *When he looked into the matter, he found he was a liar."*

C.   *"So when he went and slandered him again, how come he paid attention to it? For it is written,* 'And the king said, And where is your master's son? And Ziba said to the king, Behold, he abides at Jerusalem, for he said, Today shall the house of Israel restore me the kingdom of my father' (2 Sam. 16:3). *And how do we know that he accepted the slander from him a second time? As it is written,* 'Then said the king to Ziba, Behold, yours is all that belongs to Mephiboshet. And Ziba said, I do obeisance, let me find favor in your sight, my lord, O King' (2 Sam. 16:4)."

D.   But Samuel said, "David never paid attention to slander, *for he saw obvious things in him himself [to validate what Ziba said, and that would not constitute accepting slander], for it is written,* 'And Mephiboshet son of Saul came down to meet the king, and he had neither dressed his feet nor trimmed his beard nor washed his clothes' (2 Sam. 19:24), and further, 'And it came to pass, when he had come to Jerusalem to meet the king, the king said to him, How come you didn't go with me, Mephiboshet? And he answered, My Lord, O King, my servant deceived me; for your servant said, I will saddle an ass for myself that I may ride on it and go with the king, because your servant is lame. **[56B]**. And he has slandered your servant to my lord the king; but my lord the king is as an angel of God; do therefore what is good in your eyes; for all my father's house were but dead men before my lord the king; yet you set your servant among them that ate at your own table. What right therefore do I have yet that I should cry any more to the king? And the king said to him, Why do you speak any more of your matters? I say, you and Ziba divide the land. And Mephiboshet said to the king, Yes, let him take all, for as much as my lord the king is come in peace unto his own house' (2 Sam. 19:25-30). He said to him, 'I said, when will you come back in peace? Yet you treat me so! Not against you do I have resentment, but against Him who restored you in peace.' So it is written, 'And the son of Jonathan was Meribbaal' (1 Chr. 8:34, 9:40). Now was his name really Meribbaal? Surely it was Mephiboshet. But because he brought about a quarrel [meribah] with his master, an echo came forth and rebuked him: 'You man of strife son of a man of strife!' Man of strife as we just said. Son of a man of strife: 'And Saul came to the city of Amalek and strove in the valley' (1 Sam. 15:5)."

E.   Said R. Manni, "...concerning the matter of the valley."

BAVLI SHABBAT 5:1

XII.26. A.   Said R. Judah said Rab, "At the moment that Rab said to Mephiboshet, 'you and Ziba divide the land,' an echo came forth and said to him, 'Rehoboam and Jeroboam shall divide the kingdom.'"

BAVLI SHABBAT 5:1
XII.27. A. Said R. Judah said Rab, "Had David not accepted slander, the
kingdom of the house of David would not have been divided, and
the Israelites would not have worshipped idols, and we should
never have been exiled from our land."

BAVLI SHABBAT 5:1
XII.24. A. *Said Rab, "When you look into the case of David, you find nothing
against him except the matter of Uriah, for it is written, 'except
only in the matter of Uriah the Hittite' (1 Kgs. 15:5)."*

B. *Abbayye the Elder pointed out this contradiction to what Rab said,
"To the contrary? Did Rab say any such thing? Didn't Rab say,
'David paid attention to slander'?"*

C. *That's a problem.*

BAVLI SHABBAT 5:1
XII.25. A. *Reverting to the body of the foregoing:*

B. Rab said, "David paid attention to slander, as it is written, 'And
the king said to him, Where is he? And Ziba said to the king, Behold,
he is in the house of Machir the son of Ammiel, [but while
Mephiboshet makes disloyal accusations against him, David found
that] there was nothing to it' (2 Sam. 9:5). And it is written, 'Then
David sent and brought him out of the house of Machir the son of
Ammiel from "there was nothing to it."' *When he looked into the
matter, he found he was a liar."*

C. *"So when he went and slandered him again, how come he paid
attention to it? For it is written,* 'And the king said, And where is
your master's son? And Ziba said to the king, Behold, he abides at
Jerusalem, for he said, Today shall the house of Israel restore me
the kingdom of my father' (2 Sam. 16:3). *And how do we know
that he accepted the slander from him a second time? As it is
written,* 'Then said the king to Ziba, Behold, yours is all that belongs
to Mephiboshet. And Ziba said, I do obeisance, let me find favor
in your sight, my lord, O King' (2 Sam. 16:4)."

D. But Samuel said, "David never paid attention to slander, *for he
saw obvious things in him himself [to validate what Ziba said,
and that would not constitute accepting slander], for it is written,*
'And Mephiboshet son of Saul came down to meet the king, and
he had neither dressed his feet nor trimmed his beard nor washed
his clothes' (2 Sam. 19:24), and further, 'And it came to pass,
when he had come to Jerusalem to meet the king, the king said to
him, How come you didn't go with me, Mephiboshet? And he
answered, My Lord, O King, my servant deceived me; for your
servant said, I will saddle an ass for myself that I may ride on it
and go with the king, because your servant is lame. [56B]. And he
has slandered your servant to my lord the king; but my lord the
king is as an angel of God; do therefore what is good in your eyes;
for all my father's house were but dead men before my lord the
king; yet you set your servant among them that ate at your own

table. What right therefore do I have yet that I should cry any more to the king? And the king said to him, Why do you speak any more of your matters? I say, you and Ziba divide the land. And Mephiboshet said to the king, Yes, let him take all, for as much as my lord the king is come in peace unto his own house' (2 Sam. 19:25-30). He said to him, 'I said, when will you come back in peace? Yet you treat me so! Not against you do I have resentment, but against Him who restored you in peace.' So it is written, 'And the son of Jonathan was Meribbaal' (1 Chr. 8:34, 9:40). Now was his name really Meribbaal? Surely it was Mephiboshet. But because he brought about a quarrel [meribah] with his master, an echo came forth and rebuked him: 'You man of strife son of a man of strife!' Man of strife as we just said. Son of a man of strife: 'And Saul came to the city of Amalek and strove in the valley' (1 Sam. 15:5)."

E. Said R. Manni, "...concerning the matter of the valley."

BAVLI SHABBAT 5:1

XII.26. A. Said R. Judah said Rab, "At the moment that Rab said to Mephiboshet, 'you and Ziba divide the land,' an echo came forth and said to him, 'Rehoboam and Jeroboam shall divide the kingdom.'"

BAVLI SHABBAT 5:1

XII.27. A. Said R. Judah said Rab, "Had David not accepted slander, the kingdom of the house of David would not have been divided, and the Israelites would not have worshipped idols, and we should never have been exiled from our land."

BAVLI SHABBAT 5:1

XII.28. A. Said R. Samuel bar Nahmani said R. Jonathan, "Whoever says Solomon sinned errs, for it is said, 'And his heart was not perfect with the Lord his God as was the heart of David his father' (1 Kgs. 11:4) — *it was like the heart of David his father that it was not the same, but he also never sinned!"*

B. Then how do I read, "For it came to pass, when Solomon was old, that his wives turned away his heart" (1 Kgs. 11:4)?

C. That is to be read in accord with R. Nathan, for R. Nathan contrasted verses as follows: "'For it came to pass, when Solomon was old, that his wives turned away his heart' (1 Kgs. 11:4), as against, 'And his heart was not perfect with the Lord his God as was the heart of David his father' (1 Kgs. 11:4) — *it was like the heart of David his father that it was not the same, but he also never sinned!*

D. *"This is the sense of the matter:* 'For it came to pass, when Solomon was old, that his wives turned away his heart' (1 Kgs. 11:4) to go after other gods, but he didn't go."

E. *But isn't it written,* "Then would Solomon build a high place for Chemosh the abomination of Moab" (1 Kgs. 11:7)?

F. He wanted to build but he didn't build.

G. *What about the following:* "Then Joshua built an altar to the Lord" (Josh. 8:30) — here, too, does it mean he wanted to build but he didn't build? *What it means is that he did build, and here, too, he did build it!*

H.   *Rather, it is in accord with that which has been taught on Tannaite authority:* R. Yosé says, "'And the high places that were before Jerusalem, which were on the right hand of the mount of corruption, which Solomon the king of Israel had built for Ashtoreth the abomination of Moab' (2 Kgs. 23:13) — is it possible that Assa came along and didn't destroy them; then came Jehoshaphat and he didn't destroy them, but only Josiah came and destroyed them?! But isn't it the fact that every idol in the Land of Israel Assa and Jehoshaphat destroyed? But the former ones are compared to the latter: Just as the latter didn't do it, but it was ascribed to them to their glory, so the former ones didn't do it, but it is ascribed to them to their shame."

I.   But isn't it written, "And Solomon did that which was evil in the sight of the Lord" (1 Kgs. 11:6)?

J.   He had the power to stop his wives from doing those things but he didn't stop them, so Scripture regards him as though he personally had sinned."

Bavli Shabbat 5:1

XII.29. A.   Said R. Judah said Samuel, "It would have been better for that righteous man had he served 'something else' but that Scripture should not say of him, 'And Solomon did that which was evil in the sight of the Lord' (1 Kgs. 11:6)."

Bavli Shabbat 5:1

XII.32. A.   Said R. Samuel bar Nahmani said R. Jonathan, "Whoever says that Josiah ever sinned errs, as it is said, 'And he did that which was right in the eyes of the Lord and walked in all the ways of David his father' (2 Kgs. 22:2). Then how do I read, 'and like unto him there was no king before him, who returned to the Lord with all his heart' (2 Kgs. 23:25)? [If he returned to the Lord, it means he had sinned and so had to repent.] It means, ever judgment he made between the age of eight and eighteen he reviewed. [He wanted to see whether he had made any mistakes.] Might you suppose he took from one and gave to another? Scripture says, 'He took from his own might,' meaning, he restored a judgment out of his own property."

Bavli Shabbat 15:2D-F

I.18.A.   "And he handed her parched grain and she ate and had enough and some left over " (Ruth 2:14)

B.   Said R. Eleazar, "'she ate' — in the time of David; 'and had enough' — in the time of Solomon. 'And some left over' — in the time of Hezekiah."

C.   *There are those who say,* "'she ate' — in the time of David and Solomon; 'and had enough' — in the time of Hezekiah. 'And some left over '— in the time of Rabbi."

D.   *For a master said, "The house steward of Rabbi was richer than King Shapur."*

E.   In a Tannaite statement it was repeated: "'she ate' — in this world; 'and had enough' — in the days of the Messiah. 'And some left over' — in the age to come

This is one of the most elaborate topical composites of David-statements,

BAVLI ERUBIN

BAVLI ERUBIN 1:2

V.8. A.   Said R. Hisda, "Expounded Mari bar Mar, 'What is the meaning of the verse of Scripture, "I have seen an end to every purpose, but your commandment is exceedingly broad" (Ps. 119:96)? David said this but didn't spell it out. Job said it but didn't spell it out. Ezekiel said it but didn't spell it out. Until Zechariah b. Iddo came along and spelled it out.

B.   "'David said this but didn't spell it out: "I have seen an end to every purpose, but your commandment is exceedingly broad" (Ps. 119:96).

C.   "'Job said it but didn't spell it out: "The measure thereof is longer than the earth and broader than the sea" (Job 11:9).

D.   "'Ezekiel said it but didn't spell it out: "And he spread it before me and it was written within and without and there was written therein lamentations, and meditation of joy and woe" (Ezek. 2:10).

E.   ""'Lamentation" speaks of retribution of the just in this world, in line with the verse, "This is the lamentation wherewith they shall lament" (Ezek. 32:16).

Ps. 119:96 is stated by David.

BAVLI ERUBIN 4:3

II.3. A.   R. Dosetai of Biri expounded, "What is the meaning of the verse: 'And they told David saying, Behold the Philistines are fighting against Keilah and they rob the threshing floors' (1 Sam. 23:1)? A Tannaite statement [clarifies this matter]: Keilah was a town close to the frontier, and they came only for straw and fodder, as it is written, 'And they rob the threshing floors.' And it is written nonetheless, 'Therefore David inquired of the Lord, saying, Shall I go and smite these Philistines? And the Lord said to David, Go and smite the Philistines and save Keilah' (1 Sam. 23:2). Now what was he asking about? Should I say whether it is permitted or forbidden to beat back the attack? But then there was the court of Samuel of Ramah [whom he should have asked, instead of the Lord]! So what he wanted to know is, would he succeed or not? A close reading of the language of the verse supports this view: 'Go and smite the Philistines and save Keilah.'"

David's statement is expounded.

BAVLI ERUBIN 5:1 I.

10. F.   *"David set forth in public the tractate he was studying, Saul didn't.*
Of David, who set forth in public the tractate he was studying, it is
written in Scripture, 'They who fear you shall see me and be glad'
(Ps. 119:74). Of Saul, who didn't set forth in public the tractate he
was studying, it is written in Scripture, 'And wherever he turned
himself [53B] *he acted wrongly' (1 Sam. 14:47)."*

David carried out study of Torah in the proper manner.

BAVLI YOMA

BAVLI YOMA 7:3

I:1. B.   How do people consult the Urim and Thummim?

J.   They do not present two questions simultaneously, and if one did
so, only the first one of the questions is answered, as it is said,
"Will the men of Keilah deliver me up into his hand? Will Saul
come down...? And the Lord said, He will come down" (1 Sam.
23:11).

K.   But you just said, and if one did so, only the first one of the questions
is answered!

L.   David presented his questions [73B] not in the right order, but got
his answers back in the right order.

M.   And when he realized he had asked in the wrong order, he went
and asked in the right order: "Will the men of Keilah deliver up
me and my men into the hand of Saul? And the Lord said, They
will deliver you up" (1 Sam. 23:12).

N.   But if the occasion really required two questions, two questions
will indeed be answered: "And David inquired of the Lord, saying,
Shall I pursue after this troop? Shall I overtake them? And he
answered him, Pursue, for you shall surely overtake them and you
shall without fail recover all" (1 Sam. 30:8).

O.   And even though the decree of a prophet may be revoked, the
decree of the Urim and Thummim is never revoked: "By the
judgment of the Urim" (Num. 27:21).

4. A.   Why are they called Urim and Thummim?

B.   "Urim" because they made enlightening statements [the word for
enlighten uses the same letters as Urim].

C.   Thummim, because what they say is fully achieved [the word for
fulfil or fully achieve using the same letters as Thummim].

D.   And if you object, then why did they not carry out what they said
in Gibeah Benjamin [Judges 20]? the answer is, because they did
not really ask [their question clearly, whether it would be] victory
or defeat. But when they conquered, the Urim and Thummim

approved their action: "And Phinehas the son of Eleazar the son of Aaron stood before it in those days, saying, Shall I yet go out to battle against the children of Benjamin my brother or shall I cease, and the Lord said, Go up, for tomorrow I will deliver him into your hand" (Judges 20:28).

David asked questions and was answered.

BAVLI YOMA 8:1

IV.1. A.   ...(5) put on a sandal:

B.   *How on the basis of Scripture do we know that refraining from putting on sandals is a form of affliction?*

C.   As it is written, "And David went up by the ascent of the Mount of Olives and wept as he went up and he had his head covered and went bare" (2 Sam. 15:20) —*for what? Would you not say, because of not wearing sandals?*

D.   *How so? Maybe it means, bare of horse and whip?*

E.   *Rather, said R. Nahman bar Isaac, "Proof derives from here:* 'Go and loose the sack-cloth from off your loins and put your shoe from off your foot' (Is. 20:2). And it is written, 'And he did so, walking naked and bare' (Is. 20:2). *Now, bare of what? Obviously bare of sandals."*

F.   *How so? Maybe it means, he was wearing patched up shoes. For if you don't take that position, then you also would have to say that "naked" means, literally bare-assed! Rather, it means in torn garments, and here too, it means, in patched up shoes.*

G.   *Rather, said R. Nahman bar Isaac, "Proof derives from here:* 'Withhold your foot from being unshod and your throat from thirst' (Jer. 2:25) — keep yourself from sin, lest your food become unshod, and keep your tongue from idle gossip, lest your throat become dry with thirst."

David is the model for a ruing,

[1] IS DAVID AN ACTIVE PLAYER OR A ROUTINE AND SCARCELY ANIMATE ONE? David is the topic of a massive exposition. There is no comparable composite in the prior documents.

[2] WHAT COMPONENTS OF THE COLLECTION MAKE ROUTINE GLOSSES OF THE RECEIVED SCRIPTURES and which ones provide more than minor glosses of the tradition? The Bavli contains both types of composites but the bulk of the writing carries us deep into the exposition of David's particular characteristics,

[3] CAN WE IDENTIFY A PRONOUNCED BIAS OR A POLEMIC in the utilization of David? I do not perceive a pronounced bias engaged with David,

[4] HOW IS DAVID COMPARABLE TO OTHER SAGES IN THIS DOCUMENT? He is separate from the standard sage.

21

David in Bavli Nashim

BAVLI SOTAH

M. BAVLI TRACTATE SOTAH 1:7

I: B. *Our rabbis have taught on Tannaite authority:*

C. Absalom rebelled through his hair, as it is said: "There was none so to be praised as Absalom for his beauty. And when he cut off his hair — for it was at every year's end that he cut it, because the hair was heavy on him, therefore he cut it — he weighed the hair of his head at two hundred shekels after the king's weight" (2 Sam. 14:25f.).

E. Therefore he was hung by his hair, as it is said, "And Absalom happened to meet the servants of David. And Absalom rode on his mule, and the mule went under the thick boughs of a great oak, and his head caught hold of the oak, and he was taken up between heaven and earth, and the mule that was under him went on" (2 Sam. 18:9).

F. He took a sword to cut himself loose [Cf. T. Sot. 3:16].

G. *A Tannaite authority of the house of R. Ishmael [stated],* "At that moment Sheol opened up underneath him."

H. "And the king was much moved, and went up to the chamber over the gate, and wept, and, as he went, he said, 'O my son, Absalom, my son, my son, Absalom, would God I had died for you, O Absalom, my son, my son'" (2 Sam. 19:1) [18:33]. "And the king covered his face, and the king cried with a loud voice, 'O my son, Absalom, O Absalom, my son, my son'" (2 Sam. 19:5) [4].

I. *Why these eight references to "my son"?*

J. *Seven served to raise him up from the seven levels of Gehenna, and as to the eighth — some say it was to bring his severed head to his body, and others say it was to bring him into the world to come.*

2. A. "Now Absalom in his lifetime had taken and reared up" (2 Sam. 18:18):

B. *What is the meaning of* "taken"?

C. Said R. Simeon b. Laqish, "He had made a poor purchase for himself."

D. "The pillar which is in the king's valley" (2 Sam. 18:18):

E. Said R. Hanina bar Pappa, "It was in the deep plan of the King of the world."

F. [11A] So it is written, "Lo, I shall raise up evil against you out of your own house" (2 Sam. 12:11).

The exposition is accentuated but not elaborated

BAVLI SOTAH 8:1

IV.1. A. The Philistines came with the power of Goliath [M. 8:1P]:

B. "The sense of the name Goliath," said R. Yohanan, "is that he arose with arrogance [GYLWY PNYM] before the Holy One, blessed be he.

C. "So it is said, 'Choose a man for you and let him come down to me' (1 Sam. 17:8).

D. "Now the word 'man' refers only to the Holy One, blessed be he, as it is said, "The Lord is a man of war' (Ex. 15:3).

E. "Said the Holy One, blessed be he, "Lo, I shall bring him down through the power of a son of a man, as it is said, 'And David, son of this man of Ephrat' (1 Sam. 17:12)."

BAVLI SOTAH 8:1

IV 2. A. Said R. Yohanan in the name of R. Meir, "At three points the statements of that wicked man entrapped him.

B. "First: 'Choose a man for you and let him come down to me' (1 Sam. 17:8).

C. "Further: 'If he is able to fight with me and kill me' (1 Sam. 17:9) [which David did do].

D. "And finally: 'Am I a dog, that you come against me with staves' (1 Sam. 17:43).

E. "David, for his part, said to him, 'You come against me with sword, spear, and javelin,' (1 Sam. 17:45), and then he said to him, 'But I come against you with the name of the Lord of hosts, God of the armies of Israel, whom you have defied' (1 Sam. 17:45)."

BAVLI SOTAH 8:1

IV 3. A. "The Philistine drew near morning and evening" (1 Sam. 17:16):

B. Said R. Yohanan, "It was so as to interrupt them from reciting the Shema morning and evening."

H. "And presented himself for forty days" (1 Sam. 17:16):

I. Said R. Yohanan, "It was to match the forty days on which the Torah was given."

BAVLI SOTAH **8:1**

IV 4. A. And a champion (BYNYM) came forth from the camps of the Philistines" (1 Sam. 17:4):

B. *What is the meaning of the word used for champion?*

C. Said Rab, "He was highly developed (MBYNH) and not at all blemished."

D. Samuel said, "He was the middle one among his brothers (BYNYN)."

E. *A member of the house of R. Shila said,* "He was built like a stronghold [building]."

5. A. R. Yohanan said, "He was son of a hundred fathers and one mother, 'And Goliath from Gath was his name' (1 Sam. 17:4).

B. *R. Joseph repeated on Tannaite authority,* "For all men pressed against his mother, as on a winepress (GT)."

C. It is written, Maaroth [out of the ranks], (1 Sam. 17:23) but we read maarakhoth.

D. *R. Joseph repeated on Tannaite authority,* "For all men had sexual relations (hearu) with his mother."

BAVLI SOTAH **8:1**

IV 6. A. It is written both Harafah and Orpah (2 Sam. 21:18, Ruth 1:4).

B. Rab and Samuel:

C. One said, "Her name was Harafah, and why was she called Orpah? Because everybody had sexual relations with her doggie-style."

D. The other said, "Her name was Orpah, and why was she called Harafah? Because everybody ground her like ground grain (*harifoth*).

E. "So Scripture says, 'And the woman took and spread the covering over the well's mouth and spread ground grain on it' (2 Sam. 17:19).

F. *"If you prefer, I shall propose proof from the following verse:* 'Though you should bray a fool in a mortar with a pestle among ground grain' (Prov. 27:22)."

BAVLI SOTAH **8:1**

IV 7. A. "These four were born to Harafah in Gath, and they fell by the hand of David and by the hand of his servants" (2 Sam. 21:22):

B. *Who are they?*

C. Said R. Hisda, "Saph, Madon, Goliath, and Ish Bibenob" [2 Sam. 21:18, 20].

D. "And they fell by the hand of David and by the hand of his servants" (2 Sam. 21:22):

E. As it is written, "And Orpah kissed her mother-in-law, but Ruth embraced her" (Ruth 1:14).

F. Said R. Isaac, "Said the Holy One, blessed be he, 'Let the ones who kissed her come and fall at the hand of the sons of the one who embraced her [and Goliath was son of Orpah, Naomi's daughter-in-law].'"

G. Raba expounded, "As a reward for the four tears that Orpah wept for her mother-in-law, she had such merit that four heroes came forth from her,

H. "as it is said, 'And they lifted up their voice and wept again' (Ruth 1:14). [They thus wept twice, each time two tears from the two eyes, hence, four.]"

BAVLI SOTAH 8:1

IV. 8. A. It is written, "The arrow (HS) of his spear," but we read, "The staff (cS) of his spear" (1 Sam. 17:7).

B. Said R. Eleazar, "We have not yet reached even half (HSY) of the power of that wicked man."

C. On the basis of the passage at hand [we learn that] it is forbidden to recount the prowess of wicked men.

D. *In that case, why bring up the subject at all?*

E. *It is to make known the [still greater] prowess of David.*

The narrative is elaborated in its details,

BAVLI SOTAH 9:12

II.1. A. **When the former prophets died out [M. 9:12A]:**

B. *Who are the former prophets?*

C. Said R. Huna, "These are David, Samuel, and Solomon."

D. *R. Nahman said, "In the time of David, sometimes things worked out [when the Urim and Thumim were consulted], sometimes they did not work out,* for lo, he asked Zadoq and things worked out, then he asked Abiathar and things did not work out for him,

E. "as it is said, 'And Abiathar went up' (2 Sam. 15:24). [At issue is consultation with the Urim and Thumim]."

F. Rabbah bar Samuel raised the objection, "'And he set himself to seek God all the days of Zechariah who had understanding in the vision of God' (2 Chr. 26:5).

G. *"Does this not refer to consultation with the Urim and Thummim?"*

H. No, it was consultation through the prophets.

J. Come and take note: [T.:] **When the first Temple was destroyed, the kingship was removed from the House of David.**

K. **The Urim and Thummim ceased [M. 9:12A].**

L. **The cities of refuge came to an end.**

M. **And if someone wants you to cite, "The governor told them that they were not to partake of the most holy food until there should be a priest to consult Urim and Thummim" (Ezra 2:63),"**

N. **say to him, "This is like a man who says to his friend, 'Until the dead will live,' or, 'Until Elijah will come'" [T. Sot. 13:2].**

O. *Rather, said R. Nahman bar Isaac, "What is meant by 'former' prophets? It is used to distinguish Haggai, Zechariah, and Malachi, who are the latter prophets."*

P. *For our rabbis have taught on Tannaite authority:*

Q. **When the latter prophets died, that is, Haggai, Zechariah, and Malachi, then the Holy Spirit came to an end in Israel.**

DAVID IN BAVLI GITTIN

BAVLI GITTIN 4:6

VII.1. A. **R. Haninah b. Antigonos says, "Also: Whoever was recorded in the king's army":**

B. Said R. Judah said Samuel, "This speaks of those who served in the armies of the house of David."

C. *Said R. Joseph, "What verse of Scripture makes that point?* 'And they who were reckoned by genealogy for service in war' (1 Chr. 7:40)."

D. *How come?*

E. Said R. Judah said Rab, "So that the acts of supererogatory grace that they have performed as well as the inherited merit of their ancestors will help them."

F. *But isn't there Zelek the Ammonite (2 Sam. 23:37) – surely he descended from Ammon [but fought for David]!*

G. *No, he just lived there.*

H. *But isn't there Uriah the Hittite (2 Sam. 23:39) – surely he descended from Heth!*

I. *No, he just lived there.*

J. *And what about Ittai the Gittite (2 Sam. 15:19), and should you reply here, too, no, he just lived there, didn't* R. Nahman say, "Ittai the Gittite came and destroyed Gath"? And furthermore, said R. Judah said Rab, "David had four hundred sons, all of them born of beautiful captive women. All grew long locks plaited down the back. All of them seated in golden chariots. And they went forth at the head of troops, and they were the powerful figures in the house of David." [Being offspring of captives of war, they didn't have such fine genealogy.]

K. *They just went forth to frighten the other army [but they were not the main force of David's army].*

The scriptural narrative is clarified but not materially changed.

[1] IS DAVID AN ACTIVE PLAYER OR A ROUTINE AND SCARCELY ANIMATE ONE? David stands at the center of the scriptural narrative but does little to change the story or expand it.

[2] WHAT COMPONENTS OF THE COLLECTION MAKE ROUTINE GLOSSES OF THE RECEIVED SCRIPTURES and which ones provide more than minor glosses of the tradition? The bulk consists of minor glosses.

[3] CAN WE IDENTIFY A PRONOUNCED BIAS OR A POLEMIC in the utilization of David? I identify no pronounced bias.

[4] HOW IS DAVID COMPARABLE TO OTHER SAGES IN THIS DOCUMENT? David figures in the ordinary framework of the Torah-sages.

22

David in Bavli Neziqin

BAVLI BABA QAMMA

BAVLI BABA QAMMA 4:3

II.7. A. Said R. Hiyya bar Abba said R. Joshua b. Qorha, "One should always give precedence to a matter involving a religious duty, since, on account of the one night by which the elder daughter of Lot came prior to the younger, she came prior to her by four generations:

B. "Obed, Jesse, David, and Solomon [via Ruth]. As to the younger, she had none until Rehoboam: 'And the name of his mother was Naamah the Ammonitess' (1 Kgs. 14:31)."

A reference to David does not produce important data.

BAVLI BABA BATRA

BAVLI BABA BATRA 1:3

IV.43. A. Said R. Abbahu, "Said Moses before the Holy One, blessed be He, 'Lord of the world, how will the horn of Israel be exalted?'

B. "He said to him, 'It is through taking their census [by collecting a coin from each, and this was given to charity].'"

C. And said R. Abbahu, "They asked Solomon son of David, 'To what extent is the power of charity?'

D. "He said to him, 'Go see what my father, David, has to say about it: 'He has dispersed, he has given to the needy, his righteousness endures for ever' (Ps. 112:9)."

E. R. Abba said, "Here is the correct verse: 'He shall dwell on his, his place of defense shall be the munitions of the rocks, his bread is given him, his waters are reliable' (Isa. 33:16). Why shall he dwell

161

on high with his place with the munitions of the rocks? 'Because his bread is given to the poor and his waters are reliable.'"

F.   And said R. Abbahu, "They asked Solomon son of David, 'Who is going to inherit the world to come?

G.   "He said to him, 'He to whom the following applies: "...and before his elders shall be glory" (Isa. 24:23).'"

David is represented by Ps. 112:9 and Isa. 33;16.

Bavli Sanhedrin 1:5

XXIV.1 A.   **They bring forth the army to a war fought by choice only on the instructions of a court of seventy-one [M. 1:5B]:**

B.   *What is the scriptural source for this rule?*

C.   Said R. Abbahu, "Scripture says, 'And he shall stand before Eleazar the priest, [who shall inquire for him by the judgment of the Urim before the Lord. At his word shall they go out and at his word they shall come in, both he and all the children of Israel with him, even all the congregation]' (Num. 27:21-22).

D.   "'He' speaks of the king.

E.   "'And all the children of Israel with him' refers to the priest anointed for war.

F.   "'And even all the congregation' refers to the sanhedrin."

G.   *But perhaps it is the sanhedrin that is instructed by the All-Merciful to inquire of the Urim and Thummim?*

H.   *Rather, the proof derives from what R. Aha bar Bizna said R. Simeon the Pious said,* "There was a harp suspended over David's bed. At midnight a north wind would blow through it, and it would play on its own. David would get up right away and take up Torah-study until dawn. At dawn the sages of Israel would come in to him. They said to him, 'Our lord, king, your people Israel need sustenance.'

I.   "He said to them, 'Make a living off one another.'

J.   "They said to him, 'A handful of meal is not enough for a lion, and a pit cannot be filled up by its own dirt.'

K.   "He said to them, 'Go and organize marauders.'

L.   "Forthwith they took counsel with Ahitophel and ask advice of the sanhedrin and address questions to the Urim and Thummim."

M.   *Said R. Joseph, "What verse of Scripture shows this?*

N.   "'[16B] 'And after Ahitophel was Benaiah, son of Jehoiada, and Abiathar, and the captain of the king's host was Joab' (1 Chr. 27:34).

O.   "'Ahitophel' is the adviser, and so it is written, 'And the counsel of Ahitophel which he counseled in those days was as if a man inquired from the word of God' (2 Sam. 16:23).

P.   "'Benaiah son of Jehoiada' speaks of the Sanhedrin.

Q.   "'Abiathar' refers to the Urim and Thummim.

R.   "And so it is written, 'And Benaiah, son of Jehoiada, supervised the Kerethites and Pelethites' (1 Chr. 18:17).

S.   "Why were they called 'Kerethites' and 'Pelethites'?

T.   "Because they gave definite instructions [a play on the word KRT, which is the root for cut, hence, 'speak decisively,' and also for the name of the group], and because they did wonderful deeds [a play on the root PL', wonder], respectively.

U.   "After this: 'And the captain of the king's host was Joab'" (1 Chr. 27:34). [Schachter, p. 80, n. 13: Only after the Sanhedrin had authorized a war was there any need for Joab, the chief general.]"

V.   *Said R. Isaac, son of R. Ada, and some say R. Isaac bar Abodimi, "What verse of Scripture, [supports the view that there was a harp over David's bed]?* 'Awake my glory, awake psaltery and harp, I will wake the dawn' (Ps. 57:9)."

David gets up in the middle of the night to study the Torah. He is represented as a sage.

BAVLI SANHEDRIN

BAVLI SANHEDRIN 2:1-2

VIII.1. A.   The king does not judge, and others do not judge him [M. 2:2A]:

B.   Said R. Joseph, "That law applies only to Israelite kings. But as to the kings of the house of David, such a king judges and others judge them. For it is written, 'House of David, thus says the Lord, execute justice in the morning' (Jer. 21:12)."

C.   *Now if others do not judge him, how can they judge others?* And has it not been written, 'Ornament yourselves and be ornamented' (Zeph. 2:1), interpreted by R. Simeon b. Laqish to mean, 'Adorn yourself and then adorn others'?"

BAVLI SANHEDRIN 2:1-2

X.1. A.   Others do not marry his widow [M. 2:2G]:

B.   *It has been taught on Tannaite authority:*

C.   They said to R. Judah, "[David] married women of the royal family who were permitted to him, Merab and Michal, [but these were not his widows]."

D.   **His disciples asked R. Yosé, "How did David marry two sisters while both were yet alive?"**

E.   **He said to them, "He married Michal after the death of Merab."**

F.   **R. Joshua b. Qorha says, "His act of betrothal of Merab was made in error, as it is said, 'Give me my wife, Michal, whom I betrothed at a price of a hundred foreskins of the Philistines' (2 Sam. 3:14). [T. adds: Just as his act of betrothal was not a completely valid one, so his marriage was not a completely valid one]"** [T. Sot. 11:18-19].

G.   *From what sort of scriptural proof is this conclusion to be derived?*

H.   Said R. Pappa, "Michal is my wife, and Merab is not my wife."

I.   *And what sort of error in the betrothal was there?*

J.   It is as it is written, "And it shall be that the man who kills him the king will enrich him with great riches and will give him his daughter" (1 Sam. 17:25).

K.   *David went and killed him. [Saul] said to him, "You have a debt with me [which I owe to you], and* **one who betroths a woman by forgiving a debt does not accomplish the woman's betrothal."** *[Saul] went and gave her instead to Adriel, as it is written,* "But it came to pass at the time when Merab, Saul's daughter, should have been given to David, that she was given to Adriel the Meholathite to wife" (1 Sam. 18:19).

L.   *[Saul] said to [David], "If you want me to give you Michal, go and bring me a hundred foreskins of Philistines."*

M.   *He went and brought him a hundred foreskins of Philistines.*

N.   *He said to him, "Now you have with me an unpaid debt [which I owe you], and also a perutah [coin]."*

O.   *Saul had the notion that, where there is a loan and a small coin, [the creditor] is thinking about the loan [in any transaction or exchange with the debtor, hence David will be thinking about the loan and his act of betrothal once more would be null]. But David was thinking that where there is a loan and a coin, one's thought is about the coin.*

P.   *And if you wish, I shall propose that all parties concurred that where there is a loan and a coin owing, one's thought is on the coin. But Saul took the view that [the foreskins] were worthless anyhow, while David took the view that they were fit for dog- or cat-food.*

Q.   *And how does R. Yosé interpret the language, "Give me my wife, Michal" (2 Sam. 3:14)?*

R.   *R. Yosé interprets it in a way consistent with his reasoning in general. For it has been taught on Tannaite authority:* **R. Yosé would interpret confused verses of Scripture: "It is written, 'But the king took the two sons of Rizpah the daughter of Ayah whom she bore to Saul, Armoni and Mephiboshet, and the five sons of Michal, the daughter of Saul, whom she bore to Adriel the son of Barzillai the Meholathite (2 Sam. 21:8).**

S.   **"Now where do we find that Michal was given to Adriel the son of Barzillai the Meholathite? Was she not given only to Plait the son of Latish who was of Gallium, as it is said, 'And Saul had given Michal, his daughter, David's wife, to Plait, the son of Latish, who was of Gallium' (1 Sam. 25:44).**

T.   **But Scripture thereby links the marriage of Merab to the marriage of Michal. Just as the marriage of Michal to Plait the son of Latish was in transgression, so the marriage of Merab to Adriel was in transgression" [T. Sot. 11:17A-C].**

U.   *And as to R. Joshua b. Qorhah, is it not written,* "And the five sons of Michal, the daughter of Saul, whom she bore to Adriel" (2 Sam. 21:8)?

V. R. Joshua can say to you: **But did Michal produce them? And is it not so that Merab produced them? But Merab gave birth to them and Michal raised them, so they were called by Michal's name, [T. adds: as it is said, 'And the women of the neighborhood gave him a name, saying, A son has been born to Naomi' (Ruth 4:17)]** [T. Sot. 11:20].

W. [T. lacks:] "This serves to teach you that whoever raises an orphan in his house is regarded by Scripture as if he had given birth to him.

BAVLI SANHEDRIN 2:1-2

X.2. A. *R. Hanina says, "Proof [of the proposition just now cited] derives from the following verse of Scripture:* 'And the women of the neighborhood gave him a name, saying, A son has been born to Naomi' (Ruth 4:17)."

B. "Now did Naomi give birth to the child? Was it not Ruth? But Ruth gave birth to the child, and Naomi raised him, so he bore Naomi's name."

C. R. Yohanan said, "Proof [of the same proposition] derives from here: 'And his wife, the Judahite [Bithia, the daughter of Pharaoh] bore Yered, father of Gedor [and Heber, father of Soco, the child, and Naomi raised him, so he bore Naomi's name."

D. *R. Yohanan said, "Proof [of the same proposition] derives from here:* 'And his wife, the Judahite [Bithia, the daughter of Pharaoh] bore Yered, father of Gedor [and Heber, father of Soco, and Jekuthiel, father of Zanoah], and these are the sons of Bithia, daughter of Pharaoh, whom Mered took' (1 Chr. 4:18). ("Mered was Caleb, and why was he called Mered? Because he rebelled (MRD) against the counsel of the spies.)

E. "And did Bithia give birth [to Moses], and did not Jochebed do so?

F. "But while Jochebed gave birth to him, Bithia raised him, therefore he bore her name."

G. *R. Eleazar said, "Proof derives from here:* 'You have with your arm redeemed your people, the sons of Jacob and Joseph, Selah' (Ps. 77:16). Did Joseph beget [the people]? Was it not Jacob? But Jacob begot them and Joseph kept them alive, therefore they bore his name."

H. Said R. Samuel bar Nahmani said R. Jonathan, "Whoever teaches Torah to his fellow's son is credited by Scripture as if he begat him,

I. "as it is said, 'Now these are the generations of Aaron and Moses' (Num. 3:1), and later, 'These are the names of the sons of Aaron' (Num. 3:1), so teaching the lesson that Aaron begat them and Moses taught them [Torah], and therefore they bore his [Moses'] name."

J. "Therefore thus says the Lord to the house of Jacob, who redeemed Abraham' (Is. 29:22):

K. Now where in Scripture do we find that Jacob redeemed Abraham?

L. Said R. Judah, "He redeemed him from the trouble of raising children [because Abraham had few children, while Jacob had many]. That is in line with what is written, 'Jacob shall not now be ashamed, neither shall his face now wax pale' (Is. 29:22).

M. "'He shall not now be ashamed' — of his father.

N. "'Neither shall his face now become pale' — because of his grandfather."

Bavli Sanhedrin 2:1-2

X.3. A. It is written "Plait" (at I Sam. 25:44), and it is written "Paltiel" (2 Sam. 3:15) [so the second husband of David's undivorced wife had two names].

B. Said R. Yohanan, "He was really called Plait, and why was he later called Paltiel? Because God (el) saved him from transgression [namely, marrying an already-married woman].

C. "What did [God] do? He put a sword between him and her [so they did not have sexual relations], saying, 'Whoever gets involved in this matter will be pierced by this sword.'"

D. But is it not written, "And her husband Plait went with her" (2 Sam. 3:16)?

E. That he became like her husband [but he was not in fact ever he husband].

F. But is it not written, "He went weeping" (2 Sam. 3:16)?

G. It was on account of the loss of the religious duty [Schachter: of self-restraint]."

H. "He followed her to Bahurim" (2 Sam. 3:16): Both of them [Plait and his wife] were like youths [bahurim], who had not tasted the flavor of sexual relations [having remained celibate for their marriage].

I. Said R. Yohanan, "The strong desire affecting Joseph [Gen. 39:7-13] was modest for Boaz, and the strong desire affecting Boaz [Ruth 3:8-15] was modest for Plait ben Latish.

J. "The strong desire affecting Joseph was modest for Boaz, in line with that which is written, 'And it came to pass at midnight, and the man was startled' (Ruth 3:8)."

K. What is the meaning of "was startled"?

L. Said Rab, "His penis became as hard as a turnip top. [A play on the consonants for 'was startled' which are shared with the word for turnip.]"

M. [20A] [Yohanan continues], "And the strong desire affecting Boaz was modest for Plait ben Latish" — as we have said.

N. Said R. Yohanan, "What is the meaning of the verse of Scripture, 'Many daughters have done valiantly, but you excel them all' (Prov. 31:29)?

O. "'Many daughters have done valiantly' refers to Joseph and Boaz.

P. "'And you excel them all' speaks of Plait, son of Latish."

Q. Said R. Samuel bar Nahman said R. Jonathan, "What is the meaning of the verse of Scripture: 'Grace is deceitful and beauty is vain, but a woman who fears the Lord shall be praised' (Prov. 31:30)?

R. "'Grace is deceitful' speaks of Joseph.

S. "'Beauty is vain' speaks of Boaz.

T. "'A woman who fears the Lord shall be praised' speaks of Plait ben Latish.

U. "Another interpretation: 'Grace is deceitful' speaks of the generation of Moses.

V. "'Beauty if vain' speaks of the generation of Joshua.

W. "'A woman who fears the Lord shall be praised' speaks of the generation of Hezekiah.

X. "Another interpretation: 'Grace is deceitful' speaks of the generation of Moses and Joshua.

Y. "'Beauty is vain' speaks of the generation of Hezekiah.

Z. "'A woman who fears the Lord shall be praised' speaks of the generation of R. Judah b. R. Ilai.

AA. "They said concerning R. Judah b. R. Ilai that six disciples [in his time] would cover themselves with a single cloak but [nonetheless] would spend their time studying Torah [despite gross want]."

A huge composite conducts the analysis of David's relationship to the daughters of Saul.

BAVLI SANHEDRIN 2:3

A. [If] [the king] suffers a death in his family, he does not leave the gate of his palace.

B. R. Judah says, "If he wants to go out after the bier, he goes out,

C. "for thus we find in the case of David, that he went out after the bier of Abner,

D. "since it is said, 'And King David followed the bier' (2 Sam. 3:31)."

E. They said to him, "This action was only to appease the people."

F. And when they provide him with the funeral meal, all the people sit on the ground, while he sits on a couch.

I.1. A. *Our rabbis have taught on Tannaite authority:*

B. In a place in which women are accustomed to go forth after the bier, they go forth in that way. If they are accustomed to go forth before the bier, they go forth in that manner.

C. R. Judah says, "Women always go forth in front of the bier.

D. "For so we find in the case of David that he went forth after the bier of Abner.

E. "For it is said, 'And King David followed the bier' (2 Sam. 3:31)."

F. They said to him, "That was only to appease the people [M. 2:3D-E].

G. "They were appeased, for David would go forth among the men and come in among the women, go forth among the women and come in among the men,

H. "as it is said, 'So all the people and all Israel understood that it was not of the king to slay Abner' (2 Sam. 3:37)."

I.2.A. *Raba expounded, "What is the meaning of that which is written, 'And all the people came to cause David to eat bread' (2 Sam. 3:35)?*

B. "It was written, 'to pierce David' [with a K], but we read, 'to cause him to eat bread' [with a B].

C. "To begin with they came to pierce him but in the end to cause him to eat bread."

I.3.A. Said R. Judah said Rab, "On what account was Abner punished? Because he could have prevented Saul but did not prevent him [from killing the priest of Nob, 1 Sam. 22:18]."

B. R. Isaac said, "He did try to prevent him, but he got no response."

C. And both of them interpret the same verse of Scripture: "And the king lamented for Abner and said, Should Abner die as a churl dies, your hands were not bound or your feet put into fetters" (2 Sam. 2:33).

D. *He who maintains that he did not try to stop Saul interprets the verse in this way:* "Your hands were not bound nor were your feet put into fetters" — *so why did you not try to stop him?* "As a man falls before the children of iniquity so did you fall" (2 Sam. 3:33).

E. *He who maintains that he did try to stop Saul but got no response interprets the verse as an expression of amazement:* "Should he have died as a churl dies? Your hands were not bound and your feet were not put into fetters."

F. *Since he did protest, why* "As a man falls before the children of iniquity, so did you fall"?

G. *In the view of him who has said that he did protest, why was he punished?*

H. Said R. Nahman bar Isaac, "Because he held up the coming of the house of David by two and a half years."

David forms the center of another exegesis of the law in light of David's example,

BAVLI SANHEDRIN 2:4E

I.2.A. *As to the number of eighteen [specified at M. 2:4E], what is the source for that number?*

B. *It is from the following verse of Scripture:* "And unto David were sons born in Hebron, and his first-born son was Amnon, of Ahinoam the Jezreelites, the second, Chileab, of Abigail, the wife of Nabal the Carmelite, the third Absalom, son of Maacah; the fourth, Adonijah, son of Haggith; and the fifth, Shefatiah, son of Abital, and the sixth, Ithream, of Eglah, David's wife. These were born to

David in Hebron" (2 Sam. 3:2-5). *And the prophet said to him,* "And if that were too little, then would I add to you the like of these and the like of these" (2 Sam. 12:8). *Each "like of these" means six more [since the referent is the original six], so eighteen in all.*

C. *Rabina objected, "Might I say that* 'Like of these' *stands for twelve, and the second such reference means twenty-four* [Schachter, p. 113, n. 3: He increased the number in geometrical progression, 6, 12, 24]?"

D. *So it has been taught on Tannaite authority:* "He should not multiply wives to himself" (Deut. 17:17) — more than twenty-four.

E. *In the view of him who interprets the "and," the number is forty-eight.*

F. *It has been taught on Tannaite authority along these very lines:* "He should not multiply wives to himself" (Deut. 17:17) — more than forty-eight.

G. *And what is the reason for the view of the Tannaite authority who framed the Mishnah-passage at hand?*

H. *Said R. Kahana, "He draws an analogy between the first 'and the like' and the second 'and the like.' Just as the former refers to six, so the latter refers to the six."*

I. *But there was Michal [beyond the six wives who are listed]?*

J. Rab said, "Eglah is Michal, and why was she called Eglah? Because she was as beloved of him as a calf [eglah] is of its mother.

K. "And so it is said, 'If you had not ploughed with my heifer' (Jud. 14:18)."

L. *But did Michal have children? And is it not written,* "And Michal, daughter of Saul, had no child to the day of her death" (2 Sam. 6:23)?

M. Said R. Hisda, "To the day of her death she had none, but on the day of her death she had one."

N. *Now where, in point of fact, is the number of sons reckoned? It is in Hebron. But the case involving Michal took place in Jerusalem, for it is written,* "Michal, daughter of Saul, looked out at the window and saw King David leaping and dancing before the Lord, and she despised him in her heart" (2 Sam. 6:16).

O. And R. Judah, and some say R. Joseph, said, "Michal took her due punishment, which was childlessness."

P. *Rather, one might propose, prior to that event she had children, but afterward she had none.*

Q. [Referring to the issue of the number of eighteen specified in the Mishnah-paragraph], is it not stated, "And David took concubines and wives out of Jerusalem" (2 Sam. 5:13)?

R. It was to reach the number of eighteen [wives].

S. *What is the difference between wives and concubines?*

T. Said R. Judah said Rab, "Wives are with a marriage contract and a rite of betrothal, concubines are without a marriage contract and without a rite of betrothal."

Bavli Sanhedrin 4:2

XII.2. A. And said Rabbah, son of Raba, and some say, R. Hillel, son of R. Vallas, "From the time of Moses to Rabbi, we do not find the combination of foremost status in learning in Torah and preeminence in worldly greatness joined in a single person."

B. *And is that not so? And there was the case of Joshua?*

C. *With him was Eleazar [equal in learning].*

D. *There was Phineas? With him were the elders.*

E. *There was Saul? With him was Samuel.*

F. *But lo, [Samuel] died before him? We refer to the entire lifetime [of such a unique figure].*

G. *There was David? With him was Ira the Jairite [2 Sam. 20:26].*

H. *But lo, [Ira] died before him? We refer to the entire lifetime [of such a unique figure].*

I. *There was Solomon? With him was Shimei, son of Gera [2 Sam. 19:18].*

J. *But lo, [Solomon] killed [Shimei]? We refer to the entire lifetime.*

K. *There was Hezekiah? With him was Shebnah.*

L. *But he was killed [during Hezekiah's lifetime]? We refer to the entire lifetime.*

M. *There was Ezra? No, with him was Nehemiah, son of Hachaliah.*

N. Said R. Ada bar Ahbah, "I too say, 'From the time of Rabbi to R. Ashi, we do not find the combination of learning in Torah and worldly greatness joined in a single person."

O. *Do we not? And lo, there was Huna bar Nathan.*

P. *Huna bar Nathan was subordinate to R. Ashi.*

David supplies a fact for a proposition.

Bavli Sanhedrin 4:2

I.46.A *Said R. Tanhum, "In Sepphoris, Bar Qappara interpreted the following verse: 'These six [grains] of barley gave he to me' (Ruth 3:17).*

B. *"What are the six of barley? If we should say that* they were actually six of barley, was it the way of Boaz to give out a gift of only six barley grains?

C. "[93B] Rather it must have been six seahs of barley?

D. "And is it the way of a woman to carry six seahs?

E. "Rather, this formed an omen to her that six sons are destined to come forth from her, each of whom would receive six blessings, and these are they: David, the Messiah, Daniel, Hananiah, Mishael, and Azariah.

F. "David, as it is written, 'Then answered one of the servants and said, Behold I have seen the son of Jesse, the Bethlehemite, who is cunning in playing and a mighty, valiant man, and a man of war, and understanding in matters, and a handsome man, and the Lord is with him' (1 Sam. 16:18). [Freedman, p. 626, n. 1: The six epithets, viz., cunning in playing, mighty, valiant, etc., are regarded as blessings applicable to each of the six persons mentioned]."

G. And said R. Judah said Rab, "The entire verse was stated by Doeg only as vicious gossip.

H. "'Cunning in playing' — skillful in asking questions;

I. "'a mighty valiant man' — skillful in answering them;

J. "'a man of war' — skillful in the battle of Torah-learning;

K. "'understanding in matters' — understanding in learning one thing from another;

L. "'and a comely person' — who argues for his position with considerable reasons;

M. "'and the Lord is with him' — the law everywhere follows his opinion.

N. "'And in all regards, 'he said to him, 'my son Jonathan is his equal.'

O. *"When he said, 'The Lord is with him'— something which did not apply to himself— he was humbled and envied him.*

P. "For of Saul it is written, 'And wherever he turned about, he vexed them' (1 Sam. 14:47), while of David it is written, 'And wherever he turned about he prospered.'"

Q. *How do we know that this was Doeg?*

R. *It is written here,* "then one of the servants answered," meaning, "one who was distinguished from the other young men," and there it is written, "Now a man of the servants of Saul was there that day, detained before the Lord, and his name was Doeg, an Edomite, head herd man that belonged to Saul" (1 Sam. 21:8). [Freedman, p. 626, n. 8: Thus "a man" that is, "one distinguished" is the epithet applied to Doeg.]

S. [Reverting to Bar Qappara's statement:] "The Messiah, as it is written, 'And the spirit of the Lord shall rest upon him, the spirit of wisdom and understanding, the spirit of counsel and might, the spirit of knowledge of the fear of the Lord, and shall make him of quick understanding in the fear of the Lord' (Is. 11:2-3)."

T. And R. Alexandri said, "The use of the words 'for quick understanding' indicates that he loaded him down with good deeds and suffering as a mill [which uses the same letters] is loaded down."

U. [Explaining the same word, now with reference to the formation of the letters of the word to mean "smell,"] said Raba, "[The Messiah] smells and judges, for it is written, 'And he shall judge not after the sight of his eyes nor reprove after the hearing of his ears, yet with righteousness shall he judge the poor' (Ex. 11:3-4)."

V. *Bar Koziba ruled for two and a half years. He said to rabbis, "I am the Messiah."*

W. *They said to him, "In the case of the Messiah it is written that he*
    smells a man and judges. Let us see whether you can smell a man
    and judge."

X. *When they saw that he could not smell a man and judge, they*
    killed him.

Y. [Reverting again to Bar Qappara's statement:] "Daniel, Hananiah,
    Mishael, and Azariah, as it is written, 'In whom there was no
    blemish, but well favored, skillful in all wisdom, and cunning in
    knowledge, understanding science, and such as had ability in them
    to stand in the king's palace, and whom they might teach the
    learning and the tongue of the Chaldeans' (Dan. 1:4)."

Z. *What is the meaning of,* "In whom there was no blemish" (Dan.
    1:4)?

AA. Said R. Hama bar Hanina, "Even the scar made by bleeding was
    not on them."

BB. *What is the meaning of,* "And such as had ability in them to stand
    in the king's palace" (Dan. 1:3)?

CC. Said R. Hama in the name of R. Hanina, "This teaches us that they
    restrained themselves from laughing and chatting, from sleeping,
    and they held themselves in when they had to attend to the call of
    nature, on account of the reverence owing to the king."

David figures on a list for exegetical purposes.

BAVLI SANHEDRIN 4:2

I.50.A. "Of the increase of his government and peace there shall be no
        end" (Is. 9:6):

B. R. Tanhum said, "In Sepphoris, Bar Qappara expounded this verse
    as follows:

C. "'On what account is every M in the middle of a word open, but
    the one in the word "increase" is closed?

D. "'The Holy One, blessed be he, proposed to make Hezekiah
    Messiah, and Sennacherib into Gog and Magog.

E. "'The attribute of justice said before the Holy One, blessed be he,
    "Lord of the world, Now if David, king of Israel, who recited how
    many songs and praises before you, you did not make Messiah,
    Hezekiah, for whom you have done all these miracles, and who
    did not recite a song before you, surely should not be made
    Messiah."

F. "On what account the M was closed.

G. "'Forthwith, the earth went and said before him, "Lord of the world,
    I shall say a song before you in the place of this righteous man, so
    you make him Messiah."

H. "'The earth went and said a song before him, as it is said, "From
    the uttermost part of the earth we have heard songs, even glory to
    the righteous" (Is. 24:16).

I.   "'Said the prince of the world before him, "Lord of the world,
      [The earth] has carried out your wish in behalf of this righteous
      man."

J.   "'An echo went forth and said, "It is my secret, it is my secret" (Ps.
      24:16).

K.   "'Said the prophet, "Woe is me, woe is me" (Is. 24:16). How long?'

L.   "'How dealt treacherously, yes, the treacherous dealers have dealt
      very treacherously" (Is. 24:16).'"

M.   *And said Raba, and some say, R. Isaac, "Until spoilers come, and
      those who spoil spoilers."*

David figures as the Messiah.

BAVLI SANHEDRIN 4:2

I.67.A. "And Ishbi-benob, who was of the sons of the giant, the weight of
         whose spear weighed three hundred shekels of brass in weight,
         being girded with a new sword, thought to have slain David" (2
         Sam. 21:16):

B.   *What is the sense of "Ishbi-be-nob"?*

C.   Said R. Judah said Rab, "It was a man [ish] who came on account
      of the matter of [the sin committed at] Nob.

D.   "Said the Holy One, blessed be he, to David, 'How long will the
      sin committed [against Nob] be concealed in your hand. On your
      account, Nob was put to death, the city of priests, on your account,
      Doeg the Edomite was sent into exile; on your account, Saul and
      his three sons were killed.

E.   "'Do you want you descendents to be wiped out, or do you want to
      be handed over into the power of an enemy?'

F.   "He said to him, 'Lord of the world, It is better that I be handed
      over to an enemy but that my descendents not be wiped out.'"

G.   *One day, when he went out to Sekhor Bizzae [Freedman, p. 640, n.
      7: literally: "your seed to cease"]. Satan appeared to him in the
      form of a deer. He shot an arrow at it, and the arrow did not reach
      [the deer]. It drew him until he came to the land of the Philistines.
      When Ishbi-benob saw him, he said, 'This is the one who killed
      Goliath, my brother.'*

H.   *He bound him, doubled him up, and threw him under an olive
      press. A miracle was done for [David], in that the earth underneath
      him became soft. This is in line with the following verse of Scripture:*
      "You have enlarged my steps under me, that my feet did not slip"
      (Ps. 18:37).

I.   *That day was the eve of the Sabbath [Friday]. Abishai ben Zeruiah
      [David's nephew] was washing his head in four casks of water.
      He saw stains of blood [in the water].*

J.   *Some say a dove came and slapped its wings before him.*

K.   *He said, "The congregation of Israel is compared to a dove, for it
      is said, 'You are as the wings of a dove covered with silver' (Ps.*

68:14). *This then bears the inference that David, king of Israel, is in trouble."*

L. *He came to his house and did not find him. He said, "We have learned in the Mishnah:* **People are not to ride on his horse or sit on his throne or hand his scepter [M. San. 2:5].**

M. *"What is the rule about a time of crisis?"*

N. *He came and asked at the school house. They said to him, "In a time of crisis it is all right."*

O. *He mounted his mule and rode off and the earth crumbled up [to make the journey quick]. While he was riding along, he saw Orpah, mother of [Ishbi-benob] who was spinning. When she saw him, she broke off the spindle." He threw it at her head and killed her.*

P. *When Ishbi-benob saw him, he said, "Now there are two against me, and they will kill me."*

Q. *He threw David up and stuck his spear [into the ground], saying, "Let him fall on it and be killed."*

R. *[Abishai] shouted the Name [of God], so David was suspended between heaven and earth.*

S. *But why should David himself not have said it?*

T. Because one who is bound cannot free himself from his chains.

U. *He said to him, "What do you want here?"*

V. *He said to him, "This is what the Holy One, blessed be he, has said to me, and this is what I said to him."*

W. *He said to him, "Take back your prayer. May your son's son sell wax, but may you not suffer."*

X. *He said to him, "If so, help me."*

Y. *That is in accord with what is written,* "But Abishai, son of Zeruiah, helped him" (2 Sam. 21:17).

Z. Said R. Judah said Rab, "He helped him in prayer."

AA. *Abishai pronounced the Name and brought [David] down.*

BB. *He pursued the two of them. When they came to Kubi, they said, "Let us stand against him."*

CC. *When they came to Bethre, they said, "Will two whelps kill a lion?"*

DD. *They said to him, "Go find Orpah, your mother, in the grave."*

EE. *When they mentioned the name of his mother to him, he grew weak, and they killed him.*

FF. *So it is written,* "Then the men of David swore to him, saying, You shall no more go out with us to battle, that you not put out the light of Israel" (2 Sam. 21:17).

The narrative of David amplifies the account of his life.

Bavli Sanhedrin 4:2

I.81.A. *Said R. Nahman to R. Isaac, "Have you heard when the son of 'the fallen one' will come?"*

B. *He said to him, "Who is the son of 'the fallen one'?"*

C. *He said to him, "It is the Messiah."*

D. *"Do you call the Messiah 'the son of the fallen one'?"*

E. *He said to him, "Yes, for it is written, 'On that day I will raise up* [97A] *the tabernacle of David, the fallen one' (Amos 9:11)."*

F. *He said to him, "This is what R. Yohanan said, 'The generation to which the son of David will come will be one in which disciples of sages grow fewer,*

G. *"'and, as to the others, their eyes will wear out through suffering and sighing,*

H. *"'and troubles will be many, and laws harsh, forever renewing themselves so that the new one will hasten onward before the old one has come to an end.'"*

I.82.A. *Our rabbis have taught on Tannaite authority:*

B. The seven year cycle in which the son of David will come:

C. As to the first one, the following verse of Scripture will be fulfilled: "And I will cause it to rain upon one city and not upon another" (Amos 4:7).

D. As to the second year, the arrows of famine will be sent forth.

E. As to the third, there will be a great famine, in which men, women, and children will die, pious men and wonder-workers alike, and the Torah will be forgotten by those that study it.

F. As to the fourth year, there will be plenty which is no plenty.

G. As to the fifth year, there will be great prosperity, and people will eat, drink, and rejoice, and the Torah will be restored to those that study it.

H. As to the sixth year, there will be rumors.

I. As to the seventh year, there will be wars.

J. As to the end of the seventh year [the eighth year], the son of David will come.

K. *Said R. Joseph, "Lo, how many septennates have passed like that one, and yet he has not come."*

L. *Said Abbayye, "Were there rumors in the sixth year and wars in the seventh year? And furthermore, did they come in the right order?"*

I.83. A. *It has been taught on Tannaite authority:*

B. R. Judah says, "In the generation in which the son of David will come, **the gathering place will be for prostitution, Galilee will be laid waste, Gablan will be made desolate, and the men of the frontier will go about from town to town, and none will take pity on them; and the wisdom of scribes will putrefy; and those who fear sin will be rejected; and the truth will be herded away** [M. Sot. 9:15AA-GG].

C. "For it is said, 'And the truth will be herded away' (Is. 59:15)."

D. *What is the meaning of the statement,* "The truth will be herded away" (Is. 59:15)?

E. *Said members of the house of Rab,* "This teaches that it will be divided into herds and herds, each going its way."

F.   *What is the meaning [of the concluding passage of the same verse],*
"And he who departs from evil makes himself a prey" (Is. 59:15)?

G.   *Said members of the house of R. Shila,* "Whoever departs from
evil will be treated as a fool [using the same letters as those for
prey] by other people."

I.87.A.   *Our rabbis have taught on Tannaite authority:*

B.   "For the Lord shall judge his people and repent himself of his
servants, when he sees that their power has gone, and there is none
shut up or left" (Deut. 32:36).

C.   The son of David will come only when traitors are many.

D.   Another matter: Only when disciples are few.

E.   Another matter: Only when a penny will not be found in anyone's
pocket.

F.   Another matter: Only when people will have given up hope of
redemption, as it is said, "There is none shut up or left" (Deut.
32:36), as it were, when there is none [God being absent] who
supports and helps Israel.

G.   *That accords with the statement of R. Zira, who, when he would
find rabbis involved in [figuring out when the Messiah would
come], would say to them, 'By your leave, I ask you not to put it
off.*

H.   *"For we have learned on Tannaite authority:* Three things come
on the spur of the moment, and these are they: the Messiah, a lost
object, and a scorpion."

BAVLI SHABBAT 11.1

I.108 A.   Said Rab, "The world was created only for David."

B.   And Samuel said, "For Moses."

C.   And R. Yohanan said, "For the Messiah."

D.   What is his name?

E.   *The house of R. Shila said,* "His name is Shiloh, as it is said, 'Until
Shiloh come' (Gen. 49:10)."

F.   *Members of the house of R. Yannai say,* "His name is Yinnon, for
it is written, 'His name shall endure forever, before the sun was,
his name is Yinnon' (Ps. 72:17)."

G.   *Members of the house of R. Haninah said,* "It is Haninah, as it is
said, 'Where I will not give you Haninah' (Jer. 16:13)."

H.   Others say, "His name is Menahem, son of Hezekiah, for it is
written, 'Because Menahem that would relieve my soul, is far'
(Lam. 1:16)."

I.   *Rabbis said, "His name is 'the leper of the school house,' as it is
written,* 'Surely he has borne our griefs and carried our sorrows,
yet we did esteem him a leper, smitten of God and afflicted' (Is.
53:4)."

I.109. A.   *Said R. Nahman, "If he is among the living, he is such as I, as it is
said,* 'And their nobles shall be of themselves and their governors
shall proceed from the midst of them' (Jer. 30:21)."

B. *Said Rab, "If he is among the living, he is such as our Holy Rabbi [Judah the Patriarch], and if he is among the dead, he is such as Daniel, the most desirable man."*

C. Said R. Judah said Rab, "The Holy One, blessed be he, is destined to raise up for [Israel] another David, as it is said, 'But they shall serve the Lord their God and David their king, whom I will raise up for them' (Jer. 30:9).

D. "'Raised up' is not what is said, but rather, 'will raise up.'"

E. *Said R. Pappa to Abbayye, "But lo, it is written, 'And my servant David shall be their prince forever' (Ez. 37:25) [with the title for prince standing for less than the title for king]."*

F. [He said to him,] "It is like a king and a viceroy [the second David being king]."

Here we find yet another massive exposition on when will the Messiah come.

Bavli Sanhedrin 11:4

XII.9. A. Said R. Judah said Rab, "One should never put himself to the test, for lo, David, king of Israel, put himself to the test and he stumbled.

B. "He said before him, 'Lord of the world, on what account do people say, "God of Abraham, God of Isaac, and God of Jacob, "but they do not say, "God of David"?'

C. *"He said to him, 'They endured a test for me, while you have not endured a test for me.'*

D. "He said before him, 'Lord of the world, here I am. Test me.'

E. "For it is said, 'Examine me, O Lord, and try me' (Ps. 26:1).

F. *"He said to him, 'I shall test you, and I shall do for you something that I did not do for them. I did not inform them [what I was doing], while I shall tell you what I am going to do. I shall try you with a matter having to do with sexual relations.'*

G. "Forthwith: 'And it came to pass in an eventide that David arose from off his bed' (2 Sam. 11:2)."

H. Said R. Judah, "He turned his habit of having sexual relations by night into one of having sexual relations by day.

I. "He lost sight of the following law:

J. "'There is in man a small organ, which makes him feel hungry when he is sated and makes him feel sated when he is hungry.'"

K. "And he walked on the roof of the king's palace, and from the roof he saw a woman washing herself, and the woman was very beautiful to look upon" (2 Sam. 11:2):

L. *Bath Sheba was shampooing her hair behind a screen. Satan came to [David] and appeared to him in the form of a bird. He shot an arrow at [the screen] and broke it down, so that she stood out in the open, and he saw her.*

M. Forthwith: "And David sent and inquired after the woman. And one said, Is not this Bath Sheba, the daughter of Eliam, the wife of

Uriah the Hittite? And David sent messengers and took her, and she came to him, and he lay with her; for she was purified from her uncleanness; and she returned to her house; (2 Sam. 11:203).

N.   *That is in line with what is written:* "You have tried my heart, you have visited me in the night, you have tried me and shall find nothing; I am purposed that my mouth shall not transgress" (Ps. 17:3).

O.   *He said, "Would that a bridle had fallen into my mouth, that I had not said what I said!"'*

BAVLI SANHEDRIN 11:4 KING DAVID: HIS SIN AND ATONEMENT

XII.10.A   *Raba interpreted Scripture, asking,* "What is the meaning of the following verse: 'To the chief musician, a Psalm of David. In the Lord I put my trust, how do you say to my soul, Flee as a bird to your mountain?' (Ps. 11:1)?

B.   "Said David before the Holy One, blessed be he, 'Lord of the world, Forgive me for that sin, so that people should not say, "The mountain that is among you [that is, your king] has been driven off by a bird."'"

C.   *Raba interpreted Scripture, asking, "What is the meaning of the following verse:* 'Against you, you alone, have I sinned, and done this evil in your sight, that you might be justified when you speak and be clear when you judge' (Ps. 11:1)?

D.   *"Said David before the Holy One, blessed be he, 'Lord of the world. It is perfectly clear to you that if I had wanted to overcome my impulse to do evil, I should have done so. But I had in mind that people not say, "The slave has conquered the Master [God, and should then be included as 'God of David'].""'*

E.   *Raba interpreted Scripture, asking, "What is the meaning of the following verse:* 'For I am ready to halt and my sorrow is continually before me' (Ps. 38:18)?

F.   "Bath Sheba, daughter of Eliam, was designated for David from the six days of creation, but she came to him through anguish."

G   *And so did a Tannaite authority of the house of R. Ishmael [teach],* "Bath Sheba, daughter of Eliam, was designated for David, but he 'ate' her while she was yet unripe."

H.   *Raba interpreted Scripture, asking, "What is the meaning of the following verse:* 'But in my adversity they rejoiced and gathered themselves together, yes, the abjects gathered themselves together against me and I did not know it, they tore me and did not cease' (Ps. 35:15)?

I.   "Said David before the Holy One, blessed be he, 'Lord of the world, it is perfectly clear to you that if they had torn my flesh, my blood would not have flowed [because I was so embarrassed].

J.   Not only so, but when they take up the four modes of execution inflicted by a court, they interrupt their Mishnah-study and say to me, "David, he who has sexual relations with a married woman — how is he put to death?"

K. "'I say to them, "He who has sexual relations with a married woman is put to death through strangulation, but he has a share in the world to come," while he who humiliates his fellow in public has no share in the world to come."'"

BAVLI SANHEDRIN 11:4 KING DAVID: HIS SIN AND ATONEMENT

XII.11.A. Said R. Judah said Rab, "Even when David was sick, he carried out the eighteen acts of sexual relations that were owing to his [eighteen] wives, as it is written, 'I am weary with my groaning, all night I make my bed swim, I water my couch with my tears' (Ps. 6:7)."

B. And said R. Judah said, Rab, "David wanted to worship idols, as it is said, 'And it happened that when David came to the head, where he worshipped God' (2 Sam. 15:32), and 'head' only means idols, as it is written, 'This image's head was of fine gold' (Dan. 2:32).

C. "'Behold, Hushai, the Archite came to meet him with his coat rent and earth upon his head' (2 Sam. 15:32):

D. "He said to David, 'Are people to say that a king such as you have worshipped idols?'

E. "He said to him, 'Will the son of a king such as me kill him? It is better that such a king as me worship an idol and not profane the Name of heaven in public.'

F. *"He said, 'Why then did you marry a woman captured in battle?* [Freedman, p. 732, n. 7: Absalom's mother, Maachah, the daughter of Talmai, king of Geshur, was a war captive.]"

G. *"He said to him, 'As to a woman captured in battle, the All-Merciful has permitted marrying her.'*

H. *"He said to him, 'You did not correctly interpret the meaning of the proximity of two verses. For it is written,* 'If a man has stubborn and rebellious son' (Deut. 21:18).

I. "'[The proximity teaches that] whoever marries a woman captured in battle will have a stubborn and rebellious son.'"

BAVLI SANHEDRIN 11:4 KING DAVID: HIS SIN AND ATONEMENT

XII.12. A. R. Dosetai of Biri interpreted Scripture, "To what may David be likened? To a Samaritan merchant.

B. "Said David before the Holy One, blessed be he, 'Lord of the world, "Who can understand his errors?" (Ps. 19:13).'

C. *"He said to him, 'They are remitted for you.'*

D. "'"Cleanse me of hidden faults" (Ps. 19:13).'

E. *"'They are remitted to you.'*

F. "'"Keep back your servant also from presumptuous sins" (Ps. 19:13).'

G. *"'They are remitted to you.'*

H. "'"Let them not have dominion over me, then I shall be upright" (Ps. 19:13), *so that the rabbis will not hold me up as an example.'*

I. *"'They are remitted to you.'*

J. "'"And I shall be innocent of great transgression" (Ps. 19:13), *so that they will not write down my ruin.'*

K. "He said to him, 'That is not possible. Now if the Y that I took away from the name of Sarah [changing it from Sarah to Sarah] stood crying for so many years until Joshua came and I added the Y [removed from Sarah's name] to his name, as it is said, "And Moses called Oshea, the son of Nun, Jehoshua" (Num. 13:16), how much the more will a complete passage of Scripture [cry out if I remove that passage from its rightful place]!'"

Bavli Sanhedrin 11:4 King David: His Sin and Atonement

XII.13. A. "And I shall be innocent from great transgression: (Ps. 19:13):

B. He said before him, "Lord of the world, forgive me for the whole of that sin [as though I had never done it]."

C. He said to him, "Solomon, your son, even now is destined to say in his wisdom, 'Can a man take fire in his bosom, and his clothes not be burned? Can one go upon hot coals, and his feet not be burned? So he who goes in to his neighbor's wife, whoever touches her shall not be innocent' (Prov. 6:27-29)."

D. *He said to him, "Will I be so deeply troubled?"*

E. He said to him, "Accept suffering [as atonement]."

F. He accepted the suffering.

Bavli Sanhedrin 11:4 King David: His Sin and Atonement

XII.14. A. Said R. Judah said Rab, "For six months David was afflicted with saraat, and the Presence of God left him, and the sanhedrin abandoned him.

B. "He was afflicted with saraat, as it is written, 'Purge me with hyssop and I shall be clean, wash me and I shall be whiter than snow/ (Ps. 51:9).

C. "The Presence of God left him, as it is written, 'Restore to me the joy of your salvation and uphold me with your free spirit' (Ps. 51:14).

D. "The sanhedrin abandoned him, as it is written, 'Let those who fear you turn to me and those who have known your testimonies' (Ps. 119:79).

E. "How do we know that this lasted for six months? As it is written, 'And the days that David rules over Israel were forty years: [107B] Seven years he reigned in Hebron, and thirty-three years he reigned in Jerusalem' (1 Kgs. 2:11).

F. "Elsewhere it is written, 'In Hebron he reigned over Judah seven years and six months' (2 Sam. 5:5).

G. *"So the six months were not taken into account. Accordingly, he was afflicted with saraat [for such a one is regarded as a corpse].*

H. "He said before him, 'Lord of the world, forgive me for that sin.'

I. "'It is forgiven to you.'

J. "'"Then show me a token for good, that they who hate me may see it and be ashamed, because you, Lord, have helped me and comforted me" (Ps. 86:17).'

K. "He said to him, 'While you are alive, I shall not reveal [the fact that you are forgiven], but I shall reveal it in the lifetime of your son, Solomon.'

L. "When Solomon had built the house of the sanctuary, he tried to bring the ark into the house of the Holy of Holies. The gates cleaved to one another. He recited twenty-four prayers [Freedman, p. 734, n. 4: in 2 Chr. 6 words for prayer, supplication and hymn occur twenty-four times], but was not answered.

M. "He said, 'Lift up your head, O you gates, and be lifted up, you everlasting doors, and the King of glory shall come in. Who is this King of glory? The Lord strong and might, the Lord mighty in battle' (Ps. 24:7ff.).

N. "And it is further said, 'Lift up your heads, O you gates even lift them up, you everlasting doors/ (Ps. 24:7).

O. "But he was not answered.

P. "When he said, 'Lord God, turn not away the face of your anointed, remember the mercies of David, your servant'(2 Chr. 6:42), forthwith he was answered.

Q. "At that moment the faces of David's enemies turned as black as the bottom of a pot, for all Israel knew that the Holy One, blessed be he, had forgiven him for that sin."

BAVLI MAKKOT

BAVLI MAKKOT 2:6G-I

I:4. A. Said R. Judah said Rab, "The curse of a sage, even for nothing, comes about. How do we know that fact? It is shown by the case of Ahitophel.

B. "When David dug the pits for the Temple's foundations, the waters of the deep welled up and were going to flood the world.

C. *"David said, 'Is there anyone who knows whether or not it is permitted to write the divine name on a piece of pottery and to toss it down into the deep so that the water will subside?'*

D. *"No one was around to tell him.*

E. "Said David, "Whoever knows how to rule but does not state [the rule], will be strangled by the throat.'

F. "Ahitophel reasoned a fortiori on his own [not from tradition] as follows: "Now if in order to make peace between a man and his wife, the Torah has said, "My name, which is written in a state of sanctification, may be blotted out by water," so as to make peace for the entire world, how much more so [may the divine name be written down and blotted out]!"

G. *""Ahitophel] said to [David], 'It is permitted [to do so].'*

H. *"[David] wrote the divine name on a piece of pottery and tossed it into the deep, and the waters subsided by sixteen thousand cubits.*

I. "Nonetheless: 'And when Ahithophel saw that his counsel was not followed, he saddled his ass and arose and went home to his house and to his city, and he put his household in order and hanged himself and died' (2 Sam. 17:23)."

5. A. Said R. Abbahu, "How do we know that a curse of a sage, even if it is subject to a condition, will in any event come about? It is shown by the case of Eli.

   B. *"For Eli said to Samuel, 'God to this to you and more also if you hide anything from me of all the things he said to you'* (1 Sam. 3:17).

   C. *"And even though it is written, 'And Samuel told him every whit and hid nothing from him'* (1 Sam. 3:18), *nonetheless it is written,* 'And Samuel's sons did not walk in his ways' (1 Sam. 8:3)."

BAVLI MAKKOT 3:15

II.1. A. **Therefore he gave them abundant Torah and numerous commandments:**

   B. R. Simelai expounded, "Six hundred and thirteen commandments were given to Moses, three hundred and sixty-five negative ones, corresponding to the number of the days of the solar year, and two hundred forty-eight positive commandments, corresponding to the parts of man's body."

   C. *Said R. Hamnuna, "What verse of Scripture indicates that fact?* 'Moses commanded us Torah, an inheritance of the congregation of Jacob' (Dt. 33:4). *The numerical value assigned to the letters of the word Torah is* [24A] *six hundred and eleven, not counting, 'I am' and 'you shall have no other gods,' since these have come to us from the mouth of the Almighty."*

   D. [Simelai continues:] "David came and reduced them to eleven: 'A Psalm of David: Lord, who shall sojourn in thy tabernacle, and who shall dwell in thy holy mountain? (i) He who walks uprightly and (ii) works righteousness and (iii) speaks truth in his heart and (iv) has no slander on his tongue and (v) does no evil to his fellow and (vi) does not take up a reproach against his neighbor, (vii) in whose eyes a vile person is despised but (viii) honors those who fear the Lord. (ix) He swears to his own hurt and changes not. (x) He does not lend on interest. (xi) He does not take a bribe against the innocent' (Psalm 15)."

The topic is King David: his sin and atonement The exposition is massive.

BAVLI MAKKOT 3:15

I.26. A. That is in line with what R. Yohanan said in the name of R. Simeon b. Yohai: "David was really not so unfit as to do such a deed [as he did with Beth Sheva]: 'My heart is slain within me' (Ps. 109:22) [Mishcon: David's inclinations had been completely conquered by himself]. And the Israelites were hardly the kind of people to commit such an act: "O that they had such a heart as this always, to fear me and keep my commandments' (Dt. 5:26). So why did they do it?

B.   "[5A] It was to show you that if an individual has sinned, they say to him, 'Go to the individual [such as David, and follow his example], and if the community as a whole has sinned, they say to them, 'Go to the community [such as Israel].'

C.   *And it was necessary to give both examples. For had we been given the rule governing the individual, that might have been supposed to be because his personal sins were not broadly known, but in the case of the community, the sins of which will be broadly known, I might have said that that is not the case.*

D.   *And if we had been given the rule governing the community, that might have been supposed to be the case because they enjoy greater mercy, but an individual, who has not got such powerful zekhut, might have been thought not subject to the rule.*

E.   *So both cases had to be made explicit.*

I.27. A.   *That is in line with what R. Samuel bar Nahmani said R. Jonathan said, "What is the meaning of the verse of Scripture, 'The saying of David, son of Jesse, and the saying of the man raised on high' (2 Sam. 23:1)?*

B.   "It means, 'The saying of David, son of Jesse, the man who raised up the yoke of repentance.'"

I.28. A.   Said R. Samuel bar Nahmani said R. Jonathan, "Whoever does a religious duty in this world — that deed goes before him to the world to come, as it is said, 'And your righteousness shall go before you' (Isa. 58:8).

B.   "And whoever commits a transgression in this world — that act turns aside from him and goes before him on the Day of Judgment, as it is said, 'The paths of their way are turned aside, they go up into the waste and perish' (Job 6:18)."

C.   R. Eliezer says, "It attaches to him like a dog, as it is said, 'He did not listen to her to lie by her or to be with her' (Gen. 39:10).

D.   "'To lie by her' in this world.

E.   "'Or to be with her' in the world to come."

David illustrates the process of atonement,

BAVLI ABODAH ZARAH

BAVLI ABODAH ZARAH 1:1

I.26.A.   That is in line with what R. Yohanan said in the name of R. Simeon b. Yohai: "David was really not so unfit as to do such a deed [as he did with Beth Sheva]: 'My heart is slain within me' (Ps. 109:22) [Mishcon: David's inclinations had been completely conquered by himself]. And the Israelites were hardly the kind of people to commit such an act: "O that they had such a heart as this always, to fear me and keep my commandments' (Dt. 5:26). So why did they do it?

B.   "**[5A]** It was to show you that if an individual has sinned, they say to him, 'Go to the individual [such as David, and follow his example], and if the community as a whole has sinned, they say to them, 'Go to the community [such as Israel].'

C.   *And it was necessary to give both examples. For had we been given the rule governing the individual, that might have been supposed to be because his personal sins were not broadly known, but in the case of the community, the sins of which will be broadly known, I might have said that that is not the case.*

D.   *And if we had been given the rule governing the community, that might have been supposed to be the case because they enjoy greater mercy, but an individual, who has not got such powerful zekhut, might have been thought not subject to the rule.*

E.   *So both cases had to be made explicit.*

I.27.A.   *That is in line with what R. Samuel bar Nahmani said R. Jonathan said, "What is the meaning of the verse of Scripture, 'The saying of David, son of Jesse, and the saying of the man raised on high' (2 Sam. 23:1)?*

B.   "It means, 'The saying of David, son of Jesse, the man who raised up the yoke of repentance.'"

The theme is the sinful ancestor of the Messiah and God's forgiveness of him and of Israel

[1] IS DAVID AN ACTIVE PLAYER OR A ROUTINE AND SCARCELY ANIMATE ONE? The massive exegetical topical expositions show David as the active player.

[2] WHAT COMPONENTS OF THE COLLECTION MAKE ROUTINE GLOSSES OF THE RECEIVED SCRIPTURES and which ones provide more than minor glosses of the tradition? The topical composites do more than gloss the received tradition.

[3] CAN WE IDENTIFY A PRONOUNCED BIAS OR A POLEMIC in the utilization of David? The paramount theme is the forgiveness of sin.

[4] HOW IS DAVID COMPARABLE TO OTHER SAGES IN THIS DOCUME ? David is much more than a sage, he is the reaization of the Messiah,

23

David in Bavli Qodoshim and Niddah

BAVLI MENAHOT

BAVLI MENAHOT 11:2

II.1. A.   R. Judah says, "All acts of preparing them are inside." R.
Simeon says, "One should always be accustomed to state [the
rule as follows]: 'The two loaves and the show bread are valid
[if made] in the courtyard and are valid [if made] in Bethpage:'"

B.   *Said R. Abbahu bar Kahana, "And both authorities interpret the
same verse of Scripture:* 'And it is in a manner common, yes, though
it were sanctified this day in the utensil' (1 Sam. 21:6). *R. Judah
takes the view that David found the priests baking the show bread
on a weekday, and said to them, 'Are you baking it on a weekday?
Since it will then have been sanctified today by being kept in a
utensil of service, it will then be invalidated by being kept overnight
[so it is wrong to bake it on a weekday].' R. Simeon maintains that
David found the priests baking the show bread on the Sabbath
and said to them, 'Should you not have baked it on a week day?
For in any event it is not the oven that sanctifies the bread but the
table [and the bread will be put there only on the Sabbath].'"*

C.   *But can you really say that he found them while they were baking
it? And lo, is it not written,* "So the priest gave him holy bread, for
there was no bread there but the show bread that was taken from
before the Lord" (1 Sam. 21:7).

D.   *But what is the sense of the statement,* "And it is in a manner
common, yes, though it were sanctified this day in the utensil' (1
Sam. 21:6)? *They said to him,* "There is no bread here except for
the show bread that is taken from before the Lord." *And David
said to them,* "There is no question concerning that bread, since it

> *is not subject to the law of sacrilege [the priests' having a right to it now], it is entirely common. But even the bread that has been sanctified today in a utensil give me to eat,* [96A] *for I am in danger of losing my life [and the law may be suspended to save a life]!"*

E. *Now R. Judah and R. Simeon differ concerning the tradition on the matter, and a close reading of the language shows that this is so:* **R. Simeon says, *"One should always be accustomed to state [the rule as follows]:* 'The two loaves and the show bread are valid [if made] in the courtyard and are valid [if made] in Bethpage.'"**

F. *That's decisive.*

David figures in a detail of the narrative. The references to David yield insufficient data for responding to questions.

24

Conclusion

What at the end have I discovered in this monograph? It is the simple fact that the first exposition of the figure of Rabbi David in a program of elaboration and of *protracted* exposition of law and Scripture is found in the Bavli. Prior to the closure of that document — that is, in the Rabbinic documents that came to closure before the Bavli — we do not find an elaborate exposition of the figure of David as a rabbi. By contrast in the Bavli ample canonical evidence — such as I cite in the preceding pages — attests to the sages' transformation into a rabbi of David, King of Israel.

So while bits and pieces of Rabbi David find their way into most of the canonical documents, we find the elaborately spelled out Rabbi David to begin with in the Bavli, now as a disciple of sages and a devotee of study of the Torah. That usage attracts attention because when in Rabbinic literature as in all other Judaic canons — not only Rabbinic — we encounter "David," that signals we are meeting the embodiment of the Messiah. So the representation of the kings of Israel in the Davidic line as heirs of David forms a chapter in exposing the Messianic message of Rabbinic Judaism.

What sort of a Messiah do the sages produce? Answering this question in this manner requires a document by document study of Rabbinic Judaism, not of the historical David. That is because in line with the documentary approach to the unfolding of Rabbinic Judaism I examine the documents of formative Rabbinic Judaism in rough temporal sequence and systematically ask a uniform set of questions about the occurrence of David in those documents. In the final document of the canon of late antiquity we find the most important writing and the rarest. It is where the Messiah occurs in his own qualities.

Obviously, I do not claim to produce a secular ("critical") biography or sequence of historical narratives of David in the Rabbinic canon. I also do not characterize the post-Scriptural biography rendered accessible by the documentary approach. What we learn here concerns the uses of the figure of David in the various documents of the Rabbinic canon. The ultimate account will answer the question, does David contribute random facts or is there a concerted effort to re-present David for purposes particular to the Rabbinic canon? At stake is the definition of the program of Rabbinic Judaism, not of Scripture. To answer these questions, in line with the documentary hypothesis we examine the Rabbinic documents in approximate sequence. What I demonstrate is negative: there is no systematic program to represent David in accord with a polemical Rabbinic program.

What is at stake in the outcome? Considering the treatment of David in the Rabbinic canon asks a question of comparison and contrast. I show how Rabbinic Judaism through its reading of the figure of David confronted the conflicts between the prophet or biblical hero and the sage. The premise throughout the Rabbinic canon is that a single Judaic theological system and structure perpetually defined the heritage of Scripture and tradition. That corpus of continuous writing from the Mishnah through the Bavli and the associated Midrash-compilations both is distinguished from, and also carries forward, Scripture's law and theology. Why does this matter? Perspective on the character of Rabbinic Judaism is gained from the comparison of Scripture with later writings that carry forward, but are clearly distinct from, Scripture.

Why David in particular? Four facts point to the selection of the biblical David for an account of the canonical transformation of a Scriptural figure of David into a rabbi by the Rabbinic sages.

[1] After Moses David is the single most prominent individual figure in the heritage of the biblical narrative.

[2] The attribution of many Psalms to David's authorship endows David with self-evident prominence in the Scriptural, not only the Rabbinic, canon.

[3] His name dominates eschatological thinking in the entire repertoire of late antique Judaic documents.

[4] The protracted narrative of David in Scripture underscores his exemplary status. For these reasons the sages' figure of David exemplifies the larger context of Scripture and tradition in Rabbinic Judaism

Obviously, I do not claim to produce a secular ("critical") biography or sequence of historical narratives of David in the Rabbinic canon. I also do not characterize the post-Scriptural biography rendered accessible by the documentary approach. What we learn here concerns the uses of the figure of David in the various documents of the Rabbinic canon. The ultimate account will answer the question, does David contribute random facts or is there a concerted effort to re-present David for purposes particular to the Rabbinic canon? At stake is the definition of the program of Rabbinic Judaism, not of Scripture. To answer these questions, in line with the documentary hypothesis we examined the Rabbinic documents in approximate sequence.

What I demonstrate is negative: until the end there is no single, systematic encompassing program to represent David in accord with a polemical Rabbinic program.

The documentary outcome is familiar. The compositions in which David figures replicate in their formal program the documents in which David does not figure. The same forms predominate. a only in the later documents, mostly in the Bavli as a matter of fact. That is the protracted narrative, the extended exposition of what David thought said and did. This protracted kind of writing is particular to the Bavli and is lacking in the prior documents. That is a striking discovery, but I cannot say what it means for Rabbi David.

STUDIES IN JUDAISM
TITLES IN THE SERIES
PUBLISHED BY UNIVERSITY PRESS OF AMERICA

Judith Z. Abrams
The Babylonian Talmud: A Topical Guide, 2002.

Roger David Aus
The Death, Burial, and Resurrection of Jesus, and the Death, Burial, and Translation of Moses in Judaic Tradition, 2008.

Feeding the Five Thousand: Studies in the Judaic Background of Mark 6:30-44 par. and John 6:1-15, 2010.

Matthew 1-2 and the Virginal Conception: In Light of Palestinian and Hellenistic Judaic Traditions on the Birth of Israel's First Redeemer, Moses, 2004.

My Name Is "Legion": Palestinian Judaic Traditions in Mark 5:1-20 and Other Gospel Texts, 2003.

Alan L. Berger, Harry James Cargas, and Susan E. Nowak
The Continuing Agony: From the Carmelite Convent to the Crosses at Auschwitz, 2004.

S. Daniel Breslauer
Creating a Judaism without Religion: A Postmodern Jewish Possibility, 2001.

Bruce Chilton
Targumic Approaches to the Gospels: Essays in the Mutual Definition of Judaism and Christianity, 1986.

David Ellenson
Tradition in Transition: Orthodoxy, Halakhah, and the Boundaries of Modern Jewish Identity, 1989.

Roberta Rosenberg Farber and Simcha Fishbane
Jewish Studies in Violence: A Collection of Essays, 2007.

Paul V. M. Flesher
New Perspectives on Ancient Judaism, Volume 5: Society and Literature in Analysis, 1990.

Marvin Fox
Collected Essays on Philosophy and on Judaism, Volume One: Greek Philosophy, Maimonides, 2003.

Collected Essays on Philosophy and on Judaism, Volume Two: Some Philosophers, 2003.

Collected Essays on Philosophy and on Judaism, Volume Three: Ethics, Reflections, 2003.

Zev Garber
Methodology in the Academic Teaching of Judaism, 1986.

Zev Garber, Alan L. Berger, and Richard Libowitz
Methodology in the Academic Teaching of the Holocaust ,1988.

Abraham Gross
Spirituality and Law: Courting Martyrdom in Christianity and Judaism, 2005.

Harold S. Himmelfarb and Sergio DellaPergola
Jewish Education Worldwide: Cross-Cultural Perspectives, 1989.

Raphael Jospe
Jewish Philosophy: Foundations and Extensions (Volume One: General Questions and Considerations), 2008.

Jewish Philosophy: Foundations and Extensions (Volume Two: On Philosophers and Their Thought), 2008.

William Kluback
The Idea of Humanity: Hermann Cohen's Legacy to Philosophy and Theology, 1987.

Samuel Morell
Studies in the Judicial Methodology of Rabbi David ibn Abi Zimra, 2004.

Jacob Neusner
Amos in Talmud and Midrash, 2006.

Analytical Templates of the Yerushalmi, 2008.

Ancient Israel, Judaism, and Christianity in Contemporary Perspective, 2006.

The Aggadic Role in Halakhic Discourses: Volume I, 2001.

The Aggadic Role in Halakhic Discourses: Volume II, 2001.

The Aggadic Role in Halakhic Discourses: Volume III, 2001.

Analysis and Argumentation in Rabbinic Judaism, 2003.

Analytical Templates of the Bavli, 2006.

Ancient Judaism and Modern Category-Formation: "Judaism," "Midrash," "Messianism," and Canon in the Past Quarter Century, 1986.

Bologna Addresses and Other Recent Papers, 2007.

Building Blocks of Rabbinic Tradition: The Documentary Approach to the Study of Formative Judaism, 2007.

Canon and Connection: Intertextuality in Judaism, 1987.

Chapters in the Formative History of Judaism, 2006.

Chapters in the Formative History of Judaism: Second Series: More Questions and Answers, 2008.

Chapters in the Formative History of Judaism: Third Series: Historical Theology, the Canon, Constructive Theology and Other Problems, 2009.

Chapters in the Formative History of Judaism: Fourth Series: From-Historical Studies and the Documentary Hypothesis, 2009.

Chapters in the Formative History of Judaism: Fifth Series: Some Current Essays on the History, Literature, and Theology of Judaism, 2010.

Chapters in the Formative History of Judaism: Sixth Series: More Essays on the History, Literature, and Theology of Judaism, 2011.

Chapters in the Formative History of Judaism: Seventh Series: More Essays on the History, Literature, and Theology of Judaism, 2011.

Comparative Midrash: Sifré to Numbers and Sifré Zutta to Numbers: Two Rabbinic Readings of the Book of Numbers, Volume One: Forms, 2009.

Comparative Midrash: Sifré to Numbers and Sifré Zutta to Numbers: Two Rabbinic Readings of the Book of Numbers, Volume Two: Exegesis, 2009.

The Documentary History of Judaism and Its Recent Interpreters, 2009

Dual Discourse, Single Judaism, 2001.

The Emergence of Judaism: Jewish Religion in Response to the Critical Issues of the First Six Centuries, 2000.

Ezekiel in Talmud and Midrash, 2007.

First Principles of Systemic Analysis: The Case of Judaism within the History of Religion, 1988.

First Steps in the Talmud: A Guide to the Confused, 2010.

Habakkuk, Jonah, Nahum, and Obadiah in Talmud and Midrash: A Source Book, 2007.

The Halakhah and the Aggadah, 2001.

Halakhic Hermeneutics, 2003.

Halakhic Theology: A Sourcebook, 2006.

The Hermeneutics of Rabbinic Category Formations, 2001.

Hosea in Talmud and Midrash, 2006.

How Important Was the Destruction of the Second Temple in the Formation of Rabbinic Judaism? 2006.

How Not to Study Judaism, Examples and Counter-Examples, Volume One: Parables, Rabbinic Narratives, Rabbis' Biographies, Rabbis' Disputes, 2004.

How Not to Study Judaism, Examples and Counter-Examples, Volume Two: Ethnicity and Identity Versus Culture and Religion, How Not to Write a Book on Judaism, Point and Counterpoint, 2004.

How the Bavli is Constructed: Identifying the Forests Comprised by the Talmud's Trees: The Cases of Bavli Moed Qatan and of Bavli Makkot, 2009.

How the Halakhah Unfolds: Moed Qatan in the Mishnah, Tosefta, Yerushalmi, and Bavli, 2006.

How the Halakhah Unfolds, Volume II, Part A: Nazir in the Mishnah, Tosefta, Yerushalmi, and Bavli, 2007.

How the Halakhah Unfolds, Volume II, Part B: Nazir in the Mishnah, Tosefta, Yerushalmi, and Bavli, 2007.

How the Halakhah Unfolds, Volume III, Part A: Abodah Zarah in the Mishnah, Tosefta, Yerushalmi, and Bavli, 2007.

How the Halakhah Unfolds, Volume III, Part B: Abodah Zarah in the Mishnah, Tosefta, Yerushalmi, and Bavli, 2007.

How the Halakhah Unfolds, Volume IV, Hagigah in the Mishnah, Tosefta, Yerushalmi, and Bavli, 2009.

The Implicit Norms of Rabbinic Judaism, 2006.

Intellectual Templates of the Law of Judaism, 2006.

Isaiah in Talmud and Midrash: A Source Book, Part A, 2007.

Isaiah in Talmud and Midrash: A Source Book, Part B, 2007.

Is Scripture the Origin of the Halakhah? 2005

Israel and Iran in Talmudic Times: A Political History, 1986.

Israel's Politics in Sasanian Iran: Self-Government in Talmudic Times, 1986.

Jeremiah in Talmud and Midrash: A Source Book, 2006.

Judaism in Monologue and Dialogue, 2005.

Lost Documents of Rabbinic Judaism. 2010.

Major Trends in Formative Judaism, Fourth Series, 2002.

Major Trends in Formative Judaism, Fifth Series, 2002.

Messiah in Context: Israel's History and Destiny in Formative Judaism, 1988.

Micah and Joel in Talmud and Midrash, 2006.

Narrative and Document in the Rabbinic Canon, Vol. I: From the Mishnah to the Talmuds, 2009.

Narrative and Document in the Rabbinic Canon, Vol. II: The Two Talmuds, 2010.

The Native Category – Formations of the Aggadah: The Later Midrash-Compilations – Volume I, 2000.

The Native Category – Formations of the Aggadah: The Earlier Midrash-Compilations – Volume II, 2000.

Paradigms in Passage: Patterns of Change in the Contemporary Study of Judaism, 1988.

Parsing the Torah, 2005.

Persia and Rome in Classical Judaism, 2008

Praxis and Parable: The Divergent Discourses of Rabbinic Judaism, 2006.

The Program of the Fathers According to Rabbi Nathan A, 2009.

Rabbi David: A Documentary Catalogue, 2012.

Rabbi Jeremiah, 2006.

The Rabbinic System: How the Aggadah and the Halakhah Complement Each Other, 2011.

Rabbinic Theology and Israelite Prophecy: Primacy of the Torah, Narrative of the World to Come, Doctrine of Repentance and Atonement, and the Systematization of Theology in the Rabbis' Reading of the Prophets, 2007.

The Rabbinic Utopia, 2007.

The Rabbis and the Prophets, 2010.

The Rabbis, the Law, and the Prophets. 2007.

Reading Scripture with the Rabbis: The Five Books of Moses, 2006.

The Religious Study of Judaism: Description, Analysis, Interpretation, Volume 1, 1986.

The Religious Study of Judaism: Description, Analysis, Interpretation, Volume 2, 1986.

The Religious Study of Judaism: Context, Text, Circumstance, Volume 3, 1987.

The Religious Study of Judaism: Description, Analysis, Interpretation, Volume 4, 1988.

Sifré Zutta to Numbers, 2008.

Struggle for the Jewish Mind: Debates and Disputes on Judaism Then and Now, 1988.

The Talmud Law, Theology, Narrative: A Sourcebook, 2005.

Talmud Torah: Ways to God's Presence through Learning: An Exercise in Practical Theology, 2002.

Texts Without Boundaries: Protocols of Non-Documentary Writing in the Rabbinic Canon: Volume I: The Mishnah, Tractate Abot, and the Tosefta, 2002.

Texts Without Boundaries: Protocols of Non-Documentary Writing in the Rabbinic Canon: Volume II: Sifra and Sifre to Numbers, 2002.

Texts Without Boundaries: Protocols of Non-Documentary Writing in the Rabbinic Canon: Volume III: Sifre to Deuteronomy and Mekhilta Attributed to Rabbi Ishmael, 2002.

Texts Without Boundaries: Protocols of Non-Documentary Writing in the Rabbinic Canon: Volume IV: Leviticus Rabbah, 2002.

A Theological Commentary to the Midrash – Volume I: Pesiqta deRab Kahana, 2001.

A Theological Commentary to the Midrash – Volume II: Genesis Raba, 2001.

A Theological Commentary to the Midrash – Volume III: Song of Songs Rabbah, 2001.

A Theological Commentary to the Midrash – Volume IV: Leviticus Rabbah, 2001.

A Theological Commentary to the Midrash – Volume V: Lamentations Rabbati, 2001.

A Theological Commentary to the Midrash – Volume VI: Ruth Rabbah and Esther Rabbah, 2001.

A Theological Commentary to the Midrash – Volume VII: Sifra, 2001.

A Theological Commentary to the Midrash – Volume VIII: Sifre to Numbers and Sifre to Deuteronomy, 2001.

A Theological Commentary to the Midrash – Volume IX: Mekhilta Attributed to Rabbi Ishmael, 2001.

Theological Dictionary of Rabbinic Judaism: Part One: Principal Theological Categories, 2005.

Theological Dictionary of Rabbinic Judaism: Part Two: Making Connections and Building Constructions, 2005.

Theological Dictionary of Rabbinic Judaism: Part Three: Models of Analysis, Explanation, and Anticipation, 2005.

The Theological Foundations of Rabbinic Midrash, 2006.

Theology of Normative Judaism: A Source Book, 2005.

Theology in Action: How the Rabbis of the Talmud Present Theology (Aggadah) in the Medium of the Law (Halakhah). An Anthology, 2006.

The Torah and the Halakhah: The Four Relationships, 2003.

The Transformation of Judaism: From Philosophy to Religion, Second Edition, Revised, 2010.

The Treasury of Judaism: A New Collection and Translation of Essential Texts (Volume One: The Calendar), 2008.

The Treasury of Judaism: A New Collection and Translation of Essential Texts (Volume Two: The Life Cycle), 2008.

The Treasury of Judaism: A New Collection and Translation of Essential Texts (Volume Three: Theology), 2008.

The Unity of Rabbinic Discourse: Volume I: Aggadah in the Halakhah, 2001.

The Unity of Rabbinic Discourse: Volume II: Halakhah in the Aggadah, 2001.

The Unity of Rabbinic Discourse: Volume III: Halakhah and Aggadah in Concert, 2001.

The Vitality of Rabbinic Imagination: The Mishnah Against the Bible and Qumran, 2005.

War and Peace in Rabbinic Judaism: A Documentary Account, 2011.

Who, Where and What is "Israel?": Zionist Perspectives on Israeli and American Judaism, 1989.

The Wonder-Working Lawyers of Talmudic Babylonia: The Theory and Practice of Judaism in its Formative Age, 1987.

Zephaniah, Haggai, Zechariah, and Malachi in Talmud and Midrash: A Source Book, 2007.

Jacob Neusner and Renest S. Frerichs
New Perspectives on Ancient Judaism, Volume 2: Judaic and Christian Interpretation of Texts: Contents and Contexts, 1987.

New Perspectives on Ancient Judaism, Volume 3: Judaic and Christian Interpretation of Texts: Contents and Contexts, 1987

Jacob Neusner and James F. Strange
Religious Texts and Material Contexts, 2001.

David Novak and Norbert M. Samuelson
Creation and the End of Days: Judaism and Scientific Cosmology, 1986.

Proceedings of the Academy for Jewish Philosophy, 1990.

Risto Nurmela
The Mouth of the Lord Has Spoken: Inner-Biblical Allusions in Second and Third Isaiah, 2006.

Aaron D. Panken
The Rhetoric of Innovation: Self-Conscious Legal Change in Rabbinic Literature, 2005.

Norbert M. Samuelson
Studies in Jewish Philosophy: Collected Essays of the Academy for Jewish Philosophy, 1980-1985, 1987.

Benjamin Edidin Scolnic
Alcimus, Enemy of the Maccabees, 2004.

If the Egyptians Drowned in the Red Sea, Where Are the Pharoah's Chariots?: Exploring the Historical Dimension of the Bible, 2005.

Judaism Defined: Mattathias and the Destiny of His People. 2010.

Thy Brother's Blood: The Maccabees and Dynastic Morality in the Hellenistic World, 2008.

Rivka Ulmer

Pesiqta Rabbati: A Synoptic Edition of Pesiqta Rabbati Based Upon All Extant Manuscripts and the Editio Preceps, Volume I, 2009.

Pesiqta Rabbati: A Synoptic Edition of Pesiqta Rabbati Based Upon All Extant Manuscripts and the Editio Preceps, Volume II, 2009.

Pesiqta Rabbati: A Synoptic Edition of Pesiqta Rabbati Based Upon All Extant Manuscripts and the Editio Preceps, Volume III, 2009.

Manfred Vogel

A Quest for a Theology of Judaism: The Divine, the Human and the Ethical Dimensions in the Structure-of-Faith of Judaism Essays in Constructive Theology, 1987.

Anita Weiner

Renewal: Reconnecting Soviet Jewry to the Soviet People: A Decade of American Jewish Joint Distribution Committee (AJJDC) Activities in the Former Soviet Union 1988-1998, 2003.

Eugene Weiner and Anita Weiner

Israel-A Precarious Sanctuary: War, Death and the Jewish People, 1989.

The Martyr's Conviction: A Sociological Analysis, 2002.

Leslie S. Wilson

The Serpent Symbol in the Ancient Near East: Nahash and Asherah: Death, Life, and Healing, 2001.

Tzvee Zahavy and Jacob Neusner

How the Halakhah Unfolds, Volume V: Hullin in the Mishnah, Tosefta, and Bavli, Part One: Mishnah, Tosefta, and Bavli, Chapters One through Six, 2010.

How the Halakhah Unfolds, Volume V: Hullin in the Mishnah, Tosefta and Bavli, Part Two: Mishnah, Tosefta, and Bavli, Chapters Seven through Twelve, 2010.